Michael Brill

Spontaneous eye blinks as an alternative measure
for spatial presence experiences

Michael Brill

Spontaneous eye blinks as an alternative measure for spatial presence experiences

Würzburg
University Press

Dissertation, Julius-Maximilians-Universität Würzburg
Fakultät für Humanwissenschaften, 2018
Gutachter: Prof. Dr. Frank Schwab, Prof. Dr. Peter Ohler

Impressum

Julius-Maximilians-Universität Würzburg
Würzburg University Press
Universitätsbibliothek Würzburg
Am Hubland
D-97074 Würzburg
www.wup.uni-wuerzburg.de

© 2019 Würzburg University Press
Print on Demand

Coverdesign: Jule Petzold
Coverfoto: Bettina Schwaiger

ISBN 978-3-95826-094-8 (print)
ISBN 978-3-95826-095-5 (online)
DOI 10.25972/WUP-978-3-95826-095-5
URN urn:nbn:de:bvb:20-opus-167898

Ich möchte allen danken, die mich auf meinem Weg zur Promotion begleitet haben, insbesondere meiner Familie, meinen Freunden, meinen Kolleginnen und Kollegen sowie ganz besonders meinem Betreuer. Ich kann mir dieses Projekt nicht ohne ihre Unterstützung vorstellen.

Preface

Presence can be understood as a specific mental state, which can emerge during the reception or use of different media. Therefore, it has to be conceptualized as a process phenomenon. Given this process nature of presence, post-receptive, summative self-reports could be insufficient, and observational methods seem to be more appropriate. Consequently, theorizing and hypothesis testing in presence research should be associated with the use or development of appropriate process measures. However, observational studies are comparably rare in (media) psychology—possibly due to their immanent theoretical and methodological challenges, which are opposed by the publication pressure that frequently results in prioritizing more economical, but less sophisticated measurements.

Nevertheless, Michael Brill decided to take a close look at an observational measure: temporal-structural aspects of the media user's spontaneous blinking behavior. This ubiquitous, yet rarely considered behavior can be detected relatively simple and unobtrusive. It offers an objective process measure during the reception or use of media, be it linear film or interactive games. At the same time, however, blinking behavior shows large inter-individual variation and can be object to interference from several factors. Michael Brill's studies explore the question of how this behavior and its temporal structure can serve as an (indirect) indicator for presence experiences.

In sum, this book describes three elaborated studies in a clear, stringent and precise manner. The studies are convincingly derived from the status quo of theory and empirical findings, and address important aspects more in-depth than existing research. The author convinces in the clarity of his arguments and in the critical examination of his own approach. The project's summaries and discussions offer detailed conclusions and explanations, as well as inspiring reflections. First and foremost, the book provides suggestions for, and evaluations of the analytical opportunities of time series measures in media studies. Undoubtedly, the reader will find a solidly researched, well planned and competently analyzed piece of scientific research.

Prof. Dr. Frank Schwab

Table of Contents

Figures

Tables

Abbreviations

ADHD	Attention-deficit/hyperactivity disorder
AR	Augmented reality
ASD	Autism spectrum disorders
DA	Dopamine
DAN	Dorsal attention network
DMN	Default-mode network
ERF	Ego reference frame
FEF	Frontal eye-field
Fps	Frames per second
HMD	Head-mounted display
hMT+	Human visual area V5
IP	Internet protocol
IR/NIR	Infrared/near-infrared
MT	Middle temporal visual area
PERF	Primary ego reference frame
PMSP	Process model for the formation of spatial presence experiences
PTZ	Pan-tilt-zoom
RGB	Red, green, blue
SBR	Spontaneous blink rate
SEB	Spontaneous eye-blinks
SPES	Spatial Presence Experience Scale
SSM	Spatial situation model
VAN	Ventral attention network
VDU	Video display unit
VR	Virtual reality

1 Introduction

March 25th 2014, Menlo Park and Palo Alto, California. Mark Zuckerberg (Mark Zuckerberg, 2014) and the Facebook press division (Facebook, 2014) announce Facebook's latest acquisition: the startup Oculus VR, Inc., which was developing virtual reality hardware, most prominently a *head-mounted display* (HMD) called Oculus Rift. Facebook invested two billion US dollars (Forbes, 2014) and, as came to be known later, another one billion US dollars in "employee retention packages and goal targets" (Business Insider, 2017). Although the Oculus Rift's development had started as a successful crowdfunding campaign, this appears to be a high price for a start-up with no finished product, and, at this time, no user base except the Kickstarter backers. What convinced Facebook to secure this technology?

In his Facebook post announcing the deal (Mark Zuckerberg, 2014), Zuckerberg explicitly refers to the immersive capabilities of head-mounted displays and how the feeling of immersion might change the way we will experience gaming and social interaction in the future. He already mentions several applications for the technology (and thus several ways for Facebook to return the investment), such as gaming, social interaction, doctor house calls, or broadcasting of sports events. All these activities were supposed to benefit from more immersive media technology, thus enabling the users to engage in the content as if they were actually present in the mediated environment.

Parallel to the development of Oculus Rift, but to an even larger extent after the company's acquisition, more players emerged in the VR market and announced a series of products:

- In Cooperation with Oculus VR, Samsung offers the Gear VR, which allows using certain Samsung smartphones as screen and computing unit, thus turning the combination of smartphone and Gear VR into a stand-alone head-mounted display.
- Former games developer and now publisher Valve Software teamed up with Taiwan hardware manufacturer HTC to develop a VR ecosystem around the HTC Vive HMD, with sophisticated room scale tracking technology, trackable controllers, and connection to the Steam VR content distribution via Steam.
- Google offer their Samsung Gear VR-like device Daydream, successor to their low-cost cardboard VR headsets, using the same principle as the Gear VR.

- Optics specialist Zeiss offers their smartphone-based VR headset, the VR One Plus.
- Razer developed the open source head-mounted display HMD OSVR HDK 2.
- Sony releases their PlayStation VR HMD for the PlayStation 4 console system.
- Fove offer their FOVE VR HMD with integrated eye-tracking; this technology would allow for foveated rendering, whereby frames are rendered in high resolution only at the user's focal gaze point, and for depth-of-field effects.

This list merely covers the hardware aspect of VR technology, so these devices only represent the necessary technology for presentation (and ultimately: sale) of VR content. It is especially this emerging market for VR content, which makes several market researchers project a considerable growth in VR related revenues per year:

- TrendForce (2015) estimates the current size of the market to be 6.7 billion USD in 2016, with an expansion to 70 billion USD in the year 2020.
- Digi-Capital's (2015) projections combine the fields of virtual reality (VR) and augmented reality (AR); they estimate a combined volume of 150 billion USD in the year 2020, with a 30 billion share for VR; recent projections (Digi-Capital, 2017) estimate the VR/AR market to be 108 billion USD in the year 2021.
- KZero (2015a, 2015b) estimates a total of 9.318 billion USD for the year 2018, divided into software sales of 4.666 billion USD and hardware sales of 4.652 billion USD.
- International Data Corporation (IDC, 2016) expects an increase for the worldwide AR and VR market from 5.2 billion USD in 2016 to more than 162 billion USD in 2020.
- Juniper Research (2016) estimates that combined VR-related hardware sales could increase from about 5 billion USD in 2016 to more than 50 billion USD in the year 2021.

While these numbers are not perfectly consistent, for example regarding the specific goods that have been taken into account for the projections, it is nevertheless apparent that virtual reality has been attributed a considerable growth potential. These optimistic estimates, fueled by now widely available VR consumer hardware, also led to discussions whether the year 2016 would see the breakthrough of VR ("Is 2016 the year of virtual reality?", Fortune, 2015; "The year of

VR", Game Informer, 2015; "2016: The year of VR?", Virtual Reality Society, 2016).

With vivid VR marketing, terms like "*presence*" and "*immersion*" (Oculus VR, 2017; HTC Corporation, 2017) are now brought to the masses—terms and underlying knowledge from decades long, ongoing presence research by a large scholarly community, coming from "a wide range of academic disciplines (from computer sciences to neuro- and social sciences to philosophy)" (Wirth, et al., 2007, p. 494). Presence is seen as an experiential state which can occur during media use, and is thus regarded to be a process phenomenon (Wirth et al., 2007; see section 2.2 of this thesis). Strictly speaking, this means that in presence research, theorizing, hypothesis testing and thus understanding of the phenomenon benefits from, if not depends on adequate process measurement methods. For a process phenomenon, the necessary measurement methods go beyond post-session, summative self-report measures; they rather call for online process measures, so researchers can observe the user's ongoing presence experiences. However, observational studies in general tend to fall short in psychological research. Older estimates state that only 8% of psychological research in general was based on observational methods (Bakeman & Gottman, 1997). More specifically, relying solely on self-report measures has been criticized in the domain of presence research, as well (e.g., Liebold, Brill, Pietschmann, Schwab, & Ohler, 2017; Slater, 2004; see also section 3.2 of this thesis).

In face of this scientific need for appropriate measurement methods, several approaches have been proposed as continuous, observational measures in presence research (see section 3.3), and this thesis suggests and examines another possible measure for presence experiences: structural aspects of spontaneous eye-blink behavior. Because the primary physiological function of blinking is to maintain tear film integrity (see section 4.1 of this thesis), one could assume that this omnipresent closing of our eyelids occurs independently of external stimuli; however, there is a large theoretical and empirical foundation to suggest that cognitive, and especially attentional processes can influence blinking behavior (see section 4.2). Several existing studies have addressed influences on blinking in a variety of media use contexts, and some studies already examined blinks in a measurement context for the media use phenomena of transportation and narrative engagement (see section 4.2). The present thesis focuses on the phenomenon of spatial presence, and aims at establishing a thoroughly grounded link between blinking, modulated by attentional and cognitive processes during media use, and the phenomenon of presence.

Several features make blinks an option worth investigating (see section 5.2 of this thesis): In terms of measurement, they can be measured relatively unobtrusive and by relatively simple means. Unlike a summative, post-session self-assessment, they are recorded throughout the media use process, thus allowing for online observation of unfolding media use processes, and they are quite sensitive for disruptions. Unfortunately, there are some negative aspects as well: as will be described later (see sections 4 and 5), spontaneous eye-blinks show a large inter-individual variability, and as a consequence of their high sensitivity, they are prone to interference from several factors. As is the case for most objective, corroborative presence measures, blinks—reflecting attentional processes—can only represent an indirect indicator for presence experiences (see section 5).

To approach this complex of problems in the present thesis, we will first have a detailed look at the presence phenomenon (section 2 of this thesis), and will review the concept's development, theoretical advancements, and several theoretic approaches. This theoretical foundation for presence is then followed by a distinction from other, adjacent concepts of media use. Then, the question of presence assessment in general is addressed: different subjective measurement approaches for presence experiences are discussed, including their shortcomings, and criticism they have faced. This will lead to a review of several existing approaches for objective measurement of presence experiences, and the question how their validity can be evaluated (section 3). Having established a foundation of presence theories, subjective and objective measurement approaches, we move on to the core questions of this project: the relation between internal processes, spontaneous eye-blinks, and presence. Findings from multidisciplinary research on eye-blinks will provide the framework for the investigation of eye-blink behavior during media use (section 4). From the bodies of theory on presence and blinking, and from critically evaluated existing studies on eye-blink behavior during media use, implications for the present thesis project are derived. This foundation leads to formulation of the hypotheses to be investigated in this thesis, to the choice of stimuli, and methods for measurement and analysis (section 5). In the following sections, the three experiments conducted in this thesis project are described in detail (sections 6, 7, and 8). Results from these studies, along with their theoretical and methodological implications, are discussed in a general discussion (section 9). Finally, a synopsis concludes the thesis (section 10).

Before the presence concept is introduced in the next section, a few comments on formal features of this thesis are made to facilitate the reader's immersion in the text. Regarding gender, the female or male form is used indiscriminately. While several types of eye-blinks can be distinguished (see section 4.1 for an explanation of the different types of eye-blinks), the scope of this thesis is exclusively on spontaneous eye-blink behavior. In the interest of readability, terms like eye-blinks, eye-blink behavior, or blinks are used synonymously in this thesis, and unless otherwise specified, these terms refer to spontaneous eye-blinks. On several occasions throughout the text, I will use the term "we", for example when structuring the text as a service to the reader, or when presenting conclusions. The term "we" is used to imply that the respective information is shared between the two necessarily present persons in the reading process: myself as the author, represented by the text, and the reader. My thesis is referred to as either "this thesis" or "the present thesis".

The following section defines our understanding of what media are, and presents development of and theories for the presence concept. As has been mentioned earlier in the text, this thesis conceptualizes internal processes, and attention, in particular, as the link between observable eye-blink behavior, and subjectively reported presence experiences; therefore, a particular focus in descriptions of the respective theories lies on the role of attention in the respective conceptualization.

2 Theory

2.1 Media Definition

Because presence experiences should occur during media use (Wirth et al., 2007), it is necessary to first disambiguate the term *media*. Media can be defined as external representational systems, which are internally organized by symbolic systems (Ohler, Liebold, Pietschmann, Valtin, & Nieding, 2013; translated from German). This definition includes both traditional and digital media, and both non-interactive and interactive media. In this interpretation, new media, such as video games or virtual reality simulations, are merely an advancement of traditional media, such as paintings, photographs, books, newspapers, film, or TV. Ohler et al. (2013) explain that all media, regardless of the technology employed as a delivery system, have a common purpose: to provide an external, accessible representation of entities that would otherwise only exist as internal representations in every person's own neuronal system.

Consequently, media can be seen as a technology-assisted bridge to overcome the air gaps between human minds, both in terms of space and time. Media as an external storage device enable us to perceive the Mona Lisa's smile, expressed on canvas by Leonardo da Vinci more than 500 years ago; they give us a (limited) access to Leonardo's thoughts, and thus allow our neuronal systems to engage in a (limited) interaction process with Leonardo's neuronal system.

Processes in the media recipient are an important aspect in Ohler et al.'s (2013) understanding of media: effects of external representations in media can only emerge in interaction with the recipient's—or the user's—own internal representations. The fact that the human cognitive system is necessarily involved in media use is also a key aspect of the present thesis. We will discuss how the experience of presence as a media effect results from internal processes in the recipient or user, and how spontaneous eye-blinks, being influenced by such internal processes, could be used as a source of information about ongoing presence experiences. To approach this topic, we will now first discuss the concept of presence, and how researchers have addressed the concept in their theorizing, so far.

2.2 Presence Theories

For a long time in the history of humankind, humans have experienced narratives taking place in a different time or place, as Biocca and Levy (1995) note with the example of verbal storytelling of early Homo sapiens. What has maybe evolved more drastically than storytelling itself is the delivery device: media, and their ability to illustrate content, have made considerable technological advances in the past century. For more than three decades now, these technological advances have also fueled research on media's ability to elicit presence, which is the media's potential to let us experience the depicted environment as if we were actually present in the depicted place. When using Marvin Minsky's (1980) article on "telepresence" as a starting point for presence research, then, at the time of writing, there is a theoretical and empirical body of research from over 35 years of scholarly work. The following section describes some major conceptualizations of presence that advanced the field of presence research considerably, or describe important aspects for the reasoning of this thesis. Since this thesis aims at investigating the relation between spontaneous eye-blink distribution and presence experiences, the discussion of attention as a common factor of influence for both blinking and presence is essential. Consequently, each presence conceptualization is also evaluated in respect to the role it assigns to attentional processes.

2.2.1 Minsky (1980)

In June 1980, Cambridge computer science and robotics researcher Marvin Minsky published his article *Telepresence* in the *OMNI magazine*, in which, as the editorial note put it, he "proposes a 20-year plan that will alleviate the painful side effects of modern civilization" (Minsky, 1980, para. 1): his vision of distant working by use of sophisticated, remote controlled machines. Minsky describes that a major inspiration for this concept came from Robert A. Heinlein's short story *Waldo* (Heinlein, 1942). In this story, the protagonist suffers from a muscle weakness condition, and operates a series of mechanical hands from the comfort of zero gravity in space. Because these devices carefully mimic his movements and are optimally designed for their specific purposes, Waldo has an efficient means to operate without being physically present, and can do so even more efficiently as if he used normal human extremities. Waldo's presence is mediated by technology, and he feels present by help of a mediating technology: Minsky sees this as the essence of telepresence. The article in general mostly aims at depicting Minsky's vision of the future of working environments and the world of employment, including the question of how increasing automation with robotics and artificial intelligence will impact the need for human employees—a question still extremely up-to-date in present day. Nevertheless, along with a series of examples for available technologies and necessary developments, it was his thoughts on the mediated nature of the working experience that became seminal for presence research. As the pivotal element, Minsky identifies the fact that in order for telepresence to function properly, the technology needs to achieve "that sense of 'being there'" (Minsky, 1980, para. 19)—this expression should become the core metaphor for describing the presence phenomenon.

In Minsky's elaborations, the aspect of attention is covered implicitly, at most, since the telepresence workers necessarily attend to the mediating technology in order to perform their jobs. Minsky rather gives some statements on how to design an optimal flow of information to the users. Examples include the necessity to "incorporate new theories of human sensory pattern perception and feedback control" (para. 20), to transmit input and feedback via a broad range "of natural sensory channels" (para. 39) such as "touch, pressure, textures, and vibration" (para. 39), and the possibility to identify less important, neglectable sensory feedback.

2.2.2 Steuer (1992)

For his own conceptualization of telepresence, Steuer (1992) primarily emphasized the aspect of human experience in human-machine-interaction, and only secondarily the aspect of technological hardware (Steuer, 1992, p. 75). To begin with, he reports the distinction between the experiences of presence, defined as the natural "sense of being in an environment" (Steuer, 1992, p. 75), and telepresence, defined as "the experience of presence in an environment by means of a communication medium" (Steuer, 1992). In the latter case, the environment could be either real, but mediated, as found in work with teleoperators, or virtual and mediated, as found in virtual reality environments. Interestingly, Steuer already points out that, strictly speaking, even presence—as the natural human experience of real environments—is a mediated experience: a perception mediated by our sensory organs, supported by "automatic and controlled mental processes" (Steuer, 1992, p. 75, citing Gibson, 1979). Furthermore, Steuer states that there are more biological mechanisms involved, including "mindful attention, perceptual, and other mental processes that assimilate incoming sensory data with current concerns and past experiences" (Steuer, 1992, p. 75, citing Gibson, 1966). Steuer further suggests a distinction between the human side and the technological side of the telepresence phenomenon. He mainly addresses the effects of technological factors on user experience in his article, but also reminds the reader that subjective user factors and evaluations by the user will probably have an impact, as well. Steuer further argues that of the numerous possible technological aspects, he focuses on the aspects that will most likely have an at least similar effect across a wide range of users.

While telepresence as a human experience occurs on the human side, he identifies several key properties with influence on telepresence on the technological side, as well. First, Steuer assumes a superordinate factor of vividness, which is to what extent the technology can "produce a sensorially rich mediated environment" (p. 80). Second, a superordinate factor of interactivity describes to what extent the users are enabled to "influence the form or content of the mediated environment" (p. 80). Vividness and interactivity should represent the technological possibilities of a medium to elicit telepresence; however, as Steuer states, there might be considerable inter-individual differences in the experience of presence. As technological details in the domain of vividness, Steuer gives the two examples of a technology's sensory breadth and depth, that is the number of simultaneously presentable sensory channels, and the resolution in which input is presented on these channels. For the domain of interactivity, he names the three examples speed, range, and mapping of the possible interactions: How quickly user input can influence the mediated environment, how many possibilities are offered for doing so, and finally, how naturally and predictably these possibilities are translated to the mediated environment. In an optimal scenario, these features could be implemented in a virtual environment, such as a virtual reality system; Steuer defines virtual reality as a real or simulated environment in which a user can experience telepresence (Steuer, 1992), and thus offers a definition independent from distinct technological factors. A detailed taxonomy for mediated experiences can also be found in Robinett (1992), with emphasis on the system formed by user and technology.

Regarding the role of attention, one might refer to the parallels in the concepts of presence and telepresence; after all, Steuer defines telepresence as presence within mediated environments. For the concept of presence in the narrower understanding presented in his paper, Steuer sees controlled or mindful attention allocation as a supporting factor for the emergence of presence. However, no explicit predictions are provided for the role of attention in emergence of telepresence.

2.2.3 Lombard and Ditton (1997)

Another seminal article for presence research was published by Lombard and Ditton (1997), who explicate their understanding of presence to not only include virtual reality and other sophisticated media environments, but also "traditional media" (para. 1) like film and television. The authors first conduct a comprehensive review of presence studies and identify six major conceptualizations of presence, influenced by the background and interest of the respective researchers. Following are the original labels by Lombard and Ditton, each followed by a brief summary of their elaborations (para. 9–31):

1) Presence as social richness: Aiming at how "sociable, warm, sensitive, personal or intimate" a medium is perceived when interacting with other users via the medium.

2) Presence as realism: Aiming at how accurately a medium can depict real objects and places.

3) Presence as transportation: Aiming at how much a user experiences being transported to the depicted environment ("You are there"), or that the depicted environment and objects are transported to her ("It is here"), or that she is transported together with another user to a shared environment ("We are together").

4) Presence as immersion: Aiming at how much a medium blocks out real world stimuli, or absorbs the user's psychological resources.

5) Presence as social actor within the medium: Aiming at the experience of a "media personality" or a "virtual actor" as a real social actor by neglecting his or her mediated nature and the lack of bidirectionality.

6) Presence as medium as social actor: Aiming at the overlooking of the "mediated nature of a communication experience" when interacting with a medium that elicits social cues.

Based on their review of literature, they identify common aspects in this research, and use this concept to explicate presence as "the perceptual illusion of nonmediation" (para. 32). Lombard and Ditton derive several properties of presence experiences from this definition: First, the perceptual aspect refers to the involvement of a user's "sensory, cognitive, and affective processing systems" (para. 32). Second, the illusion of non-mediation is seen as the overlooking of the fact that the medium as a piece of technology is involved in the mediation process; in consequence, the user "responds as he/she would if the medium were not there" (para. 32). Third, depending on technology and content on hand, presence can either result in a user experience of sharing "the same physical environment" (para. 33), or in the medium being transformed to a social entity. Fourth, media use is a necessary condition for presence experiences, and it is no matter of degrees: A user either experiences presence or she does not. Lombard and Ditton state that when referring to a degree of presence during use of different media, it should be regarded as the extent to which non-mediation experiences occurred. Fifth, there should be inter-individual and even intra-individual differences, since presence should result from the interaction of "formal and content characteristics of a medium and characteristics of the media user" (para. 37).

Lombard and Ditton include a review of factors that researchers had identified as contributors to presence experiences. They cluster these factors into three facets of the media use process: Media form features, media content features, and user characteristics. Here, the factors are first listed in their original wording, and then the aspects relevant for attentional processes are briefly discussed in more detail:

- As media form features, they identify: number and consistency of sensory outputs; image quality, image size, and viewing angle; motion and color; dimensionality; camera techniques; aural presentation; stimuli for other senses; interactivity; obtrusiveness of the medium; and the number of people who are present in the virtual environment.
- As media content features, they identify: social realism; use of media conventions; and the nature of the task or activity.
- As media user characteristics, they identify: the user's willingness to suspend disbelief; his or her knowledge of and prior experience with the medium; other user variables, such as personal relevance of media content, or, where the authors refer to Mehrabian (1976), "the degree to which they 'screen' complex stimuli" (para. 97).

This thesis project primarily aims at the phenomenon that has later been labeled spatial presence experiences (e.g., Wirth et al., 2007); thus, the most relevant concepts of presence from Lombard and Ditton's overview would be presence as transportation and—to some extent—presence as immersion.

Regarding the role of attention, Lombard and Ditton name several factors on user and technology side. On the side of technology, the factors number and consistency of sensory outputs, and the viewing angle of the respective medium are listed: The more our sensory systems are occupied with virtual world stimuli, the less the amount of real-world stimuli the user could possibly attend to. Lombard and Ditton state that sensory input channels are not equally important, but "visual and aural senses dominate our perception" (para. 42). However, the illusion might be affected significantly if sensory output is not consistent for all sensory channels, thus revealing the mediated nature of the experience. This is closely related to the obtrusiveness of a medium, that is the degree to which a medium will "draw attention to itself and remind the media user that she/he is having a mediated experience" (para. 53). Lombard and Ditton further cite existing research, in which the relevance of visible devices for obtrusiveness is pointed out: users should rather not be distracted by, for example, visible displays or control devices, by malfunctions, text, TV network logos, irrelevant information, or real-world environmental cues. More formal media features with influence on attention are supposed to be motion, color, and interactivity. Interactivity of a medium, on the other hand, in most cases requires certain user actions in order to continue stimulus presentation. It can be argued that the more specific a medium's requirements for these user actions are (e.g., in terms of which action out of a range of possible actions needs to be made with a certain timing), the more a user might be required to pay attention to the medium's current requirements and his appropriate actions. As user variables, Lombard and Ditton name prior experience with and knowledge about the medium, the willingness to suspend disbelief, a person's tendency to screening of complex stimuli, and personal relevance of the content, among others.

In conclusion, it can be derived from Lombard and Ditton's elaborations that the visual sensory channel is especially important for presence experiences, and that it is important for users to pay attention to the content of a medium, and rather not to media form features or the real environment.

2.2.4 IJsselsteijn, de Ridder, Freeman, and Avons (2000)

Another overview was published in an article on presence measurement by IJsselsteijn, de Ridder, Freeman, and Avons (2000). They understand presence as "the sense of 'being there' in a mediated environment" (para. 3) and follow Freeman (1999), who clustered Lombard and Ditton's (1997) six categories of presence research into a physical domain and a social domain. The physical domain is described as "the sense of being physically located somewhere" (para. 5), and the social domain as the "feeling of being together (and communicating) with someone" (para. 5). IJsselsteijn et al. (2000) also review presence literature and identify several important factors for the emergence of presence experiences (para. 7-10). First, the authors name "the extent and fidelity of sensory information"; second, "the match between sensors and the display", meaning predictable effects of user input as in Steuer's (1992) concept of mapping; third, "content factors" such as interactivity or social elements for the depicted objects, actors and events; and, finally, "user characteristics". User characteristics comprise motor skills, cognitive and perception abilities, previous experiences, expectations, and the willingness to suspend disbelief (suspension of disbelief: Coleridge, 1817) about distracting media aspects; the authors report that those factors had "received little attention" in research at the time of writing.

IJsselsteijn et al. also acknowledge the importance of attention, and sum up that the allocation of "sufficient attentional resources to the mediated environment" (para. 10) is seen as an "important component of presence" (IJsselsteijn et al., 2000, para. 10). They follow perspectives that explicitly assume limited attentional resources during the presence process (Draper, Kaber, & Usher, 1998, cited by IJsselsteijn et al., 2000, p. 3), and argue that presence should be affected when attention is drawn away from the mediated environment and instead directed to real-world stimuli. They further explain that this can be used for assessment of presence by measuring secondary task reaction times, with longer reaction times and more errors for the secondary task indicating a higher attentional engagement in the mediated stimulus.

Based on the assumptions on limited attentional resources during presence formation, IJsselsteijn et al. (2000) see the possibility of presence assessment with secondary task reaction times as a suggestion for future research. They assume that more intense presence will lead to allocation of more attentional resources to the medium as a primary task, which should in turn impair reaction times and task accuracy for a secondary task. If, on the other hand, attentional resources are directed to a secondary task, presence should decrease with the resulting decreased attention on the medium.

2.2.5 Wirth et al. (2007)

The Process Model of the Formation of Spatial Presence Experiences (PMSP) was developed in the European research project *Presence: Measurement, Effects, Conditions* by Wirth and colleagues from Finland, Germany, Italy, Portugal, the United States, and Switzerland (Wirth et al., 2007, p. 493 and p. 519). The research project led to the development of the PMSP as a detailed theoretical foundation, as well as the MEC-SPQ (MEC-Spatial Presence Questionnaire; Vorderer et al., 2004; Wirth et al., 2008) as a measurement instrument, and the evaluation of several alternative measures for presence experiences (Böcking et al., 2008). The MEC-SPQ was later refined to the Spatial Presence Experience Scale (SPES; Hartmann et al., 2015); the SPES questionnaire was used as the subjective self-report instrument for presence in this thesis project.

The authors see several shortcomings in existing presence theories, especially redundancy "with basic concepts of general psychology" (Wirth et al., 2007, p. 494) due to conceptual similarity with "human perception of non-mediated reality" (p. 494).

For their theorizing on presence, Wirth and colleagues focus on the sub-concept of spatial presence, and define the central aspect of spatial presence as "the conviction of being located in a mediated environment" (Wirth et al., 2007, p. 495). Spatial presence could occur during use of a wide range of highly immersive, but also less immersive media (Wirth et al., 2007, p. 496). Wirth et al. (2007) define spatial presence as a two-dimensional construct. The first dimension should reflect the degree of self-location, which is the "sensation of being physically situated within the spatial environment portrayed by the medium" (Wirth et al., 2007, p. 497). The second dimension should reflect the "perceived possibilities to act"—in a state of presence, these perceived possibilities should be limited to the action possibilities offered by the mediated environment (Wirth et al., 2007, p. 497). Further, the experience of presence is regarded as a binary state, so presence should either be experienced, or be experienced not at all (p. 497). The authors define spatial presence as follows:

> "Spatial Presence is a binary experience, during which perceived self-location and, in most cases, perceived action possibilities are connected to a mediated spatial environment, and mental capacities are bound by the mediated environment instead of reality." (Wirth et al., 2007, p. 497).

To explain the process of presence formation, the model uses several existing theories from psychology and communications, and integrates them into a two-step model with a process-oriented perspective (Wirth et al., 2007, p. 495). Both technological factors and user factors are considered in the model.

To explain how presence can emerge, Wirth et al. (2007) see attention—and other cognitive processes—as a necessary foundation for "higher forms of experience" (p. 498), including presence. For attention, they distinguish involuntary, automatic attention allocation triggered by the medium from voluntary, controlled devotion of attention to the medium (Wirth et al., 2007, p. 498). Automatic attention allocation is considered to be mainly driven by orienting reactions in the sense of Posner (1980) towards media form features like novelty or rapid and surprising stimulus changes. This way, the organism's "sensory organs and information processing systems [are prepared] for input", and these and further processes, such as an elevation of the "activation level in the cortical areas", enable the organism to provide a "relatively stable stream of stimuli" to the higher levels of mental processing (Wirth et al., 2007, p. 499).

However, more factors on media and user side are supposed to influence if (a) this stream of information can be delivered by the medium continuously, (b) is transmitted to and received by the user's sensory organs successfully, and (c) is attended to by the user continuously. The authors conclude that in order to bind a user's attention to the medium, a "continuous stream of highly detailed information" should be superior to an "interrupted and/or less-detailed stream of input" (Wirth et al., 2007, p. 499). Additionally, features of media content should become more relevant when it comes to sustained attention allocation to the medium, for example regarding the fit of media content with the user's domain-specific interest. The authors are citing Krapp (1993) to define domain-specific interest as the "relationship between an individual's motivational dispositions and the content or issue of an object" (Wirth et al., 2007, p. 500). Thus, if a user is interested in the media content, she is more likely to show controlled attention allocation on the media stimulus (Wirth et al., 2007, p. 500). Further, the authors assume both types of attention to be involved to varying degrees in the formation of presence experiences, and their involvement should depend on, among other aspects, the immersive capabilities of the respective medium. Highly immersive media, for example, should elicit more automatic attention allocation, and thereby require less controlled attention allocation (Wirth et al., 2007, p. 501).

However, media stimuli are not the only factors competing for the user's attention: the PMSP is built on the premise that media use necessarily occurs as an activity in a real-world environment, and in most cases, a user will be confronted not only with stimuli from the media content at hand, but also with stimuli from the real world. The model assumes that as soon as attention has been allocated to the media stimulus, the user processes the perceived media cues in order to recognize if they depict a "space/room" and "if yes, what kind of space/room" (Wirth et al., 2007, p. 497). Based on this information, a spatial situation model (SSM) is formed by the user as a mental representation of the mediated environment. The authors conceptualize the SSM as a "mental model [...] of the spatial environment" in the sense of Johnson-Laird (1983), and Sanford and Garrod (1981). It is constructed with the help of bottom-up elements, such as spatial cues from the medium, and top-down elements, such as "relevant spatial memories and cognitions" of the user (Wirth et al., 2007, p. 501). For the media factors of SSM construction, Wirth et al. (2007, pp. 502–503) can draw on a large body of research on spatial cues in different media, for example perspective, occlusion, relative size, foreshortening, motion parallax, convergence, or spatial, haptic, and vestibular cues. Especially for sensory rich media, it is important to present the cues in a "consistent and plausible manner" (Wirth et al., 2007, p. 504) across the different sensory modalities. For user factors of SSM construction, visual-spatial imagery is seen as the most important user trait.

When an SSM of the mediated environment has been constructed, it is possible for the user to "subjectively position [her] own physical experience" (Wirth et al., 2007, p. 505) in the mediated environment, and enter a state of presence. Wirth and colleagues (Wirth et al., 2007, p. 505) model the process towards a state of presence by using the concepts of primary egocentric reference frame (PERF, Riecke & von der Heyde, 2002) and perceptual hypotheses (Bruner & Postman, 1949). According to research described by Wirth et al., an egocentric reference frame is defined as a "mental model of the world that is organized from a first-person perspective" (Wirth et al., 2007, p. 505) and serves as a point of reference for the locations of the own body and of other objects in space (Wirth et al., 2007, p. 505). It needs "permanent updating of [...] [the] spatial mental model" with visual and other sensory cues (Wirth et al., 2007, p. 505). For most media environments, the SSM and ERF created from the media cues will contradict the SSM and ERF created from the real environment, so mental processing will only focus on one of both; this ERF in focus then becomes the primary egocentric reference frame (PERF). If the media environment is chosen as PERF, spatial presence is experienced, and "perceived self-location, perceived possible actions and mental capacities are all bound to the mediated space" (Wirth et al., 2007, p. 506). The theory of perceptual hypotheses (Bruner & Postman, 1949) is used to explain this testing process of competing reference frames. The theory states that an organism's perception of its environment can be described as a "cognitive interaction", during which stimuli are received and interpreted by using "available hypotheses about the environment" (Wirth et al., 2007, p. 506). These hypotheses are generated from experiences in prior perception processes, they guide perception in the current process, and are tested using the currently perceived information (Wirth et al., 2007, p. 507); testing of these hypotheses is terminated if the hypothesis is confirmed, but is continued if the hypothesis cannot be confirmed. The authors (Wirth et al., 2007, p. 507) give the following example that might occur during the reception of a TV show: The protagonist enters a site that appears to be an old temple; being experienced with that kind of action drama content, the viewer scans for evidence to confirm the hypothesis that the site actually is a temple. If such evidence—the authors give the example of an ancient altar—is found, the temple hypothesis is confirmed; on the other hand, if contradicting evidence is found, the hypothesis is modified accordingly, and scanning for evidence is restarted until a hypothesis can be accepted. Several hypotheses, also variable in strength, can be tested simultaneously. This is the case if there are competing hypotheses regarding the current egocentric reference frame—and as we have stated earlier, this will frequently occur when mediated stimuli are perceived in a real environment: the SSMs constructed from real-world stimuli and mediated stimuli represent two rivaling options for the primary egocentric reference frame. This should lead to testing of the "medium-as-PERF-hypothesis": during processing of the medium's spatial cues, either the "reality-as-PERF-hypothesis" or the "medium-as-PERF-hypothesis" are confirmed (Wirth et al., 2007, p. 508). The authors define that "Spatial Presence occurs when the medium-as-PERF-hypothesis is confirmed repeatedly through processed information and is thus stabilized over time" (Wirth et al., 2007, p. 508). Wirth and colleagues name several media factors with influence on perceptual hypothesis testing: persistency, that is the duration of uninterrupted presentation of the depicted spatial environments; narrative, drama and plot in the media content; match of visual and vestibular information; and interactivity of the medium (Wirth et al., 2007, pp. 510–511).

User Factors

In addition to media factors, user factors might also contribute to the formation of presence experiences. Wirth and colleagues name the concepts of *involvement*, *suspension of disbelief*, and *trait absorption*. Involvement is described as the degree to which an individual connects information from the media content to her own life (Wirth et al., 2007, p. 512; see further elaborations on involvement in the next subsection on related concepts of media use). Two examples for effects of involvement with a media content are given, namely a strong motivation "to deal with the content in more depth", or involvement driven by arousal and stimulation rooted in, for example, a film's story (Wirth et al., 2007, p. 512). For the next concept, suspension of disbelief, Wirth and colleagues rely on theories from literature theory and define suspension of disbelief as "not paying attention to external stimuli and internal cognitions that (might) distract from the enjoyment of the mediated story and environment. Such distractions may be of technological kind or of the contents" (Wirth et al., 2007, p. 512). Despite the existence of distractors such as noises, haptic or olfactory cues from the real world, or despite an unrealistic narrative plot, users may not notice the distractors or, if noticed, "do not focus on them" (Wirth et al., 2007, p. 514). By neglecting information from the real environment that opposes the medium-as-PERF-hypothesis, and by readily processing information from the mediated environment that would in reality oppose a perceptual hypothesis, the user's suspension of disbelief strengthens the medium-as-PERF-hypothesis and weakens the reality-as-PERF-hypothesis; this way, suspension of disbelief can support the formation of presence experiences (Wirth et al., 2007, p. 514). Finally, trait absorption is incorporated into the model as a user characteristic. Referring to Wild, Kuiken, and Schopflocher (1995), trait absorption is defined as "an individual's motivation and skill in dealing with an object in an elaborate manner" (Wirth et al., 2007, p. 515). Wirth et al. (2007) further state that higher levels of trait absorption are related to higher levels of "attention allocation, the identification of spatial structures, involvement, and suspension of disbelief" (p. 515). The process model assumes that all of these factors contribute to the formation of a media recipient's or user's spatial presence experiences.

Role of Attention
Regarding the role of attention for presence experiences, the model makes detailed predictions. Attention is regarded as a necessary, but not sufficient condition for experiencing presence: media content needs to be perceived via the sensory organs as a requirement for the ensuing processes of presence formation. The model first distinguishes between automatic attention and voluntarily directed attention. The model further names several factors on user and media side with influence on attentional processes: Interest of the user in the mediated content, and features of media content or form that might attract attention, such as rapid stimulus changes.

As described above, the theory considers attention, or rather continuous attention on the stimulus, to be a necessary, but not sufficient condition for the emergence of presence. This represents a useful assumption for the purpose of this thesis: in order for the user to sustain a state of presence, ongoing allocation of controlled and automatic attention on the stimulus is necessary. The degree to which the two attention facets are involved during this process may vary, depending on, for example, media immersiveness. Wirth et al. (2007, p. 499) see different contributions of attentional processes throughout the reception process by "short-term orienting responses and more persistent attention allocation" (p. 499). They explain that upon a first orienting, cortical activation is increased and prepares the organism for the ensuing attentional processes (Schmidt & Thews, 1997, cited by Wirth et al., 2007, p. 499). These further processes, such as the construction of mental representations, depend on a sustained attention allocation on the medium (p. 499). With respect to media form features, a sustained attention allocation should be fostered by a "continuous stream of highly detailed information", in contrast to an "interrupted and/or less detailed stream of input" (p. 500). With respect to media content features, Wirth et al. (2007, p. 500) conclude that "enduring involuntary attention allocation is facilitated by content variables to a certain extent" (Hawkins et al., 2002, cited by Wirth et al., 2007). Consequently, content can have a significant impact on attention allocation, even without salient form features; for example, this might be the case if content matches a recipient's domain-specific interest (Wirth et al., p. 500). Wirth et al. further state that during processing of content, it might be difficult to distinguish between basal attention processes and especially the concept of higher cognitive involvement (p. 500), which is—among other processes—attributed an attentional component (Batra & Ray, 1985; Roser, 1990; cited by Wirth et al., 2007, p. 512).

On the second level of presence formation, the theory locates a stage of perceptual hypotheses testing; spatial presence should occur if the medium-as-PERF-hypothesis is "confirmed repeatedly through processed information and is thus stabilized over time" (Wirth et al., 2007, p. 508). The model thus assumes a continuous processing of information, which depends on a continuous stream of information, which in turn is provided by continuous attentional processes. This assumption of ongoing cognitive, and especially attentional processes during media use is a key aspect for the rationale of this thesis, because we will see in section 4 that these processes can influence spontaneous eye-blink behavior. However, the stream of information from the medium might include evidence supporting, but also evidence contradicting the medium-as-PERF-hypothesis. How persistent this stream needs to be—that is, how long it can be interrupted without consequences for the formation of presence—is also seen as an attention allocation problem, but is a question for further research (Wirth et al., 2007, p. 510). However, the authors state that rich SSMs might consume cognitive resources—and thus attention—more effectively, and that interactivity might support attention allocation on the stimulus, as well. The PMSP model further formulates suspension of disbelief as a process component with influence on perceptual hypotheses testing. Suspension of disbelief is explained as not paying attention to distracting internal or external stimuli, which can origin from either media content or media technology (Wirth et al., 2007, p. 513). If such aspects do elicit attention, the recipients are supposed to "not focus on them", and thus suspend them from testing of the medium-as-PERF-hypothesis (p. 514). Suspension of disbelief is thought to cause a "lack of attention to distracting information from the surrounding world" (p. 514), and by doing so allow the recipient to "weaken or delete" contradicting factors from her focus of attention (p. 514). While this conceptualization implies a top-down modulation of attentional processes, the model does not elaborate on exactly how and where during the media use process these effects occur, especially in respect to the highly automatic processes of automatic attention allocation, such as orienting responses.

For the process of presence formation as a whole, the authors conclude that absorption into a mediated environment should enhance, among others, the user's overall attention allocation, but also specific sub-processes like identification of spatial structures (p. 515). The model predictions especially relevant in the scope of this thesis concern the ongoing attention allocation during creation and updating of spatial situation models, during testing of perceptual hypotheses, the possible user actions in accordance with mental representations of the mediated environment, and the accompanied binding of cognitive resources.

2.2.6 Schubert (2009)

Schubert refers to presence as experiencing the "sense of *being there*" (Schubert, 2009, p. 161), which had been labeled in literature as telepresence, presence, spatial presence, or physical presence (Schubert, 2009, p. 161). He argues for a cognitive theory of presence, and sees a desideratum in existing presence theories concerning the link between unconscious perception and processing of spatial cues on the one hand, and the conscious experience of presence on the other hand (Schubert, 2009, p. 162). In analogy to emotions as affective feelings, Schubert suggests to understand the emergence of presence as a cognitive feeling. Cognitive feelings are defined as subjective experiences, which result from unconscious processes, and are supposed to aid in monitoring and controlling of cognitive functions: they "inform judgments, decisions and behavior" (Schubert, 2009, p. 169), and are attributed an indisputable nature, just being felt like affective feelings or perceived like sensory perceptions of the environment (Schubert, 2009). Schubert (2009) argues that such properties also characterize presence experiences, and that regarding presence as a subjective feeling also legitimizes the use of subjective self-report measures for presence assessment. Objective measures should help to shed light on the formation processes of presence experiences, although they would likely not so much depict spatial presence as conceptualized by Schubert, but rather cognitive processes leading to the experience of presence (Schubert, 2009, p. 177).

Due to his concept of presence as a cognitive feeling, Schubert (2009) attributes a different role to attention. Schubert argues that attention "does not provide useful information on whether the construction [of a situated model] was successful, or whether the own body is actually located in the virtual environment" (p. 172). Consequently, attention would not be a useful indicator for presence experiences (p. 173), and "deliberately focusing attention on aspects of the virtual environment and suppressing contradicting information from the real environment" (p. 173) would rather be supporting factors for the formation of presence. Further, if a feeling of being present is contradicted by other information, attention can be drawn to the strong presence feeling, and users who are unfamiliar with this experience might be drawn out of the state of presence (p. 174). Schubert concludes that orientation behavior, attention and explorative behavior in a virtual world should be influenced by the state of presence, but also—on a superordinate level—by a user's current goals, such as the intention to perform well in a given task in the virtual environment (p. 179).

2.2.7 Lee (2004a, 2004b)

Lee provides another categorizing of presence experiences (Lee, 2004a), and drafts an evolutionary frame to explain the emergence of presence (Lee, 2004b). Lee (2004a) situates presence experiences in between the common experiencing of reality, that is the sensory perception of real-world objects, and the experience of hallucination, that is the non-sensory perception of imagined objects. So according to his explications, presence is a psychological state in which virtual objects are perceived as real objects in either sensory or non-sensory ways; the latter aims at processes occurring during, for example, the reading of books, where only textual representations of the narrated objects are offered. Such objects in mediated environments can have varying degrees of connections to reality, ranging from para-authentic to entirely artificial objects. Lee (2004a) further distinguishes three presence categories: physical presence, social presence, and self-presence. Physical presence is characterized by the experience of sensorially or non-sensorially perceived virtual physical objects as real physical objects, so their mediated nature is neglected; apart from that, the user does not necessarily feel present in the mediated environment. Social presence is characterized by the experience of sensorially or non-sensorially perceived virtual social actors as real social actors; here, social presence extends the concept of co-presence, so these virtual actors are not necessarily representations of real persons. Self-presence is characterized by the experience of sensorially or non-sensorially perceived virtual self-representations as the real self. Lee (2004a) points out the importance of accurate sensory or social feedback for self-presence, for example regarding movement in the virtual environment, whereby the user's point of view in the virtual environment should change appropriately according to the user's input.

Lee's (2004b) suggestions for evolutionary foundations of presence are based on Darwin's (1859) work on natural selection and adaptation of organisms to their environment. Lee further builds on existing research findings, and first assumes that human beings show a tendency to regard perceived information as real, as long as there is no contradicting evidence (Gerrig, 1993, cited by Lee, 2004b). Second, Lee assumes that the environment of natural selection favors a reaction's speed over a reaction's accuracy, so the human cognitive system should have adapted to initially treat representations as real, unless proven otherwise (Mantovani, 1995, cited by Lee, 2004b). Lee (2004b) refers to modular models of the human mind, and describes the role of two such modules: Folk physics and folk psychology, which are supposed to deal with basic physical concepts such as gravity, and basic social concepts, respectively. Lee (2004b) argues that these modules of the human mind, which have evolved to react to real-world entities, are also triggered by media stimuli, including today's rich new media. Real-world reactions towards mediated objects could then occur because these evolved mechanisms process mediated stimuli the same way they would process real-world stimuli.

The role of attention is acknowledged in Lee's evolutionary concept of presence (Lee, 2004b). He cites research suggesting that big objects are strong attractors of attention, and that size judgments for real-world and mediated stimuli rely on the same evolved processes; Lee suggests that this might explain why larger screens for media presentation cause stronger effects on presence and related variables (p. 499). Attention should also be sensitive to motion in the media stimulus; Lee cites research that sees motion as a trigger for media users to orient themselves towards moving objects and pay attention to them (p. 500).

2.2.8 Riva, Mantovani, Waterworth and Waterworth (2015)

A different approach has been proposed by Riva, Mantovani, Waterworth, and Waterworth (2015), who draft a volitional approach to presence. They see presence not so much as a phenomenon exclusive to media use, but as a phenomenon with deeper roots in the "control of the individual and social activity" (Riva et al., 2015, p. 73). The key assumptions for this model are that the psychological foundations of presence are related to "human action and its organization in the environment" (p. 73), are related to the "body and embodiment processes" (p. 73), and have evolved to understand and manage the "causal texture of both the physical and social worlds" (p. 73). The authors start with a previous, broad definition of presence by IJsselsteijn and Riva (2003), which defined presence as a "complex, multidimensional perception", created by cognitive processes from sensory input (Riva et al., 2015, p. 92). This definition is detailed with regard to the role of a subject's intentions, and the actions performed to achieve these intentions. The authors see their conceptualization of presence as a "missing link" (p. 93) between two different approaches. On the one hand, cognitive approaches address the question how "action is planned and controlled in response to environmental conditions" (pp. 92–93); on the other hand, volitional approaches address how "action is planned and controlled by [a] subject's needs, motives and goals" (p.

93). Riva et al. (2015) argue that presence serves the process of transforming intentions into actions, so a subject experiences presence if she is "able to enact [her] intentions in an external world" (p. 93). Riva et al. (2015) locate various presence concepts within this framework. The aspect translating best to spatial presence is defined as presence (in contrast to social presence, another aspect within Riva et al.'s framework). Presence in the sense of Riva et al. should enable a subject to control actions by comparing the perceptual inputs from an action with her predictions of these inputs. For the use of mediated environments, the model predicts that a state of presence should be characterized by the experience that "the technology has become part of the self" (p. 93). This means that compared to the real world, there is no additional effort in the comparison process of predicted action outcomes and observed, actual action outcomes, and users "perceive and act directly, as if unmediated" (p. 93). With this heavy focus on actions in a mediated environment, Riva et al.'s model seems to primarily aim at presence experiences during use of interactive media, such as virtual reality systems.

The role of attention is mentioned throughout several stages of the model. First, attention is—in line with various other conceptualizations of presence—seen as a necessary factor for presence to occur. Riva et al. also address the selective nature of attention to identify beneficial and hindering circumstances for presence. For example, presence experiences should be hindered if real-world actions do not translate to the desired virtual-world actions, as would be the case during a technical malfunction. Then, attention would need to support "conscious efforts to perform actions" (p. 81), and would not be applied in the same way as in a state of presence. Attention is also addressed in the context of presence classification, in this case the role of selective attention for the concept of core presence (p. 85). It is further assumed that attention can be attracted by media content features (p. 90), and that directing attention to the appropriate media aspects (p. 91) can aid in the formation of presence.

2.2.9 Liebold, Brill, Pietschmann, Schwab, and Ohler (2017)

Liebold, Brill, Pietschmann, Schwab, and Ohler (2017) build upon the tradition of breaks in presence research, that is the observation of reactions towards events that disrupt the current media use, and most likely presence experiences, as well (Slater & Steed, 2000; see section 3.3.1). Liebold et al. propose a cognitive mechanism to explain breaks in presence, and to predict what reactions towards breaks in presence could be expected. The authors start from the concept of mental models in the formation of presence experiences (Wirth et al., 2007), where predictions of these models need to be consistent with actual input from a mediated environment. Liebold et al. emphasize the importance of the "availability and consistency of mental models with the VE [virtual environment]" (p. 4) for the formation of presence, and as long as consistency is given, "the user's attention is fully directed at the VE, which is perceived as if it was real" (p. 4). A break in presence might be caused by an unexpected inconsistency between perceived information and mental model predictions, so the artificial nature of the current experience becomes obvious; here, the focus is not so much on "unexpected information in general" (p. 4), since, as Liebold et al. explain, these are a common element of, for example, suspenseful narratives. Unexpected model violations, on the other hand, should cause an orienting response in the user, because an explanation for the inconsistent information is needed, and the current mental model as a reference frame has no explanatory value in this regard. As Liebold et al. elaborate further, model violations can occur on different levels, from incorporation of new or missing information, over the incorporation of placeholders for missing information, to information that is inconsistent with a placeholder, or even contradicting the whole model. The probability for elicitation of an orienting response, and the magnitude of these responses, should increase from level to level; consequently, especially the higher-level inconsistencies would more likely cause a strong enough orienting response to cause a break in presence. Since orienting responses are "a very stable reaction of the human cognitive system to unexpected stimuli" (p. 5)—in this case stimuli that are inconsistent with the current mental model—they could be used to infer information on the user's perception of the eliciting stimulus. Orienting responses are described to be elicited pre-attentively, and are involuntarily directing and focusing "all attention and cognitive resources [...] on the eliciting stimulus" (p. 5); they are influenced by stimulus novelty, stimulus magnitude, and emotional relevance. The research review by Liebold et al. further suggests that these mechanisms of automatic attention allocation can be suppressed by controlled attention allocation, and can be subject to habituation processes.

Attention is attributed a key role in this concept; detailed predictions are made for the role of attention in both the formation and the disruption of presence, and these predictions are based on a suggested cognitive mechanism explaining why orienting responses can lead to breaks in presence. In this mechanism, the intensity of an orienting response, reflecting the intensity of the underlying model violation, is seen as informative for the user's internal processes. Especially when considering attentional aspects of orienting responses, this might lead to new ways of measuring presence experiences.

Attention is attributed an even more significant role in another, innovative reconceptualization of presence experiences by Liebold, Pietschmann, Ohler (2015), who see mental models and focused attention on the content of a media stimulus with concurrent neglecting of disrupting media form features as the core aspect for not only presence, but a variety of media reception phenomena.

2.3 Related Concepts of Media Use Processes

Media research is a field involving a broad range of disciplines and research traditions, with a variety of stimuli and methods. Since processes of media use seem to be inherently complex, they have fertilized not only diverse theorizing on presence, but also on different other aspects of media use. We will now briefly review several media use concepts adjacent to presence: flow, immersion, involvement, narrative engagement, and transportation.

2.3.1 Immersion

Immersion can be defined as the "degree to which a virtual environment submerges the perceptual system of the user" (Biocca & Delaney, 1995). Especially virtual reality systems are able to effectively block out the real environment with goggles, headphones, and gloves (Biocca & Levy, 1995). Lombard and Ditton illustrate that this property of VR can create experiences that go well beyond, for example, the experience of reading a book, because it is as if "this book has stretched in all directions and wrapped itself around the senses of the reader—the reader is swallowed by the story" (Lombard and Ditton, 1997). The immersion concept is seen as distinct from the presence concept (Slater, Usoh, & Steed, 1995). Slater, Linakis, Usoh, and Kooper (1996) characterize immersion with several technology-based properties, namely the degree to which immersion is extensive (the number of sensory channels), surrounding (the directions from which stimuli can reach the user), inclusive (the blocking-out of real-world cues), vivid (the variety and richness of the sensory information, as proposed by Steuer, 1992), and matching (the user's body movements result in appropriate changes of virtual sensory input). Consequently, Slater and Colleagues (1996) see immersion as "an objective description of what any particular system does provide" (p. 74), and presence as "a state of consciousness, the (psychological) sense of being in the virtual environment, and corresponding modes of behaviour" (p. 74). Immersion can be seen as a factor of influence for presence, albeit not a direct cause, because there are still "cognitive processes leading from stimuli perception to presence" (Schubert, Friedmann, & Regenbrecht, 2001, p. 267). Research findings show that higher degrees of immersion enhance presence experiences, for example when comparing virtual reality settings with traditional media (Baños et al., 2004; Gorini, Capideville, De Leo, Mantovani, & Riva, 2011).

2.3.2 Narrative Engagement

Busselle and Bilandzic (2008) proposed a detailed model for processing of narratives in a broad range of media. Using a mental models approach, they discuss processes and effects for engagement in narratives, comprehension of narratives, perceived realism, and further phenomena like transportation or identification (Busselle & Bilandzic, 2008, p. 255). Busselle and Bilandzic (2009) further offer a questionnaire instrument to assess narrative engagement. The questionnaire uses the authors' "mental models approach to narrative processing" (Busselle & Bilandzic, 2009, p. 321) and assesses the four dimensions narrative understanding, attentional focus, emotional engagement, and narrative presence. The authors distinguish their concept from, as they put it, other "different aspects of engaging with a narrative" (p. 321), like transportation, identification, presence, or flow. Their process model of narrative engagement proposes that during comprehension of narratives, media users construct mental models to organize the mediated information about "settings, characters, and situations" (p. 322) and comprehend the sense of the mediated information. The model's focus is on information processing, not so much on the circumstances or the media of information delivery. Busselle and Bilandzic (2009) explain that the mental models are constantly updated during processing of the perceived information, and that media users are enabled to comprehend narratives by processes of perspective taking. They detail perspective taking into cognitive perspective taking, empathy, and sympathy. When users focus their attention on comprehension of a narrative, the authors see the possibility for flow and narrative presence to emerge. In a state of flow, focusing on the story is supposed to be experienced as easy, and during presence in the narrative, users are supposed to lose awareness of the real environment, of themselves, and of the course of real-world time. Engaging with narratives is thought to elicit enjoyment, and lead to formation of stronger story-consistent attitudes.

Summed up, the theory on narrative engagement explains this phenomenon of media use as a continuous process of constructing and updating mental models, for which sustained attention allocation on the stimulus is necessary. If attention is diverted by real-world stimuli or by inconsistent aspects in content, narrative engagement should be impaired.

2.3.3 Transportation

Transportation (Gerrig, 1993) or narrative transportation (Green & Brock, 2000) describes that media users who engage in a narrated story can feel themselves being transported, like a traveler on a journey. The user is transported from the "world of origin" to the narrative world, making "some aspects of the world of origin inaccessible" (Gerrig, 1993, pp. 10–11). This transported state should involve attention, imagery, and feelings, so "all mental systems and capacities become focused on events occurring in the narrative" (Green & Brock, 2000, p. 701). As a consequence, the media user neglects certain aspects of the real environment, either physically or psychologically. She can then "experience strong emotions and motivations, even when they know the events in the story are not real" (Green & Brock, 2000, p. 702); the concept predicts that such effects can occur for fictional and non-fictional narratives, which can be delivered by a wide range of media.

Transportation shares with other concepts of media use the significant role attributed to continued attention on stimulus content, while at the same time neglecting real-world stimuli.

2.3.4 Involvement

Research on the concept of involvement has yielded a wide range of conceptualizations and foci of research (Wirth, 2006). In general, involvement can be defined as the frequency of a media user making conscious bridging experiences, connections, or personal references between stimulus content and her own life (Krugmann, 1965; Wirth et al., 2007, p. 512). Involvement effects are described as the result of a voluntary and intentional information-exchange process, and they can be observed on cognitive, affective, conative, or behavioral dimensions (Wirth et al., 2007, p. 512). While some conceptualizations of presence consider involvement as a component of presence (e.g., Witmer & Singer, 1998), we will here follow Wirth et al.'s (Hofer, Wirth, Kuehne, Schramm, & Sacau, 2012; Wirth et al., 2007; Wirth, Hofer, & Schramm, 2012) approach, who define involvement and presence as separate processes. They see involvement as "the *active and intensive processing* of the mediated world", while for presence they see an emphasis on "the experience of 'being' solely within the mediated world" (Wirth et al., 2007, p. 513). Furthermore, Wirth et al. (2007, p. 513) suppose involvement to include "higher forms of information processing, such as thinking about, interpreting, elaborating, appraising, and assigning relevance to the media content". While involvement would still include processes referencing real world information, for example on the user's own biography, presence would include a more distinct detachment from real-world information (Wirth et al., p. 513). States of high involvement, where the user's "concentration and mental capacity are primarily devoted to the media", could then be seen as a facilitating factor for the emergence of presence, because users do not so much process current real-world information, but rather enrich the spatial situation model with media information (p. 513).

As can be seen, even in Wirth et al.'s concept with distinctions between presence and involvement, there is conceptual overlap, especially regarding the role of attention. Both concepts require continuous attention on the stimulus and continuous processing of the presented information: spatial cues need to be perceived and processed for the formation of presence, and perceived content is addressed by the cognitive dimension of involvement with its attentional, inferential, and elaborative components (Wirth et al., 2007, p. 512).

2.3.5 Flow

The concept of flow (Csikszentmihalyi, 1975) assumes that a flow state occurs if there is balance between the difficulty of a task and the skills of an individual engaging in this task. Csikszentmihalyi (e.g., Nakamura & Csikszentmihalyi, 2014) characterizes flow as a state with "intense and focused concentration on what one is doing in the present moment", as "merging of action and awareness", as "loss of reflective self-consciousness", with "a sense that one can control one's actions", "distortion of temporal experience", and "experience of the activity as intrinsically rewarding, such that often the end goal is just an excuse for the process" (p. 240). Recent research on flow offers, for example, further conceptualizations with a focus on video games and media enjoyment (Sherry, 2004), investigates antecedents and individual variables for flow (Jin, 2012) and its relation to presence experiences (Jin, 2011), analyzes neural activation patterns during flow (Klasen, Weber, Kircher, Mathiak, & Mathiak, 2012), or proposes a neuropsychological explanation for the foundation of flow as a cognitive synchronization of attentional and reward networks (Weber, Tamborini, Westcott-Baker, & Kantor, 2009). Common to these concepts is the requirement of sustained attention on the stimulus to maintain the flow state.

2.4 Conclusion: Presence, Related Concepts, and Attention

After this review of different presence theories and an overview over the adjacent concepts of flow, immersion, involvement, narrative engagement, and transportation, it can be concluded that all of these concepts attribute a central role to continued attention on the media stimulus. In most cases, the target of attention is required to be media content, and not form features, technical aspects, or inconsistencies in the stimulus. Several theories use a mental models approach (Wirth et al., 2007; Busselle & Bilandzic, 2008; Liebold et al., 2017), and for the domain of presence, for example Liebold et al.'s (2017) recent approach offers detailed predictions for the interplay between mental model construction, model violation, attention, and presence.

For now, we note that ongoing attention on the media stimulus is indispensable to the formation of presence. In section 5, we will integrate the presented theorizing with further necessary aspects to finalize the rationale of this thesis. These further necessary aspects concern measurement of presence experiences and research on eye-blink behavior, and will be addressed in the two following sections.

3 Presence Measurement

The scope of this thesis is the evaluation of stimulus dependent structure in blinking behavior—caused by attentional and cognitive processes during media use—as an indicator for presence experiences. To justify the use of blinking behavior as a measure, we need to explain how blinking behavior should be related to presence. As we have seen in the previous section, it has been theorized that several attentional and cognitive processes contribute to the formation of presence experiences; such predictions are especially detailed in mental model approaches to the presence phenomenon. Before we discuss the influence of several attentional and cognitive processes to blinking behavior in the next section, and finally relate blinking to presence, we now review several existing presence measures, and will see what standards are to meet for a new measurement approach. Two major distinctions can be made to categorize existing approaches for assessment of presence experiences: (a) a distinction regarding the data source, in this case subjective self-report measures versus objective measures; and (b) a distinction regarding the time of measurement, be it real-time and online measurements, thus accompanying media use, or measurements taken at a single, often post-session moment. In the scope of this thesis, all of these facets are of interest, since an objective, continuous measure is to be related to a subjective, post-session self-report measure. The major distinction in the following presentation of measurement methods will be subjective versus objective measures, and aspects of time of measurement will be discussed within these categories.

We will first have a look at several self-report measures, of which most are post-session questionnaires, and then address inherent, methodological shortcomings of such measures. These reflections will be complemented with considerations on the basic requirements for an objective measure for spatial presence. Following this, we will address several existing approaches for presence assessment by means of objective, instrument-based measurements, and see how their quality has been evaluated in existing research. A comprehensive compendium of subjective and objective measurement approaches for presence, as they existed in 2004, can be found in van Baren and IJsselsteijn (2004).

3.1 Self-Report Measures

When regarding presence as a subjective experience, asking users for self-report ratings of this experience is a straight-forward way of evaluating this experience

(Wirth et al., 2008; Schubert, 2009, p. 164). Such evaluations are commonly collected using survey methods after media use, as is the case for most questionnaire measures.

A large selection of subjective questionnaire instruments has been proposed. Kim and Biocca (1997) suggest a self-report measure that distinguishes the "two factors 'arrival,' for the feeling of being there in the virtual environment, and 'departure,' for the feeling of not being there in the physical environment". Witmer & Singer (1998) created the Presence Questionnaire (PQ) with subscales labeled as involvement/control, natural, auditory, haptic, resolution, and interface quality (p. 233). Schubert, Friedmann, and Regenbrecht (2001) created a questionnaire incorporating "presence, immersion, and interaction factors" (p. 266). Baños, Botella, et al. (2004) propose a questionnaire incorporating scales for assessment of presence and reality judgement. Lombard et al. (2000) propose a questionnaire for spatial presence and social presence with the dimensions social richness, realism, transportation, immersion, social actor within the medium, and medium as social actor. Researchers Slater, Usoh, and Steed used a short questionnaire with a conservative measurement approach that does not require ordinal-scaled questionnaire scores to be treated like interval-scaled scores (e.g., Slater, McCarthy, & Maringelli, 1998; Usoh, Catena, Arman, & Slater, 2000). Lessiter, Freeman, Keogh, and Davidoff (2001) introduced the ITC-Sense of Presence Inventory with the four facets sense of physical space, engagement, ecological validity, and negative effects. Hartmann et al. (2015) developed the Spatial Presence Experience Scale (SPES), which is in accordance with the process model for the formation of spatial presence experiences (Wirth et al., 2007), and thus offer a self-report measure with a sophisticated theoretical foundation. The SPES is a refined successor to the MEC-SPQ (Vorderer et al., 2004), which was developed in the same international project as the process model. In accordance with the PMSP model, spatial presence is operationalized with two facets, addressing the aspect of feeling present in the mediated environment (*spatial presence: self-location*), and the aspect of feeling able to act in accordance with the action possibilities offered by the mediated environment (*spatial presence: possible actions*). Further scales assess the presence model's antecedent processes of attention, domain-specific interest, visual-spatial imagery, aspects of the mediated spatial situation model, and involvement. Since the SPES questionnaire is based on the PMSP model, it is the self-report measure of choice in this thesis. The SPES will be discussed in more detail in section 5.

Compared to a large number of questionnaires with only one point of measurement, fewer subjective measures with a higher temporal resolution have been developed, for example video-supported, continuous slider responses for rating the experience (Chung & Gardner, 2012).

3.2 Criticism on Self-Report Measures

While subjective assessment of presence is a very direct and economical way of data collection, researchers have criticized certain shortcomings of this approach. Freeman, Avons, Pearson, & IJsselsteijn (1999), for example, could show that a self-report measure of presence did not deliver stable assessments of the user's presence experiences; the ratings rather seemed to be influenced by prior experience with the same or comparable stimuli, which likely directed the user's attention on different aspects of the stimulus. The authors suggest that because "direct subjective assessment of presence in naive observers is potentially unstable and subject to prior experience and task expectations" (p. 12), self-report measures should be corroborated by objective measurement approaches.

Usoh, Catena, Arman, and Slater (2000) suggest that self-report measures might struggle to differentiate between different reference environments. They compared two different questionnaires' ability to discriminate between a virtual and a real setting, and found that only one questionnaire was able to do so, with a very small effect and only on some of its scales. Usoh et al. suggest that researchers should be careful when comparing measures across different virtual environments.

Slater (2004) even raises the suspicion that "postexperience presence questionnaires alone" (p. 484) might be unable to depict presence experiences in virtual environments reliably. Mimicking questionnaire approaches in presence research, Slater confronted participants with a questionnaire about the made-up construct of yesterday's colorfulness, and found relations between variables that are typically also observed in research with presence questionnaires. Ultimately, Slater suggests that researchers should not rely on self-report ratings of presence alone, because it is not possible to prove a meaningful connection to the actual experience in the mediated environment. Slater and Garau (2007) also call for a corroboration of subjective presence measures with behavioral and psychophysiological measures.

However, even when assuming that questionnaires are perfectly reliable and valid instruments, another challenge for post-session self-report measures is to depict the fluctuations of ongoing presence experiences during media use. Presence theories, such as the model by Wirth et al. (2007), predict fluctuations of presence, in this case as a binary state: either the user is in a state of presence, or he is not. Even when treating presence as a binary state—thus circumventing the problem of how to assess different intensities of presence—it is not perfectly clear how exactly users construct their self-reports from the recollection of a given media use situation. Self-report scores may reflect the frequency of transitions into a state of presence, or the duration of presence states as a proportion of the overall media use duration, or an especially memorable instance of the media experience (see Bacherle, 2015, pp. 130–140, on the formation of post-reception user judgments). Apart from that, while a summative score for a given interval may yield an estimate of overall presence experiences, it would certainly fail to indicate when exactly during media use presence occurred, and when it did not. Especially in the domain of interactive stimuli, structural aspects or "patterns of the user-media-interaction that unfold over the course of time" (Brill, Jonsson, Magnusson, & Schwab, 2016, p. 184) can be more informative than a measure reflecting the period of interaction as a whole, and serve researchers to gain "deeper insight into the mental processing of interactive media" (p. 192).

Subjective measures that aim at a more fine-grained description of the media use process, such as repeatedly presented short scales or continuous slider responses, necessarily interrupt the "unmediated" media experience, and thus the state of presence (Liebold et al., 2017). For mid-session assessments, but also for the use of distracting secondary tasks, careful timing of interruptions could be planned, but in any case, these measures rely on recall of the previous experience from memory, and are thus potentially prone to memory effects and response biases.

An example for the importance of a measure's ability to portray dynamic process features of media use unobtrusively can be found in research on a related concept of media use, namely narrative transportation. Bezdek and Gerrig (2017) analyzed modulation of attentional focus in viewers of suspenseful movie segments. By means of secondary task reaction times and cued recall of movie stills, they found that viewers directed more attention towards the stimulus during highly suspenseful scenes, providing "evidence for changes in attentional tuning as people view film narratives" (p. 60). This is in line with neuropsychological research results (Bezdek, Gerrig, Wenzel, Shin, Pirog Revill, & Schumacher, 2015), where it has been found that neural processing of peripheral cues decreased during suspenseful moments of movies, whereas processing of central stimuli increased at the same time. For a detailed elucidation of such ongoing, dynamic attention processes, online process measures with appropriate temporal resolution are necessary.

3.3 Objective Measures

Objective measures involve observational measures, and in most cases, technology-assisted methods are used to continuously record indicators for a user's internal state; this higher temporal resolution allows for a more fine-grained analysis of media use processes than post-session questionnaires. Rey, Parkhutik, and Alcañiz (2011) categorize objective measures for presence into behavioral, psychophysiological, and neurophysiological measures (p. 274). Another possibility for classification of measures is whether the focus is on continuous processes during media use, or on measuring indicators during rather discrete events during media use. Several approaches of the latter kind can be found in research on so-called breaks in presence, that is occasions where the user disengages from feeling present in the mediated environment (Slater & Steed, 2000). The focus of the present thesis is on structures in blinking behavior during media use, and thus on behavior during an extended observation period; nevertheless, we will first present findings from breaks in presence research, since it has yielded several objective measurement methods. After that, we will review continuous process measures for presence.

3.3.1 Focus on Discrete Instances

Breaks in presence occur when users do no longer favor the mediated environment in the interpretation of their sensory input (Slater & Steed, 2000). Slater and Steed argue that focusing on breaks in presence, defined as transitions out of a state of presence, allows for a more precise observation of user experiences, whereas transitions into a state of presence are more complicated in assessment. Even if participants could reliably report their transitions into presence, it would only be possible at the cost of immediately terminating the state of presence. In addition, the transitions into presence may occur at different times during media use. On the other hand, if the researcher induces breaks in presence, they can be precisely defined, controlled, and salient transitions from a state of presence "back" to the real world.

Slater, Brogni, and Steed (2003) asked users to explore a virtual environment, and immediately report the occurrence of breaks in presence. Measurements of galvanic skin responses and heart rate changes were analyzed around breaks in presence, and showed reproducible reactions time-locked to these disruptive events.

Rey, Parkhutic, and Alcañiz (2011) evaluate cerebral blood flow velocity in VR users during breaks in presence, and during recovery from breaks in presence. The authors describe that the general rationale for objective measures is the observation of reactions that would be expected if the media content was real, such as a stress response when facing stressful stimuli. If such a reaction can be observed, the conclusion is plausible that the user experienced the stimuli as if they were unmediated, and thus experienced presence. As Slater, Lotto, Arnold, and Sanchez-Vives (2009) phrase it, presence can be described as "the sense of being there signalled by people acting and responding realistically to virtual situations and events" (p. 193).

Liebold, Brill, Pietschmann, Schwab, and Ohler (2017) propose a cognitive model for the explanation of breaks in presence, and see breaks in presence as "special cases of orienting responses" (Liebold et al., 2017, p. 19). They first identified externally valid types of breaks in presence for the domain of video games. These breaks in presence were implemented in a commercial video game, and several behavioral and psychophysiological measures were analyzed during occurrences of breaks in presence: blinking behavior, electrocardiogram (ECG) for calculation of heart rate variability, electromyogram (EMG) of trapezius and corrugator, and skin conductance responses (SCR). Results show that half of the types of breaks in presence elicited the hypothesized responses in line with the orienting response assumption: SCR responses, cardiac responses, and longer inter-blink intervals for those breaks in presence "with strong psychophysiological responses" (Liebold et al., 2017, p. 21). The delayed occurrence of blinks after a break in presence is assumed to reflect blink inhibition during an orienting response. Measures of EMG were found to be less informative. The authors conclude that while not all orienting responses will lead to a break in presence, most breaks in presence induced in this study could nevertheless be seen as a result of orienting responses. The findings underline the importance of a cognitive perspective on media use processes and the usefulness of a mental models approach (Liebold et al., 2017, pp. 22–23).

Comparable efforts have been made in research on the processing of narratives, where it can be assumed that inconsistencies, such as unknown or surprising aspects of the narrative, can affect situation models (Valtin, Liebold, Pietschmann, & Ohler, 2011). Sukalla, Shoenberger, and Bolls (2016) address such instances of inconsistency from a process-oriented perspective on narrative engagement. They used heart rate and skin conductance measures to analyze orienting responses towards narrative surprise structure. Orienting responses were then related to the level of narrative engagement to gain insights into cognitive processing of narratives.

For the media use phenomenon of flow, Núñez Castellar, Antons, Marinazzo, and van Looy (2016) investigated attentional engagement of video game users. The researchers used a secondary task paradigm, and found converging evidence from behavioral and electroencephalogram (EEG) measures indicating that in a state of flow, more attentional resources need to be re-allocated from the game to the secondary task stimulus. This re-allocation was observable as longer reaction times towards secondary task stimuli, and co-occurred with distinct EEG activity. Another approach to objective, online flow measurement in video games comes from Weber, Huskey, Craighead, and Terrazas (2016), who also found prolonged reaction times towards secondary task stimuli, and conclude that in a state of flow, attention is highly focused on the media stimulus.

3.3.2 Focus on Continuous Intervals

As has been described in the introduction of this section, research on breaks in presence focuses on discrete events during the media experience, namely the transitions out of a state of presence. The following approaches for objective measurement do not focus primarily on single instances during media use, but on continuous periods of media use. To this end, the whole duration of media use, or at least longer intervals, are observed. This widening of the scope of observation, a "bird's eye view" (Magnusson, 2005), is important for this thesis project, because it better allows for the investigation of structural aspects of behavior. While these periods of media use should in theory include breaks in presence, their influence on these measurement approaches is usually not discussed.

Process-oriented presence research could show that several objectively measured variables vary depending on the current media content; for example Brogni, Vinayagamoorthy, Steed, and Slater (2006) observed users in a virtual environment, and found changes in heart rate between different phases of the experiment. If such variations show reactions towards virtual stimuli that could also be expected for real stimuli, the reactions can be interpreted in the sense of behavioral realism (Slater, Lotto, Arnold, and Sanchez-Vives, 2009). A behavioral realism approach has also been used in the interpretation of postural responses or bodily sway, which have been suggested as an objective measure for presence (Freeman, Avons, Meddis, Pearson, & IJsselsteijn, 2000; IJsselsteijn, Ridder, Freeman, Avons, & Bouwhuis, 2001). In a series of studies, effects of screen size, stereoscopic presentation, and image motion on postural responses and subjective self-report measures were observed. Results of the first study show that stereoscopic presentation elicited greater postural responses and higher subjective ratings of presence (Freeman, Avons, Meddis, Pearson, & IJsselsteijn, 2000); however, on an individual level, there was no correlation between subjective and objective measures. In the second study (IJsselsteijn, de Ridder, Freeman, Avons, & Bouwhuis, 2001), stereoscopic presentation, but not screen size had an effect on postural responses, leading the authors to a cautious conclusion about the validity of the postural responses measure.

Wiederhold et al. (2001) found correlations between measures for heart rate and skin conductance with presence questionnaire scores in a simulated airplane setting.

A selection of alternative measurement approaches has been evaluated in the international research project around Wirth et al.'s (2007) presence theory. The evaluation results are presented in Böcking et al. (2008) and will be discussed in more detail later in this section. For now, the following overview provides a description of the measures and their theoretical grounding.

The first measure employs a think aloud method. Participants were asked to verbalize their thoughts during media use, thus allowing insights into their cognitive processes (Böcking et al., 2008, p. 358). Participants were considered to be in a state of presence if the expressed thoughts suggested that the participants located themselves in the mediated environment; the frequency of such presence statements was used as an indicator for presence.

Second, eye-tracking was used to quantify attention allocation on the medium in terms of fixation durations (Böcking et al., 2008, pp. 359–360). As Laarni, Ravaja, and Saari (2003) explain, information obtained from eye-tracking can be interpreted in three ways. First, the intensity of attention allocation on the stimulus could possibly reflect the processing of the stimulus, because attention allocated to the stimulus cannot be used to process real-world stimuli. Second, fixations can reveal which media information is paid attention to, and is thus probably being processed. And, third, fixations can indicate whether users are focusing their attention on certain details of the stimulus, or are rather scanning the stimulus cursorily. The study reported by Böcking et al. defined the intense processing of media information, operationalized as longer fixation durations on the stimulus, as a presence indicator.

Third, secondary task reaction time (STRT) was tested (Böcking et al., 2008, p. 360), derived from a limited resources model of attention (p. 360; Lang, 2000). With media use as the primary task, users are asked to also engage in a secondary task, in this case reaction towards a real-world stimulus. The longer reaction times for the secondary task are, the more attentional resources should have been directed to the medium (Böcking et al., 2008, p. 361). As Böcking et al. concede, such a measure may not be exclusively indicative for attention, since involvement processes could also cause prolonged reaction times. Böcking et al. (2008, p. 361) argue that their theory considers both attention and involvement as antecedents of presence, and prolonged response times could either way be interpreted as a result of more presence experiences. The authors assume that more media-absorbed attention should lead to facilitation and longer duration of presence experiences. Ultimately, focusing attention on mediated spatial information should result in more relative relevance of media stimuli compared to rivaling real-world stimuli, thus leading to presence (pp. 361–362).

Fourth, functional magnetic resonance imaging was related to subjective presence measures (Böcking et al., 2008, p. 362). Baumgartner et al. (Baumgartner et al., 2006; Böcking et al., 2008, p. 362) proposed three possibilities to relate fMRI measurements to presence experiences: by measuring activity in brain areas related to (a) emotional involvement, (b) to processing of spatial information, or (c) to control of experience and behavior.

Two additional studies that related spontaneous eye-blink behavior to media use phenomena are especially relevant in the scope of this thesis: Bacherle (2015) investigated blinking as an indicator for narrative engagement and transportation in movie audiences, and Nomura, Hino, Shimazu, Liang, and Okada (2015) investigated blinking as an indicator for transportation experiences in recipients of comedy performances. These studies will be presented after we have established the theoretical and empirical foundation for blinking behavior (section 4).

Evidently, researchers have investigated a series of possible objective indicators for presence and other phenomena of media use. Using these indicators, researchers can gain access to the underlying processes of the phenomena of interest; due to conceptual limitations, subjective measures are unable to provide this degree of access. However, objective measures are not free from conceptual limitations, either. Such limitations can result from the complex nature of human experiencing during reception of complex, natural stimuli; after all, we have addressed nothing but a fraction of the body of research on media use in the theory section of this thesis. Three conceptual limitations should be discussed here: first, attention is modeled as a necessary, but not sufficient condition for the emergence of presence; second, attention is modeled as a necessary, but not sufficient condition for the emergence of other reception phenomena, as well; and third, media users will probably experience not only one reception phenomenon in an experimental session.

3.3.2.1 Attention as a Necessary, but Not Sufficient Condition for Presence

Conceptualizations of spatial presence, such as the model by Wirth et al. (2007), demand continuous attention allocation on the stimulus, so mediated spatial information can be perceived and processed as an antecedent of presence. However, once attention has been directed to the stimulus and a spatial situation model has been formed, presence can occur, but it will not do so necessarily; it is still possible that, again referring to Wirth et al.'s (2007) model, the testing of perceptual hypotheses does not favor the mediated spatial situation model, and presence does not occur. Further, as Liebold et al. (2017) have shown, attention on the stimulus does not necessarily lead to presence, because attention could also be attracted by media content inconsistencies, or by interfering formal features. Strictly speaking, the mere provision of attentional resources to the medium alone will hardly be an indicator for presence, as long as further features of media form and content remain unconsidered. As can be seen from this suggested relation between attention and presence, a definite conclusion of the kind "if and only if an individual continuously allocates attention to a media stimulus, then the individual experiences presence" is not supported by theory. For such a conclusion, it would be necessary that attention on a media stimulus always and only leads to presence, so one is able to infer the current existence of presence from the current existence of attention. Since attention on a stimulus may or may not lead to a state of presence, inferences of this kind seem problematic.

This inference problem is rarely addressed in presence research. To increase the indicatory capabilities for attentional processes as a presence measure, it would be beneficial to use more detailed assumptions on the nature of allocated attention. For example, Liebold et al. (2017) have made such assumptions on presence and attention with respect to orienting responses. In this thesis, we detail our assumptions by considering structure in ongoing attention allocation. As we have seen in the previous section on presence theories, presence is conceptualized as a process phenomenon unfolding over time during media use; it thus seems reasonable to observe processes of attention in their unfolding over time, as well. Other research on attention towards continuous, natural stimuli, namely studies on attentional inertia in TV research, has shown that the longer attention is allocated on TV content, the higher is the probability that viewers will keep their attention allocated to the TV, probably due to their cognitive processing of interesting content (e.g., Anderson, Alwitt, Lorch, & Levin, 1979; Anderson & Lorch, 1983). It could be interpreted that the duration of ongoing attention allocation on the medium—and thus the proportion of attention allocation relative to the whole media use duration—already is of informative value. Why sustained attention allocation could become evident as structured blinking behavior will be detailed further in section 4.

3.3.2.2 Attention Is Not Exclusively a Part of the Presence Concept

As has been detailed in the previous section on presence theories, sustained attention allocation is not only seen as an important component of presence, but also of other reception phenomena, such as involvement, narrative engagement, and transportation. By neglecting possible interdependencies between these media use phenomena, researchers would also neglect that changes in attention allocation could not only indicate changes in presence processes, but also in, for example, flow, involvement, or transportation. This means that inferences based on attentional processes alone will hardly be indisputably attributable to presence.

3.3.2.3 Participants in Presence Studies Will Most Likely Not Only Experience Presence

As has been detailed in section 2, the diverse reception processes in themselves are most likely not disjoint; there rather exists considerable conceptual overlap between different reception processes, especially regarding the role of attention. When using natural stimuli, presence will probably not occur isolated during media use: for example, narratives might induce involvement, narrative engagement, or transportation, and in video game settings, flow experiences might result from gameplay. Strictly speaking, attention on a stimulus may or may not lead to presence, and at the same time may or may not lead to other, more or less presence-related phenomena of media use. It can be assumed that the respective phenomena do not occur isolated in experiments, but are rather just measured separately and isolated in most studies, while other possible reception processes are neglected. For the presence domain, comparably few studies simultaneously assess more than one concept, as for example in Jin (2011). Unfortunately, due to the limiting frame of the present thesis, we will also provide an incomplete consideration of reception processes, and will only focus on the relation between attentional or cognitive processes and presence.

As a summary, it can be concluded from these challenges that attentional processes as a measurement approach for presence are not without limitations, either. However, other research domains in psychology face such limitations, as well, and gathering more knowledge on attentional processes should nonetheless advance our understanding of the nature of presence processes during media use.

In principle, this attention problem seems to resemble the problem of emotion specific measurements of autonomous responses in emotion research: for example, a physiological, autonomic measure alone, such as electrodermal activity, is in most cases no specific indicator for a certain basic emotion. Nevertheless, this has not hindered emotion researchers to collect an enormous body of evidence, and has for example led to suggestions to combine several psychophysiological measures to infer a participant's emotional state (e.g., Collet, Vernet-Maury, Delhomme, & Dittmar, 1997). The present thesis intends to add to the body of research by focusing on structural aspects of blinking behavior during media use. To this end, the predictive quality of blink indicators needs to be evaluated; the next subsection presents pertinent research, and addresses how objective measures can be related to established self-report measures.

3.3.3 Assessing the Quality of Objective Measures

As an example for the evaluation of alternative presence measurement approaches, we will now review research by Böcking et al. (2008) that relates four different objective indicators to self-report scores of the MEC-SPQ presence questionnaire (Vorderer et al., 2004; Wirth et al., 2008).

The MEC-SPQ—and its recent successor, the SPES questionnaire (Hartmann et al., 2015)—are a result of the MEC (Measurement, Effects, Conditions) research project on presence (Wirth et al., 2007). During creation and validation of the PMSP process model (Wirth et al., 2007), the project partners conducted a series of evaluation studies for alternative presence measures. Four different measurement methods (think aloud, secondary task reaction times, eye-tracking, and fMRI) were compared to MEC-SPQ scores across seven different media environments with varying immersive capabilities: an internally and an externally valid version of each linear text, hypertext, and virtual reality, and an internally valid film condition. For each media environment, different conditions were designed as mediated environments supporting lower or higher presence experiences, either by manipulating the instruction and/or by varying the amount of spatial cues (Böcking et al., 2008, pp. 363–364). The internally valid stimulus depicted a virtual Mozart museum, and different manipulations were applied to create the respective versions. For the (a) linear text condition, three conditions were created with either less spatial cues in the text, more spatial cues in the text, or more spatial cues in the text with an additional instruction to imagine the described environment as carefully as possible. For the (b) hypertext condition, the ratio of text length to picture size was manipulated, and navigation style was either artificial or natural by clicking on the images. For (c) film and (d) virtual reality stimuli, field of view was manipulated. For the externally valid stimuli, the fields of view of (b) hypertext, (c) film and (d) virtual reality were manipulated. For the (a) linear text, participants were either instructed to read the text with a very critical attitude, or in a normal fashion, so a varying degree of suspension of disbelief would probably influence presence experiences (Böcking et al., 2008). In addition, control groups were tested without application of a secondary measurement method, so the methods' influence on presence experiences could be evaluated (Böcking et al., 2008).

To assess the secondary measures' applicability, several aspects of the secondary methods were evaluated: convergent validity with MEC-SPQ scores, sensitivity, obtrusiveness, and robustness.

For the criterion of convergent validity, or the degree to which the new objective measures and an established subjective measure are comparable in their measurements, participants were pooled across all experiments into groups for the respective secondary measure. These groups were then split into tertiles based on their scores on the MEC-SPQ's scale *spatial presence: self-location*, which is supposed to represent the user's experience of being physically present in the mediated environment (Böcking et al., 2008, p. 366). Using these tertiles, the secondary measures were then correlated to presence questionnaire scores.

To assess the criterion of sensitivity, or the degree to which the measures are able to detect different magnitudes of presence experiences, the questionnaire results were again used as the standard. It was assumed that the MEC-SPQ's five-point Likert scales are appropriate to differentiate between lower and higher levels of presence; the secondary measures needed to meet this standard, as well. To this end, the effect sizes d resulting from comparisons of presence scores between low and high presence conditions were compared to the respective effect sizes of the secondary measures (Böcking et al., 2008, p. 366).

When compared with traditional, post-session questionnaire methods, secondary measurements face the additional challenge of obtrusiveness: Because they are not just administered after the experimental session, but in most cases rather take place during presentation of the stimulus, it is important that they do not interfere with presence experiences. Especially for measures such as fMRI, it is evident that some measurement methods can make it challenging for media users to overlook the real environment. Böcking et al. (2008, pp. 366–367) examined each measure except fMRI for the degree to which application of the measurement method reduced the participants' presence experiences.

To assess the robustness of secondary measures, the correlations between secondary measures and SPSL scores were compared across the different media environments. Due to technical difficulties, robustness could not be assessed for the eye-tracking method (Böcking et al., 2008, p. 367).

For each secondary measure, it is important to derive theoretically grounded indices for the subsequent comparison with established questionnaire scores. We will now have a closer look at Böcking et al.'s (2008) elaborations on two of the four secondary measures: eye-tracking and secondary task reaction time (STRT). The rationale for these measures considers attentional processes during media use and is thus especially relevant in the scope of this thesis.

For the use of eye-tracking as a secondary presence measure, Böcking et al. (2008, pp. 369–370) present existing research suggesting that gaze durations or fixation times allow inferences about what is processed by a user's cognitive system, and on how deeply it is processed. It was assumed that longer fixation times on the stimulus indicate stronger presence experiences, because they would indicate a more intense attention allocation, and a more thorough processing of spatial information (p. 361). The authors acknowledge that fixation times might well be influenced by further aspects of media form and content, and according to their reasoning, a method comparison across different media would probably be more reliable, but also more "fragile" (p. 361) if similar stimuli with differing immersive capabilities were to be compared. While these methodological issues are addressed, it is not clear how the problem of attention being a necessary, but not sufficient condition for presence is treated in the study. Especially with regard to media form aspects, it could be possible that attention on the technical media aspects—and not the media content with its spatial cues—is generating prolonged fixation times.

For STRT, Böcking et al. (2008, p. 361) build on a limited attentional resources model. The STRT paradigm confronts participants with a dual task. For media researchers, an appropriate primary task would be the use of some kind of medium. At the same time, a rivaling secondary task (e.g., reacting to a sound by pressing a button) needs to be attended to, as well. It is assumed that the more attentional capacities are directed towards the primary task, the less attention can be directed to the secondary task; this is mostly inferred from longer reaction times and/or more errors in the secondary task. Recent, refined implementations of this paradigm, using stimulus-congruent and stimulus-incongruent cues with an externally valid stimulus, can be found in a study by Huber, Holl, Liebold, Pietschmann, and Wolfrum (2017). For the presence studies presented by Böcking et al., it is assumed that, in accordance with the PMSP model, attention is a "central antecedent" of presence experiences (p. 361); longer reaction times should thus indicate higher attention allocation on the stimulus, which should in turn facilitate experiences of spatial presence (p. 361). They further argue that if the medium is able to almost completely absorb the user's attentional resources, the acceptance of the medium-as-PERF-hypothesis should occur more likely, and if accepted, it should sustain for a longer period of time. As an additional argument, the authors presume that focusing attention on spatial media cues at the same time reduces the amount of attention directed to the real environment's spatial cues; consequently, media cues would be assigned more "relative relevance" and "dominate the users' experience quality" in a way that lets presence emerge or persist (pp. 361–362).

We conclude the presentation of Böcking et al.'s studies with their evaluation of alternative measures concerning validity, obtrusiveness, robustness, and sensitivity.

For assessment of convergent validity, participants were grouped into low, middle and high presence groups based on their SPSL scores; the alternative measures' concordance with these groups showed to what extent secondary measure and SPSL self-report were in agreement. Neither the think aloud method, eye-tracking, nor secondary task reaction time showed statistically significant correlations with questionnaire scores (correlations between $r = -0.11$ and $r = 0.28$; Böcking et al., 2008, p. 368).

For assessment of obtrusiveness, SPSL presence scores of participants in each secondary measurement group were compared with scores of participants in an otherwise identical control condition; in a factorial design, the partial η^2 of the factor secondary measurement was used as an indicator for obtrusiveness (Böcking et al., 2008, pp. 366–367). While fMRI was not assessed in this respect due to the unique setting in which these measurements were taken, the other measures were found to be not obtrusive (think aloud method: Cohen's $d = 0.00$ to 0.01; eye-tracking: $d = 0.00$ to 0.03) or only partially obtrusive (STRT: $d = 0.00$ to 0.18; Böcking et al., 2008, p. 370).

Of the secondary measures under investigation, only the think aloud method was found to be robust across different media environments, with correlations to SPSL scores of $r = 0.10$ to 0.12 (Böcking et al., 2008, p. 371). Because eye-tracking and fMRI were not analyzed, only the different implementations of STRT were left to be assessed, which proved to be not robust across media environments. Correlations to SPSL scores were found to be $r = -0.30$ to 0.41 for an auditive secondary task, $r = -0.42$ to 0.10 for a visual secondary task, and $r = -0.33$ to 0.45 for a combined auditive and visual secondary task (Böcking et al., 2008, p. 371).

The examination of sensitivity across measures yielded mixed results (Böcking et al., 2008, p. 369). Only the think aloud method for the virtual reality stimulus (Cohen's $d = 0.24$; SPSL: $d = 0.03$), and STRT for an auditive secondary task with a text stimulus as primary task proved to be sensitive (Cohen's $d = 0.41$;

SPSL: $d = 0.56$) when using externally valid stimulus material. For the internally valid stimuli, only eye-tracking with the hypertext stimulus was determined to be "hardly sensitive" (p. 369; Cohen's $d = 0.19$; SPSL: $d = 0.48$). All other measures were determined to be "not sensitive" (four measures) or "unusable" (three measures).

Overall, Böcking et al. (2008) draw a very cautious conclusion about the investigated measures' quality, and state a general lack of validity: only fMRI showed acceptable validity, but at the cost of high obtrusiveness and low robustness. The other measures—think aloud, eye-tracking, and STRT—showed in part higher robustness and lower obtrusiveness, but lacked validity and sensitivity. Böcking et al. (2008) nevertheless encourage researchers to further investigate the matter, for example with different objective indicators (p. 375).

With the foundation for presence theory and measurement established in sections 2 and 3, we will now in detail discuss blinking behavior in the next section, see how eye-blinks are influenced during media use, and thus address further theoretical foundations for this thesis.

4 Blinking Behavior

In order to use spontaneous eye-blink behavior as a presence measurement, it is necessary to explicate the mechanisms that should qualify blinking as an indicator for internal processes, so a link can be hypothesized between presence experiences and stimulus-dependent structure in blinking behavior. After we have established a theoretical and methodological background for presence in sections 2 and 3, we will now review a body of research constituting the blinking-related theoretical foundations for this thesis. To do so, we will first define what eye-blinks are in general, and spontaneous eye-blinks in particular, and then discuss factors of influence for blinking behavior. We will then review research that shows how the functions of spontaneous eye-blinks go well beyond their basic, eye-physiological function, and will see that blinking is much more than a random, ubiquitous process.

Since spontaneous eye-blinks (SEB) have gained considerable scholarly attention from a broad range of researchers, such as "psychologists, neurologists, psychiatrists, optometrists, and ophthalmologists" (Cruz, Garcia, Pinto, & Cechetti, 2011, p. 33), the studies discussed here cover a broad range of disciplines, research questions, paradigms, and methods of data acquisition. There are several possibilities to organize this body of research: studies can see alterations of blinking behavior as causes or effects of other internal processes, they can observe either mere blink frequencies or blink timing and structure, they can observe blinks in trial-based paradigms or with continuous stimuli, and they can focus on foundational research or applied research. After first describing research findings about the basics of blinking behavior, the presented studies will be grouped into two domains: research that sees blinks as (a) interfering with processes of perception or cognition, so it would be adaptive to inhibit blinks during such processes, or (b) research that sees blinks as integral parts of processes of perception or cognition. To date, there seems to be no definitive scientific consent as to if one of these two approaches holds exclusively true and how exactly internal processes are intertwined with blinking. It exceeds the scope of this thesis to determine if one of these positions, or even both, are correct. Nevertheless, both positions can contribute to the aim of this thesis: blinks would be informative if (a) structure in blinking behavior resulted from inhibitory processes during sustained attention allocation on stimulus content, but also if (b) structure in blinking behavior reflected sustained attention on and cognitive processing of stimulus content. We will review research suggesting that attentional processes during stimulus intake on the one hand, and cognitive processes during stimulus processing on the other hand, cause structural variations in blinking behavior. In addition to research on these two positions, some studies will be presented that relate alterations in blinking behavior to certain developmental and cognitive deficiencies, being another hint to the interdependence between blinking and mental processes.

4.1 Characterizing Blinking Behavior

4.1.1 Physiology

The visual sensory system is the most complex and most advanced human sensory system (Gerrig & Zimbardo, 2016). As Gerrig explains, the visual system allows organisms to discover distant prey or hunters, and enables humans to perceive and properly act upon changes in their environment (p. 119). The perception process can be organized into sensory processes, perceptual organization, and identification or recognition of objects (p. 112). The visual system provides the organism with a retinal image as a proximal stimulus that represents an actual, distal stimulus, such as a remote object (p. 114). This proximate stimulus is then transduced by sensory receptors into nerve impulses, which can be further processed by neural systems (p. 119), and, supported by bottom-up and top-down processes, enable humans to perceive for example the own body's motion in space, the motion of other objects, and spatial depth (pp. 142–150). Until the proximate stimulus is present on the retina, light reflected or emitted from the distal stimulus needs to pass several components of the eye. First, light passes the outer barrier of the eye, the cornea. From anterior to posterior, the cornea consists of the epithelium, the Bowman's membrane, the stroma, the recently discovered Dua's layer (Dua, Faraj, Said, Gray, & Lowe, 2013), the Descemet's membrane, and the endothelium (National Eye Institute, 2016a; see Figure 1). Light further passes the liquid-filled anterior eye-chamber, the pupil as the opening in the iris, the lens, and the vitreous humor, before it incides onto sensory receptors on the retina (National Eye Institute, 2012, 2016a).

The cornea is the barrier between the outer world and the anterior chamber, and together with the chamber's fluid, the transitional zone from air over cornea to fluid contributes the major proportion of the eye's refractive power (Olsen, Arnarsson, Sasaki, Sasaki, & Jonasson, 2007; Sayegh, 1996). Together with the lens, the cornea forms a sophisticated optical system, wherein each component compensates for aberrations introduced by the other component (Artal &

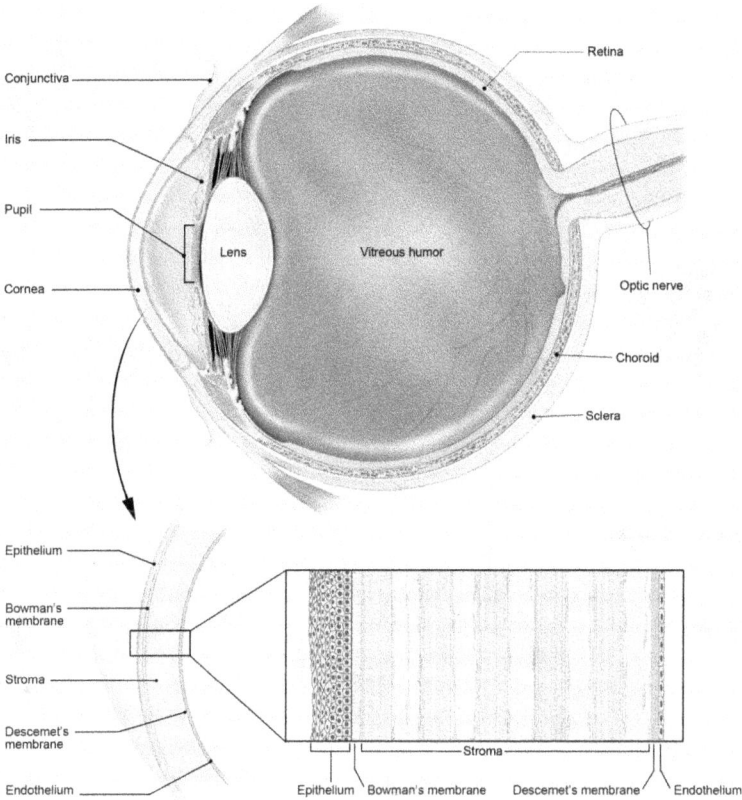

Figure 1. Eye anatomy.
Source: Picture courtesy of the U.S. National Eye Institute (NEI, 2016a; CC BY 2.0). Picture has been cropped and resized.

Guirao, 1998). At its rim, the cornea adjoins the conjunctiva, which is folded inwards into the eye-socket and covers the inner eyelids. The soft conjunctiva tissue provides mucin components for the tear film, and forms—together with the cornea—a sophisticated defense mechanism against bacterial and viral penetration (Rolando & Zierhut, 2001). While tear fluid is also present in the conjunctiva's inner folds, the fluid is only present in form of a tear film on the surface of the eyeball in the palpebral fissure (Mishima, 1965), that is the eye-ball's surface that is not covered by the eye-lids. Different components of tear fluid are produced in

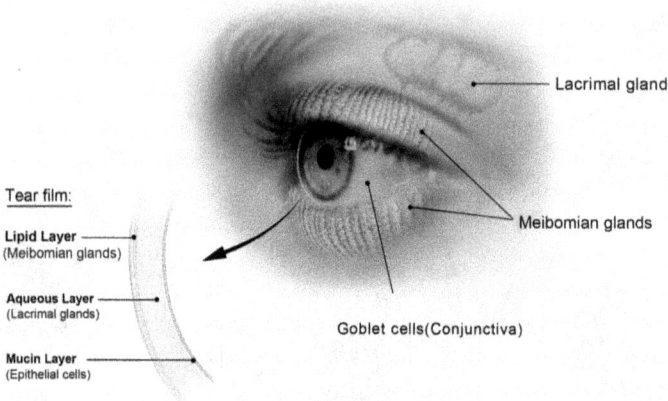

Tear film:

Lipid Layer
(Meibomian glands)

Aqueous Layer
(Lacrimal glands)

Mucin Layer
(Epithelial cells)

Lacrimal gland

Meibomian glands

Goblet cells(Conjunctiva)

Figure 2. Tear glands and tear film.
Source: Picture courtesy of the U.S. National Eye Institute (NEI, 2016b; CC BY 2.0). Picture has been cropped and resized.

the lacrimal glands, meibomian glands, epithelial cells of the ocular surface, and goblet cells of the conjunctiva (Johnson & Murphy, 2004, pp. 456–458; see Figure 2).

4.1.2 Definition of Eye-Blinks

Eye-blinks can be described as "a fast eyelid movement that closes and opens the palpebral fissure" (Cruz, Garcia, Pinto, & Cechetti, 2011, p. 29), and are commonly distinguished into three different types of eye-blinks: The first type, voluntary blinks, are controlled by will. The second type, involuntary reflex blinks, can occur after "different trigeminal, visual, and acoustic stimuli" (Cruz et al., 2011, p. 29). In a natural situation, such stimuli could be objects that approach the eye or even touch the eye; in laboratory experiments, such stimuli can be, for example, an air puff administered to the eye surface, or electrical stimulation of the supraorbital nerve (Van der Werf, Brassinga, Reits, Aramideh, & Ongerboer de Visser, 2003). The third type, which is of interest in the scope of this thesis, are involuntary, spontaneous eye-blinks, which are characterized as an "unconscious, transient, or brief closure of both upper eyelids that occurs in a highly symmetrical and coordinated fashion in the absence of any evident stimulus" (Cruz et al., 2011, p. 29).

4.1.3 Functions of Eye-Blinks

The physiological function of spontaneous eye-blinks is described as the maintenance of clarity of vision and tear film stability (Cruz, Garcia, Pinto, & Cechetti, 2011). The eyeball is protected by a "tear film composed of lipid, aqueous, and mucin layers" (Tsubota & Nakamori, 1993, p. 584) which is typically six to ten micrometers thick (Doane, 1980, p. 507), although Johnson and Murphy (2004) question such numbers due to possible measurement issues. The tear film is distributed over the ocular surface by blinking (Tsubota & Nakamori, 1993, p. 584). In addition, blinks support tear fluid production by releasing products of the meibomian glands, and support tear clearance by nasolacrimal drainage (Johnson & Murphy, 2004, p. 461). Tear film integrity is crucial for a healthy cornea, since secretory mucins protect the surfaces of eyeball and lids from damage during rapid eye-movements (Johnson & Murphy, 2004, p. 452), and bind pathogens and foreign substances (p. 453). Because the transparent cornea cannot rely on blood vessels for nutrient supply and disposal of metabolites, tear film needs to provide these functions, as well: water in the aqueous layer of the tear film "contains numerous electrolytes, proteins, peptide growth factors, vitamins, anti-microbials, cytokines, immunoglobulins, and hormones" (p. 453).

In theory, the corneal tear film would break up after about 15 to 30 seconds due to evaporation (Doane, 1980, p. 507), calling for a physiological necessary blink rate of about four blinks per minute. However, spontaneous eye-blink rates in healthy individuals are reported to be much higher. In a comprehensive review, Doughty (2001) reports mean blink frequencies from 22 studies employing different measurement methods and observation intervals during silent primary gaze conditions. The overall average was 14.5 blinks per minute (minimum: 10 blinks per minute, maximum: 22.4 blinks per minute). These rather high numbers are remarkable in face of the constant effort and loss of visual information inherent to blinking. In addition, eye-blink rates not only differ considerably between individuals, but they also differ systematically within subjects depending on the task at hand. In his review of studies, Doughty (2001) reports mean blink rates from 2.9 blinks per minute during reading to 28.6 blinks per minute during conversation.

Further research finds a large variation of mean spontaneous eye-blink rates. The following list contains several examples for eye-blink rates that have been observed during different tasks:

- 15 blinks per minute under relaxed conditions (Tsubota et al., 1996),
- 54.5 per minute for newscasters on air (Tsubota, Egami, Ohtsuki, & Shintani, 1999, p. 308),
- 12.9 blinks per minute while watching a documentary (calculated from study results; Ousler et al., 2014, p. 871),
- 14.9 blinks per minute for reading on a computer screen and 13.6 blinks per minute for reading on paper (Chu, Rosenfield, & Portello, 2014),
- 15.5 blinks per minute (median) during presentation of a picture and 4 to 11.5 blinks per minute (median) under different reading conditions (Argilés, Cardona, Pérez-Cabré, & Rodríguez, 2015),
- 22.4 blinks per minute while fixating a fixation cross and 27.0 blinks per second while watching excerpts from a TV show (Nakano, Kato, Morito, Itoi, & Kitazawa, 2013),
- 16.8 blinks per minute while watching excerpts from a TV show (Nakano, 2015),
- 2.4 to 31.8 blinks per minute during an experiment with a rapid serial visual presentation task, a cognitive psychology paradigm (Colzato, Slagter, Spapé, & Hommel, 2008),
- 2.4 to 39.2 blinks per minute during fixation of a printed fixation cross (Colzato, Slagter, van den Wildenberg, & Hommel, 2009),
- 1.4 to 14.4 blinks per minute during reading, 8.0 to 21.0 blinks per minute during primary gaze, and 10.5 to 32.5 blinks per minute during conversation (Doughty, 2001),
- 11, 13, 11 and 16 blinks per minute during primary gaze on a neutral wall at four measurement periods during one day (measured during two minutes; Barbato et al., 2000),
- 22 blinks per minute for primary gaze, 10 blinks per minute for reading a book, and 7 blinks per minute for reading on a screen (Tsubota & Nakamori, 1993),
- 13.8 blinks per minute during primary gaze in healthy males (Doughty & Naase, 2006),
- and 17 blinks per minute at rest, 26 during conversation and 4.5 while reading a text on paper (Bentivoglio et al., 1997).

While these findings are not all comparable, for example due to different implementations of a resting condition or different observation intervals, they nevertheless show the large variability even in mean values of blink rate.

4.1.4 Phases of an Eye-Blink

Malmstrom, Rachofsky, and Weber (1977) provide a literature review on differ-ent components of the blinking process, and describe the coordinated movement patterns of eye lids and eye ball during a blink. Concerning movement of the eyeball, they cite Yarbus (1967) who describes an eye-blink as being preceded by a "slight upward rotation of the eyeballs". However, newer research indicates that eyeball movement during the eye-blink sequence is more complex, and under natural viewing conditions does not show an upward rotation (Doane, 1980), but rather a downward and medial rotation (or a rotation towards the eyeball's nat-ural resting position, if the point of fixation is located off-center). This rotational movement is faster than the eyelid's closing (Riggs, Kelly, Manning, & Moore, 1987). In addition, a slight inward retraction of the eyeballs of "less than 1mm" (Riggs, Kelly, Manning, & Moore, 1987, p. 334) can be observed during blinking. The main characteristic of a blink, the rapid movement of the eyelids, has been measured with upper lid velocities of 17 to 20 cm per second, with peaks of over 40 cm per second (Doane, 1980). This rapid movement originates from com-bined actions of the orbicularis oculi muscle (OOM) and the levator palpebral superioris muscle (LPS; Cruz et al., 2011, p. 31), which are in a balance during an open eye resting state. During a blink, initial inhibition of LPS is followed by ac-tivation of OOM and closes the upper lid, supported by passive force from stretched ligaments. At the end of downward movement, which can occur upon or before complete closure of the palpebral fissure, both muscles are relaxed; as the maximum amplitude is reached, LPS is reactivated and OOM remains deac-tivated, resulting in immediate reopening of the eye. If upper and lower lid touch, the maximum of this movement results in a phase of complete eye closure, the "blackout period"; however, the blackout period can also be defined as the period of pupil occlusion. Including the following re-opening process, the total duration of a blink can be up to 200 ms (Yarbus, 1967); the blackout period itself may last 30 ms to 100 ms (Lawson, 1948) or even 100 to 150 milliseconds (Volkmann, 1986, p. 1407), depending on measurement and definition.

4.1.5 Preserving Perception Continuity

In face of the ubiquitous interruptions and modifications of our binocular, visual input by saccades, blinking, focusing and vergence, Volkmann (1986, p. 1413) emphasizes the importance of evolved mechanisms that ensure a stable and per-sistent perception. Such mechanisms enable organisms to distinguish "image motion on the retina that is produced by movements of the eyes and image motion that is produced by movements of external objects" (Volkmann, 1986, p. 1413); these omnipresent mechanisms have the "effect of selectively discarding information that might lead to maladaptive responses" (p. 1413). As Volkmann (1986) states further, especially the blackout period of "100–150 msec" (p. 1407) has a considerably greater luminance change and duration than a typical saccade of only about 50 ms (p. 1407), and should thus pose a significant challenge to neuronal suppression mechanisms. Such mechanisms of visual suppression are an aspect of blinks that has attracted researchers' attention, and numerous studies have moved from treating blinks as mere artefacts to investigating the complex mechanisms around human visual perception during blinking. Nevertheless, blinks in general have received relatively little attention in research for considerable time: in many cases, such as fMRI or EEG studies, blinking is usually an artefact that hinders analysis of very sensitive measures (Shultz, Klin, & Jones, 2011, p. 21270). For example, blinking during fMRI studies causes significant changes in the BOLD signal in different brain areas. While these changes seem to have a signature distinct to eye-blinks, they could nevertheless contaminate fMRI measurements if blinks do not occur balanced across experimental conditions (Hupé, Bordier, & Dojat, 2012).

The necessary steps for a visual suppression mechanism have been detailed by Bonfiglio et al. (2011). From their examination of EEG changes during the course of an eye-blink, they infer three distinct processes that can be observed as typical electrophysiological processes in the EEG signal (p. 44): First, short-term memory needs to hold the visual information of the perceived environment prior to the blink. Second, after the blink's blackout phase, the perceived new image of the environment is compared to the representation of the earlier environment in short-term memory; and third, the neural systems recover from this task.

In a series of experiments, researchers Volkmann, Riggs, Ellicott and Moore investigated the mechanisms of visual suppression. Riggs, Volkmann, and Moore (1981) first tried to replicate luminance changes during blinks as an external stimulus, so they temporarily darkened the visual field with the objectively same parameters that characterize a spontaneous eye-blink. Results showed that the three participants in this study perceived the artificial, external blink to be "much stronger" (p. 1075) than a natural blink; to attain subjectively identical ratings, the external blink's luminance change had to be reduced in both magnitude and duration. The authors conclude from these results that neural suppression mechanisms prevent us from perceiving the momentary blackout completely, leading us to perceive the blink's visual effect as "extremely small" (p. 1078). Volkmann, Riggs, Ellicott, and Moore (1982) describe the mechanism as a central neural inhibition "linked primarily to the efferent discharge to close the eye", which, apart from masking the blackout period, also enables us to "[recapture] the visual scene as the eyes reopen" (p. 995).

Bristow, Haynes, Sylvester, Frith, and Rees (2005) further studied the neural correlates of these processes during blinking in an fMRI study, and tried to decompose the involved neural structures into correlates of luminance change, motoric activity, and the actual suppression effect. To do so, they asked participants to insert a fiber-optic light source into the oral cavity, which directly illuminated the retina with light-bursts through the palatine bone (p. 1296). Because the participants wore opaque goggles, interfering luminance changes during the blinking process in a lit environment—which would also influence regular processing of visual input in the neural systems—could be ruled out. Results suggest that a suppression mechanism becomes active along with the blink-eliciting motor signals, and influences different neuronal networks in early visual areas (V3 area), as well as parietal and prefrontal areas (p. 1299). The authors argue that the suppression mechanism during blinking "may indeed share common neural mechanisms" (p. 1299) with the suppression mechanism observed during saccades, and serves the purpose of masking information loss during blinks. However, as findings by Morrone, Ross, and Burr (2005) suggest, the neural mechanisms are indeed not entirely identical, because compression effects that occur in the perception of time and space around saccades do not accompany (at least voluntary) blinks.

Bristow, Frith, and Rees (2005) also used fMRI to search for neural correlates of blinking in the human brain, and identified the V5 area to be supposedly engaged in visual suppression during blinks, whereas a brain area corresponding to the V6A in macaques presumably becomes active to ensure apparent continuity of the interrupted visual input. The V5 or hMT+ area was also identified in fMRI research by Tse, Baumgartner, and Greenlee (2010), who suggest that it may play a role in masking the image motion caused by microsaccades and eye-blinks. Nakano (2015) sees decreased activity of the superior colliculus as the neural correlate of visual suppression during blinking (pp. 57–58).

It seems that natural selection has produced sophisticated mechanisms to prevent distraction of the perceptual system during the rapid visual changes of eye-blinks: despite the momentary blindness caused by the transient closure of our eyes, we are able to perceive an apparently continuous stream of visual information. However, this does not change the fact that no update of visual information can be provided by the visual system during blinks. We will later review findings suggesting that further, highly automated mechanisms modulate the timing of blinks to minimize loss of relevant information. However, in order to deepen our understanding of spontaneous eye-blinks, the following three sub-sections will first address a common example of blinking dysfunction, the mechanisms of blink elicitation in the organism, and evolutionary aspects of blinking.

4.1.6 Blinking During VDU Work

The importance of spontaneous eye-blinks becomes most evident when blinking fails to fulfill its physiological function; in this case, ocular symptoms occur because the cornea is not provided sufficiently with water and nutrients. Especially the prevalence of conditions such as dry eye when working in front of computer screens (or video display units, VDU) has directed research to the causes for such physiologically insufficient blinking. Results show that two major reasons can be identified for ocular symptoms: reduction of spontaneous eye-blink rate, and proportion of incomplete blinks. Especially the phenomenon of incomplete blinks has received attention, because despite apparent satisfaction of ocular needs, the tear film may not be distributed properly across the whole ocular surface; this effectively doubles the time for tear evaporation for some areas of the ocular surface, and thus makes tear film break-up more likely (McMonnies, 2007).

Researchers Argilés, Cardona, Pérez-Cabré, and Rodríguez (2015) compared blink rates and percentage of incomplete blinks under six different reading conditions with a baseline condition; they found that reading in general reduced spontaneous eye-blink rate significantly, with the magnitude depending on presentation aspects like text size; again, reading on a screen led to more incomplete eye-blinks.

Tsubota and Nakamori (1993) compared conditions of primary gaze, reading a book at table level, and reading on a screen, and found that spontaneous eye-blink rate was lowest for reading on a screen. In addition, the researchers measured the size of the palpebral fissure, because the size of the uncovered ocular surface is relevant for tear film evaporation, and thus formation of dry eye conditions. They found that ocular surface was clearly reduced during reading of a book due to the down-shifted gaze; in contrast, ocular surface during reading on a screen showed a palpebral fissure size comparable to primary gaze, but with a drastically reduced blink rate. The authors conclude that this might pose the main reason for dry eye symptoms during video display work.

As Chu, Rosenfield, and Portello (2014) found, blink rates in their study did not differ drastically for reading of texts on a computer screen (14.9 blinks per minute) or paper (13.6 blinks per minute; $N = 25$ participants, $p = .58$). However, number of incomplete blinks was significantly higher for the screen condition (7.02% for screen, 4.33% for paper, $p = .02$), although no significant correlation was found between incomplete blinks and self-report on ocular symptoms. The authors assume that reduced blink rates found in previous studies might have been caused by different "cognitive demands" (p. 297). Rosenfield, Jahan, Nunez, and Chan (2015) compared blinking while reading texts with low and high cognitive demand on a tablet or in print. They found that blinking was more influenced by nature of the task, and concluded that possibly due to recent enhancements of screen technology, impact of presentation methods was lower.

Since maintenance of tear film integrity is a core function of blinking, it may appear surprising that this vital function is not fulfilled under certain conditions of visual information intake. To investigate the circumstances of this potentially severe dysfunction, several other studies considered not just low-level stimulus properties, but also the nature of the task at hand. Cardona, García, Serés, Vilaseca, and Gispets (2011) compared the impact of different scenarios of VDU use on blinking and relevant medical parameters. By comparing a baseline condition and two video games varying in difficulty, they found that blink rate decreased significantly during the game conditions, while the number of incomplete blinks increased. Tear volume was not affected by the changed blinking behavior, but quality of the corneal tear film was lower than baseline for the slow-paced game, and reduced even more for the fast-paced game. The authors conclude that not only VDU work in itself, but also "the rate at which visual information is presented" (p. 190) determine blinking behavior; however, it should be noted that the games apparently confounded amount of visual information and cognitive load from the game's difficulty. Skotte, Nøjgaard, Jørgensen, Christensen, and Sjøgaard (2006) found for a small sample of 10 participants, but with a sufficient observation duration of 10 minutes, that an active video display task decreased spontaneous eye-blink rate significantly compared to a passive video display task; in addition, putting the screen in a 25° lower position reduced blink rates on average by 13 percent. Change in blink rate for a lowered screen was not significant in another study (Nielsen, Søgaard, Skotte, & Wolkoff, 2008), but an active task again reduced blink rate significantly compared to a passive task. Results further showed blink bursts after completion of the active task, which the authors interpreted as a "compensatory blinking process" (p. 1) following a shift "from periods of high visual and cognitive demand to periods of low visual and cognitive demand" (p. 5). This let the authors suggest to alternate tasks with different cognitive loads during office work in order to support a balanced level of blinking.

The latter findings already point out that blinking behavior is systematically influenced by the nature of a task, and that this influence might go beyond basic stimulus characteristics. Remarkably, the effects of these influences may even interfere with the physiologically necessary functions of blinks. We will get back to such modulating processes after a closer look on the mechanisms that generate the spontaneous blinking behavior in the first place, and an overview about evolutionary aspects.

4.1.7 Blink Generation

Researchers have tried to determine the mechanisms behind elicitation of blinks, and to this end have focused on blink-eliciting neural mechanisms. In a study on this "blink generator", Moraitis and Ghosh (2014, p. 285) asked participants to inhibit their blinks during an auditory stimulus of variable, unpredictable length. The rather short and constant intervals at which blinks occurred after inhibition offset suggested that the blink generator was deactivated during voluntary inhibition; afterwards, it apparently restarted from an off-state and elicited a blink. Other possible assumptions about the modus operandi of the blink generator were not congruent with findings. If the blink generator had been just paused instead of stopped, or if muscular actions had merely counteracted elicited blinks, or if regular blink generator motor commands had been blocked, then the interval of the first blink would have been more variable, because the blink generator would have resumed its action at a random point in its operation (p. 280). The authors also conclude that afferent input from the cornea can be only one of several inputs for the blink generator, because intervals of the first blink did not differ after short periods of inhibition with little tear film evaporation and longer periods of inhibition with more tear film evaporation. As we will see in section 4.2, the interval of the first spontaneous blink was with about five to six seconds on average considerably longer than latencies of spontaneous eye-blinks that occur after, for example, task completion in trial-based paradigms. Further, these findings on voluntary blink inhibition are informative about the nature of the blink generator, but it remains open to what extent alteration of blink timing will occur in media research studies, where active, voluntary inhibition will rarely be enacted.

To establish an animal model of the blink generator, Kaminer, Powers, Horn, Hui, and Evinger (2011) compared spontaneous blinking behavior in rats and humans and found that the temporal organization of behavior shows comparable features. By applying a dopamine agonist or antagonist, Kaminer et al. could show a dopamine dependency of blinking behavior in the rat model. The authors assume that a "blink generator circuit" (p. 11265), involving the spinal trigeminal complex and afferent signals from the cornea, generates spontaneous blinking behavior based on tear film integrity on the cornea; this would result in a mean blink rate of about three to four blinks per minute. Reflex blinks can then be superimposed on this behavior, for example due to irritations of the cornea.

Bentivoglio at el. (1997), who calculated blink rates during resting, reading on paper, and in conversations, also found very similar distributions of inter-blink interval durations in these different conditions, which could be best fit with a log-normal distribution for most data. Oh, Jeong, and Jeong (2012) found in a trial-based experiment that "the occurrence of spontaneous eye blinking has a scale-free, self-similar structure"; this characteristic can be found in timing of other human behavior, as well, for example in heartbeat intervals, walking, tapping, and in response times in cognitive psychology paradigms (p. 11). The authors could find the same temporal organization on different timescales during tasks requiring attention, be it in the range of several seconds, or less than one second.

The very basic blinking behavior created by the blink generator can also be altered by basic ocular movement. When Evinger et al. (1994) investigated the relation between saccadic gaze shifts, head movement, and spontaneous eye-blinks, they found that larger saccadic shifts are predominantly accompanied by eye-blinks; the authors could show that these eye-blinks are indeed of spontaneous nature, and do not occur as a reflex to external stimulation during eye movement. In addition, eliciting a reflex eye-blink facilitated ensuing head movements, which let the authors conclude that the linkage between blinking and gaze shifts is deeply rooted in neuroanatomy. The authors further hypothesize that the structure of the rostral colliculus might be involved, which is supposed to "suppress blinks to protect fixation" (p. 343). Because such neural mechanisms were found in different species, the authors assume that evolution has either preserved this linkage in phylogenesis of different species, or has led to analogous mechanisms, meaning that "the linkage serves an important role for most species" (p. 343).

We can conclude that blinking behavior is generated by certain mechanisms in organisms, and can then be modulated: blinks can be elicited as spontaneous blinks or reflex blinks, and they can be elicited, inhibited or suppressed by means of neural mechanisms. Hence, blinking does not occur at random, but can be subject to external influences; interestingly, some studies find a stable, self-similar structure in blinking behavior, comparable to structure found in other human behavior. This non-random, purposeful variability in blinking behavior could indicate an informative value of blink timing, and—arguing from an evolutionary perspective—one could assume that this variability results from an organism's sensitivity for certain external signals. We use this occasion for a brief evolutionary excursus on blinking in different species and possible social aspects of blinking.

4.1.8 Evolutionary and Social Aspects of Blinking

As the research presented in the previous subsection shows, blinking behavior has a similar temporal organization in humans and rats (Kaminer et al., 2011). With regard to mere blink frequencies across different species, Tada, Omori, Hirokawa, Ohira, and Tomonaga (2013) observed spontaneous blinking behavior in individuals of 71 primate species, and related blink rate to variables such as body size, body mass, and social group size. It should be noted that accuracy of species blink rate estimates and generalizability are possibly limited, because Tada et al. observed only a limited number of individuals for each species; nevertheless, the researchers could replicate findings showing that diurnal primates have a higher blink rate than nocturnal primates (p. 5). In addition, blink rates correlate with a species' typical social group size; based on existing research, the authors propose a possible social function of blinking (pp. 6–8). They support this argument by pointing out the eyes' significant role in social coexistence: some primate species have brightly colored eyelids, clearly signaling closure of the eyes (p. 8), and the very social homo sapiens is the only primate species with a white sclera, greatly enhancing the signaling quality of gazing behavior and eye-related facial expressions (p. 8).

For gazing behavior in humans and primates, researchers have found cross-species similarities in trial-based paradigms, and these findings could be extended to natural video stimuli, as well (Shepherd, Steckenfinger, Hasson, & Ghazanfar, 2010). Shepherd et al. found that macaques paid attention to similar social cues in videos as humans did, and that these attractors of attention could not solely be explained with low-level stimulus features; but different from monkey gaze behavior, humans also directed their attention to the "targets of [a] viewed individual's actions or gaze" (p. 649).

It could be interpreted that gazing behavior seems to be influenced by a species' cognitive abilities, and thus possibly by cognitive processes; if gazing is subject to influences from internal processes, this might apply to blinking behavior, as well. Possible relations between blinking and social functioning have been researched in numerous studies. For example, Kret (2015) suggests the use of other expression systems than facial muscles to study emotion perception, namely gaze behavior, tears, and signals influenced by the autonomous nervous system like pupil dilation or pupil mimicry, blushing, and eye-blinks. Unfortunately, the paper delivers no concrete suggestions as to how and why eye-blinks could be used in this respect. More detailed findings on social functions of spontaneous eye-blinks come from Mandel, Helokunnas, Pihko, and Hari (2014). In a MEG study, they observed brain responses of participants towards video recordings of eye-blinks at normal or reduced speed; brain activity was compared to videos without blinks, but instead two small, moving horizontal bars over eyes, which served to mimic the size and movement of blinking eyelids. Results show that neural responses were reduced for slow-motion videos of bars, but slow-motion eyelids elicited reactions comparable to the videos at original speed. Apparently, the human brain is sensitive for this type of stimulus, and is able to differentiate closing eyelids from identically moving objects; the authors conclude that eye-blinks likely "are socially relevant behavioral events" in social interaction (p. 2580). Results from another study underline a possible social function of eye-blinks: neural changes in response to a videotaped speaker's eye-blinks also occurred in an audiovisual, and thus distracting condition, and measures for the participant's empathy correlated positively with the magnitude of the neural response (Mandel, Helokunnas, Pihko, & Hari, 2015). Another finding with potential social relevance comes from Fukuda (2001), who examined distribution of spontaneous eye-blinks in research on deception. Eye-blinks could be used to distinguish between relevant and irrelevant presented information in a guilty knowledge test. It could thus be hypothesized that blinks may also play a role in the competition between enacting and counteracting of deceptive behavior.

Nakano and Kitazawa (2010) provide another attribution of social function to blinking, especially in face-to-face communication. To mimic such interpersonal interactions, they presented close-up video recordings of a talking actor's face to their participants; participants tended to blink after eye-blinks of the speaker "at the end and during pauses in speech" (p. 577). This effect was not present when participants were presented only the visual or auditory components of the video. The authors propose that entrainment of spontaneous eye-blinks might serve as "a factor that facilitates social interactions in face-to-face conversations", similar to other nonverbal or paraverbal signals like nodding or utterances (p. 581). In a follow-up study, Nakano, Kato, and Kitazawa (2011) further investigated eye-blink entrainment in artificial communication situations, and found that typically developed participants depended on simultaneous input from the eye and mouth regions of the speaker to produce such eye-blink entrainment. Participants diagnosed with autism spectrum disorders, on the other hand, showed no eye-blink entrainment under any experimental condition; the authors conclude that ASD participants might have impaired processing of the facial social cues, which also leads to a lack in eye-blink entrainment.

Ford, Bugmann, and Culverhouse (2010, 2013) even go so far as to regard blinking as a non-verbal communication channel in face-to-face conversations. They hypothesize that blinking could communicate changes in the speaker's mental state, because they found a prevalence for blinks to occur at certain moments in their experimental conversations. They occurred at the beginning and end of the participants' speeches, at the beginning of a new thought process, at the end of the counterpart's speech, and when participants disengaged from fixating their counterpart's face (p. 723). As a result of this experiment, Ford and colleagues created a blinking model for robotic agents, which mimicked a physiologically determined baseline of twelve blinks per minute, and superimposed blinks at the previously identified conversational events.

While occurrence and timing of spontaneous eye-blinks may not necessarily be an explicit signaling system, the social salience of blinks nevertheless suggests that they could be used to infer some kind of information in social interaction. In line with this argument is research on virtual avatars and in robotics, where researchers try to create lifelike artificial agents. For example, a virtual e-learning environment's perceived quality was improved when the participants' avatars depicted their respective user's spontaneous eye-blinks (Dharmawansa et al., 2014): by incorporating eye-blinks as a nonverbal feature, the participants' experience of the virtual environment could be improved, especially with respect to "effectiveness of the communication factors" in a simulated group discussion (p. 237). Cummins (2012) examined blinking and gazing behavior in human dyads, and found that an individual's blinking base rate fluctuated depending on the social interaction, because "co-varying relationships" could be found "not only in the words exchanged, but in the co-varying characteristics of gaze, and even blinking" (p. 22). For the design of avatars, Cummins concludes that an avatar exhibiting an "individual style may ultimately leap across the uncanny valley" (p. 23), while avatar behavior that is modeled to represent an average behavior might be perceived as less lifelike.

Bulling and Roggen (2011) conducted research on how to facilitate human-machine interaction; while existing approaches aimed at detecting, for example, the user's affective state or physical activity, they suggest to consider a person's cognitive context. Using machine learning, they tried to infer a user's cognitive context during watching of pictures from several indicators of ocular activity, including spontaneous eye-blink rate. Pictures from four categories were presented either once or repeatedly, and the context-sensitive algorithm should infer the type of picture from the user's gaze behavior. While the study's theoretical background is scarce, and picture presentation was with up to ten seconds too short to yield usable estimates of spontaneous eye-blink rate, Bulling and Roggen report that the majority of trained computer classifying systems nevertheless incorporated blink parameters into their models. Similar to these findings, Fritz, Begel, Müller, Yigit-Elliott, and Züger (2014) used a series of biosensors (EEG, EDA, and eye-tracking) to assess task difficulty during software development; among others, they used a baseline corrected measure of spontaneous eye-blink rate as input for their machine learning classifier, but unfortunately they do not explicitly report the influence of blinks on the predictions.

4.2 Influences on Blinking Behavior

As the findings presented in section 4.1 show, blinks are not only executed to serve a physiological function. Instead, their timing can deviate significantly from a physiologically necessary behavioral pattern, because blink rates can be both lower and higher than necessary. Blinking apparently depends on the demands of a current task, appears to be a socially salient behavior, and possibly even serves a social function. Blinking can be found in a wide range of species, it is produced by sophisticated neural circuits, and additional neural mechanisms ensure a stable perception of the organism's environment during blinks and other ocular movements. In sum, the sophistication of processes around blinking behavior suggests that blinking is not just a random, arbitrary process, but is subject to systematic influences. We will now review two research positions that try to explain such systematic influences. First, research that suggests that blinks can be inhibited so they do not interfere with processes of perception or cognition, and second, research that takes assumptions one step further, assuming that blinks might serve an active role in neural processing.

4.2.1 Blinking as Interference to Internal Processes

4.2.1.1 Trial-Based Research

We will first discuss findings on blink inhibition from trial-based research paradigms. In such studies, it is of interest if blinks occur during a trial or during inter-trial intervals, and if they occur during a trial, at what time relative to the given task. To gain insights into the structure of blinking behavior, trials and their respective tasks in an experimental paradigm can be segmented into different phases. For example, Oh, Jeong, and Jeong (2012) differentiate trials into phases of stimulus presentation, which "requires a considerable allocation of sustained attention" (p. 10), a pausing phase, and a response phase, which is indicated by an appropriate cue. They found that suppression of spontaneous eye-blinks could be found during phases of stimulus presentation and before responses; after stimulus offset and after responses, blinks occurred with increased probability, sometimes in bursts.

Ohira (1996) found effects of blink distribution in a trial-based semantic priming task. Blinks were suppressed during target presentation, and occurred in bursts after presentation offset. Additionally, higher cognitive load caused by the task was associated with longer blink suppression. Another association was found between blink frequency in bursts and cognitive load, but could not be replicated in a follow-up study. Ichikawa and Ohira (2004) observed spontaneous eye-blinks in a trial-based lexical decision task. They used occurrence of blinking bursts as an indicator for the end of cognitive processing, and found that durations of these processing intervals corresponded to the level of cognitive load that would be expected for the priming task. Siegle, Ichikawa, and Steinhauer (2008) simultaneously observed spontaneous eye-blinks and pupillary responses during cognitive tasks to determine their relations to cognitive load. Results suggest that both measures allow different inferences on current cognitive load: while the authors conclude that blinks "occur during early sensory processing and following sustained information processing", pupil dilation on the other hand indicated "sustained information processing" (p. 679). While the authors instructed participants to blink as little as possible during the task, and thus possibly distorted regular blinking patterns, the moments during trials at which blinks occurred nevertheless revealed an association with cognitive processing, as has also been found in Ohira's (1996) and Ichikawa and Ohira's (2004) study.

Thomas and Irwin (2006) observed in a series of experiments that eye-blinks between stimulus presentation and recall of an iconic memory task decreased recall performance. The authors found that this interference was not caused by motor responses or changes in light intensity; they rather assume that due to reduced activation in the V1 area during blinking, blinks caused a cognitive interference with information held in iconic memory.

4.2.1.2 Research Using Continuous Tasks

Most of the presented research used trial-based paradigms with invariant timing, so participants could reliably predict the different task segments and time their blinks accordingly. Continuous tasks, on the other hand, demand longer periods of attention and effort, and they show less explicit inherent structuring, and it could be questioned if structured blinking behavior will also occur under such unpredictable circumstances. In fact, studies with continuous stimuli have also found task-dependent changes in blinking behavior. Four studies are presented in this subsection on the blink-inhibition position; more studies with differing conclusions will be presented in the next subsection.

Wood and Bitterman (1950) asked participants in a reading task to work with either low or high effort, thus trying to manipulate cognitive load. Results show that blink frequency was reduced significantly under the high effort instruction. With a focus on traffic psychology, Drew (1951) found that spontaneous eye-blink rate in a laboratory experiment and a field experiment decreased with increasing task difficulty. In the lab experiment, participants were asked to direct a remote-controlled pencil on scrolling paper along a predefined line, whereby difficulty of the remote-control mechanism and line complexity were varied to create easy and difficult conditions. Results showed that blink rate decreased with increasing difficulty, i.e. increasing line complexity, and visual and manual control effort. The same relation could be observed in the field experiment: when participants drove a car in real traffic, blink rate decreased with increasing task demands in increasing traffic density. Poulton and Gregory (1952) used a visual tracking task and found that blink frequency increased before task onset and after task offset; during the tracking task, it was reduced and was lowest "during or immediately before the difficult periods of the course" (p. 57). Benedetto et al. (2011) examined spontaneous eye-blink rate and eye-blink characteristics during a driving task with and without additional workload. While very high blink rate variability possibly prevented them from finding significant differences between experimental conditions, they found that blink duration was shorter at first when participants were confronted with the dual task, but increased with increasing time on task (p. 207). The authors interpret this as a blink inhibition in face of increased visual load that wears off over time due to depletion of resources (p. 207). Further research in traffic psychology has related parameters of blinking behavior to vigilance or drowsiness of drivers (Galley & Andres, 1996; Galley, Andres, & Reitter, 1999; Galley, Schleicher, & Galley, 2004; Hargutt, 2003; Schleicher, Galley, Briest, & Galley, 2008).

In the aforementioned studies, cognitive demands are confounded with visual demands of the task. A study that tried to eliminate the visual aspect, and intended to focus on the impact of cognitive load alone, was conducted by Holland and Tarlow (1972). They found that increased cognitive load in non-visual memory retaining and arithmetic tasks led to decreased rates of spontaneous eye-blinks. The authors assumed that blinking might be suppressed because it could possibly interfere with cognitive processing. Further, blinking occurred within trials prior to incorrect responses; the authors interpreted these blinks as indicators for forgetting or task failure, leading to the incorrect response. The assumption that blinks interfere with cognitive processes was followed further by Holland and Tarlow (1975), where they used another non-visual cognitive task, but tried to manipulate the degree of cognitive processing while keeping cognitive load constant. Because participants suppressed blinks during phases of cognitive operation, the authors again argue that blinking might interfere with cognitive processes, possibly due to the extreme changes of activity in visual brain areas during blinks. Such a suppression would be adaptive if "operational memory and the visual imagination" (p. 503) depended on the same neural circuits.

As has been shown, structured blinking behavior has been found in trial-based and continuous paradigms with explicit tasks. However, the aim of this thesis is the observation of blinking behavior during continuous, natural stimuli rather than blinking during trial tasks. Such continuous stimuli, for example video stimuli as more or less natural recordings of real-world events, do not feature an explicit organization in distinct trials and, in most cases, do not require an explicit task. While we will in a later section discuss how findings from trial-based research could be applied to continuous stimuli (see section 4.2.4), we will now first review research observing blinking behavior towards continuous video stimuli.

Nakano, Yamamoto, Kitajo, Takahashi, and Kitazawa (2009) used a video story as a natural stimulus, in this case excerpts from a comedy TV show, to observe blinking behavior of viewers. The researchers found that participants tended to blink at similar passages of the videos; this behavior could be observed as an intra-individual synchronization effect during repeated viewing of the video, and an inter-individual synchronization effect across participants. Nakano et al.'s analyses let them conclude that blink elicitation was not primarily driven by low-level stimulus properties such as cuts, but rather appeared to be influenced by media content: blinks occurred more likely at implicit breakpoints, such as "the disappearance of the main character, during a long shot and during repeated presentations of a similar scene" (p. 3641). Such synchronization effects were not evident for a video stimulus without story, or for an audio-only narrated story. The authors thus conclude that the effects resulted from "a mechanism for controlling the timing of blinks that searches for the appropriate timing to prevent the loss of critical information from the flow of visual information" (p. 3642), and that the neural correlate of this mechanism might involve the neural structures of superior colliculus and posterior parietal cortex.

Shultz, Klin, and Jones (2011) investigated blink inhibition as a function of stimulus content and the viewer's individual interest in the stimulus content. In

this case, the researchers used recordings of two children at play; in these recordings, different events created occasions of increased movement in the frame
(moving physical objects of the environment), and occasions of increased affective magnitude (children having an argument). Two groups of participants were
chosen who were predicted to show differing interest in these physical and affective stimulus properties: typically developed children, and children diagnosed
with an autism spectrum disorder. The authors hypothesized that autistic toddlers would, due to an impaired processing of emotional stimuli, show different
patterns of attention allocation, and thus different patterns of blink inhibition.
While both groups showed a stimulus-dependent organization of blink intervals,
typically developed toddlers inhibited their blinks before affective events, possibly in anticipation of "the unfolding of salient events" (p. 21273), while inhibition
in ASD toddlers occurred shortly after the affective events. This assumption is
supported by eye-tracking data, which showed that ASD toddlers fixated more
on physical objects, especially when the objects moved. While typically developed
toddlers also paid attention to the videotaped children's affective and social signals preceding the affective apex, ASD toddlers seemed to not anticipate this
apex, and only directed their attention on the videotaped children after the affective peak. The authors conclude that in this study, inhibition of spontaneous eye-
blinks helped to reveal not only what toddlers were paying attention to, but also
how engaged toddlers were with the stimulus content (p. 21273).

In these studies, as in the other studies in this subsection, Nakano et al. (2009)
and Shultz et al. (2011) see blinking as a hindrance to other processes. In subsequent studies, Nakano et al. refined their understanding of blinking, and assumed blinking to have a distinct function in internal processes.

4.2.2 Blinking as Component of Internal Processes

The research described in this subsection either sees blinking as an indicator of
attentional or cognitive processes, or even attributes blinking a dedicated role in
these processes. Especially the former is not always entirely distinct from positions in the previous subsection, which described blinks as interfering events that
need to be suppressed; however, the classification was made to best reflect the
assumed intentions of the respective authors.

Fogarty and Stern (1989) observed blinking behavior during an identification
task with peripherally presented letters. The authors conclude from the results
that blinks do not necessarily and always occur after information processing, but

"if a blink is to be made, it will most likely be made at a specific time in the information-processing chain" (p. 39). This suggests that a structured blinking behavior could be an indicator for ongoing information processing.

Malmstrom, Rachofsky, and Weber (1977) investigated a "masking hypothesis", stating that blinks during information processing are inhibited to avoid impairment of ongoing processing of visual information. In their review of blink research, they cite studies implying that frequency of spontaneous eye-blinks (SEBs) varies "with the type of mental task" (p. 163; Telford & Thompson, 1933), and with task difficulty (Gregory, 1952; Holland & Tarlow, 1972, 1975; Luckiesh, 1944). For research conducted with trial-based paradigms, they report a "U-shaped curve across the time course of a single trial" with a frequency drop from baseline during episodes of "presentation and processing of information", and a subsequent increase "at the completion of the mental task", manifesting as "a flurry of eyeblinks" (p. 163). The latter is characterized as a possible "catch up" process with a blink rate often exceeding the individual baseline (p. 163). The masking hypothesis was tested under well-lit conditions and dark conditions. During analysis of the data, the authors faced a very high interpersonal variability of spontaneous eye-blink rates, with many participants even not blinking at all during the measurement interval. The results did not support the masking hypothesis; the authors rather conclude that "inhibition of spontaneous blinking appears to be an excellent and robust indicator of cognitive activity" (p. 165).

Oh, Han, Peterson, and Jeong (2012) used a visual and an auditory Stroop task to observe eye-blink behavior in an attentional task. The researchers found that independent of modality or task difficulty, blinks occurred shortly before or after responses. Participants could be clustered into three groups, who consistently blinked either before responses, after responses, or both. The authors assume that blinking might indicate a shift in cognitive state, such as decision making or "the shift from sustained attention to the stimuli to a motor response" (p. 9), and that blinking might be "involved in, or at least is a marker of, a cognitive process that the tasks engage." (p. 11).

Wascher, Heppner, Möckel, Kobald, and Getzmann (2015) observed blinking behavior of participants engaged in a series of cognitive tasks with and without need for manual response. The researchers argue beyond Nakano et al.'s (2009) previous notion of blink inhibition, and conclude that "blinks provide a reliable measure for cognitive processing beyond (or rather additional to) manual responses" (p. 1207), because "the core trigger of blink execution appears to be the finalization of stimulus evaluation" (p. 1216). According to their results, "blinks appear to be synchronized with manual responses" in trials (p. 1214) and occur about 200 ms after button presses, what in the first place might suggest a relation with motor processes. However, the same pattern of blinking was evident in a task demanding inhibition, not execution of manual responses, suggesting that the blinking behavior was actually influenced by stimulus processing prior to the motor response. The authors conclude that blink timing might serve as a "reliable marker of cognitive processing speed even in no-go situations" (p. 1216).

Goldstein, Bauer, and Stern (1992) analyzed spontaneous eye-blink rate, blink duration, and blink latency under different low or high demanding conditions, namely memorization of two- or six-digit spans, with shorter or longer inter-stimulus intervals. By observing blink parameters before, during and after stimulus presentation, the researchers tried to infer on processes of mental task preparation, visual information intake, and mental information processing. According to the authors' conclusion, "both blink rate and blink duration reflect the anticipation of an imperative stimulus" (p. 116), but only blink rate, not blink duration is "affected by the actual encoding of that stimulus" (p. 116).

Pivik and Dykman (2004) even go so far as to assume that endogenous blinks, as they name spontaneous eye-blinks, are "a meaningful and integral component of sensory-motor processing, indexing times of facilitated attentional and motor response capability" (p. 191). They see endogenous or spontaneous blinks as especially interesting, because on the one hand, they occur more often than eye-physiologically necessary, and on the other hand, are not linked to a specific external stimulus in an obvious manner (p. 192). Pivik and Dykman argue that the question arises how organisms deal with the considerable loss of visual information during blinks, and how nevertheless a "fluid integration of [...] [visual] information into behavior" can be achieved (p. 192). In their review of existing research, Pivik and Dykman describe that (a) on a very basic level, interference of the blackout period during blinks with our perception is prevented by neuronal suppression mechanisms, possibly similar to those active during saccades (also see section 4.1.5 of this thesis). However, due to an early onset of suppression, the actual loss of visual information even exceeds the duration of the eye-blink by up to 100 ms (p. 192), so additional mechanisms seem to be necessary to minimize loss of visual information. According to studies cited by Pivik and Dykman (p. 192), blinks are (b) "decreased in frequency and strategically positioned to maximize stimulus detection" during tasks that demand a high degree of visual attention. A subsequently persisting reduction of blink frequency after stimulus offset is presumed to be determined by content features of the stimulus, with longer inhibition after stimulus presentation corresponding to higher "attentional demands and complexity of task" (Stern, Walrath, & Goldstein, 1984; Pivik & Dykman, 2004, p. 192). In addition, research suggests (c) a relation between not only blinks and processes of attention and internal processing, but also motor processes, as found frequently in pressing of response buttons (p. 193). Further studies cited by Pivik and Dykman (p. 193) showed that blinks could be delayed until button responses in complex tasks had been completed; however, this delay was not found for responses in easy tasks, and blinks could either interfere with a task when occurring too close to a response, or were inhibited for a sufficient time to not interfere. The authors aimed at replicating such relations between blinks, stimulus perception, and information processing (p. 193) with a preadolescent sample. As for adult samples in existing research, Pivik and Dykman (2004) found that blinking behavior in their predictable trial tasks was highly structured to not interfere with information intake; after visual stimuli were presented, blink timing was "further regulated beyond this time as a function of the information content and task demands associated with these stimuli" (p. 204). The authors relate blink timing to processes of selective attention, and also find an influence of priming-cues on blink elicitation after a stimulus: blinks occurred faster if the stimulus was a previously indicated non-target, what supports the idea of blinks as markers for transitions between cognitive processes (pp. 208–209).

Cong, Sharikadze, Staude, Deubel and Wolf (2010) analyzed blink timing during different tasks of finger tapping. They found increased synchronization of tapping with blinks for more difficult versions of tapping tasks, namely bimanual tapping, tapping with stronger force or impulse-like tapping. The authors argue from a motor-control point of view and especially pay attention to brain areas involved in both the production of tapping and blinking motor commands; consequently, their reasoning rather refers to timing and complexity of motor commands. While they acknowledge that the more difficult tasks may be more demanding with respect to required attention and workload, they unfortunately do not consider these factors as determinants of blink timing.

In several studies, Nakano and colleagues (Nakano, 2015; Nakano, Kato, Morito, Itoi, & Kitazawa, 2013; Nakano & Kitazawa, 2010; Nakano, Yamamoto, Kitajo, Takahashi, & Kitazawa, 2009) investigated neural processes in the human brain during spontaneous eye-blinks. Nakano, Kato, Morito, Itoi, & Kitazawa (2013) used externally valid video stimuli in an fMRI study to observe neural processes during spontaneous eye-blinks. Results show that activation in a neural network associated with attentional processes, the dorsal attention network, decreases during blinks, while at the same time activation in the so-called default mode network increases. This fMRI study was repeated with the same stimuli, but with scans including temporal and subcortical areas. Combined, it was possible to analyze activity of the dorsal attention network (DAN), which is assumed to control top-down processes of visual attention, the ventral attention network (VAN), which is assumed to control bottom-up processes of visual attention, and the default mode network (DMN; Nakano, 2015, p. 57). The results show that during blinking, activity in the DAN and VAN decreases, while activity in the

DMN increases. Nakano concludes that spontaneous eye-blinks may support switching between internal and external orienting networks, and that "internal processing, including memory retrieval, occurs during spontaneous eye-blinks by concurrently activating the brain regions connected functionally to DMN" (p. 57). This way, spontaneous blinks, which "involve a massive and dynamic alteration in brain activity between the internal and external orienting networks" (p. 58), might support the processing of information via a mechanism of attention disengagement.

In sum, the presented body of research supports the assumption that attention on, and processing of a media stimulus should affect the timing of spontaneous eye-blinks; this should hold true even more for interactive media, where properly timed motor responses are necessary. Before we conclude this section with a short summary on the implications of blink research for this thesis, two digressions will address further aspects of the topic. First, an excursus will address the neurochemistry of blinking, further underlining the relation between blinking and cognitive processes. Second, another excursus will offer possible explanations to bridge the conceptual gap between findings from trial-based research, and research with continuous tasks or stimuli.

4.2.3 Blinking and Dopamine

Another relation between cognitive processes and blinking behavior can be found in research on dopaminergic processes. Spontaneous eye-blink frequency is a commonly used, easy to acquire marker of central dopaminergic activity (e.g., Karson, 1983). It has been used to relate dopamine to personality in general (Colzato, Slagter, van den Wildenberg, & Hommel, 2009; Barbato, Della Monica, Costanzo, & De Padova, 2012), to dopamine-related traits of personality such as creativity (Chermahini & Hommel, 2010) or positive emotionality (Depue, Luciana, Arbisi, Collins, & Leon, 1994). Further, spontaneous eye-blink frequency has been discussed for monitoring both progression and treatment side-effects in Parkinson's disease (Karson, 1988), and for the diagnosis of schizophrenia and autism (Karson, 1989).

Conditions with impairment of dopaminergic transmission also affect spontaneous eye-blink rate (Esteban, Traba, & Prieto, 2004). For example, Lozoff (2011) reviews research on the consequences of iron deficiency during infancy, a condition that is supposed to have an impact on dopaminergic functioning. In line with an impairment of "dopaminergic function in the nigrostriatal pathway"

(p. 743), iron-deficient children show a lower eye-blink rate than healthy controls, but show a normalizing eye-blink rate when under iron therapy. For another condition, the fragile X syndrome, Roberts, Symons, Johnson, Hatton, and Boccia (2005) used blink rate as an indicator of dopamine level in typically developed boys and same age boys with the fragile X syndrome. The condition often leads to "mental retardation [and] symptoms including anxiety, social avoidance, sensory processing dysfunction [...] and aggression" (p. 648). The authors see fragile X syndrome as a "unique model for exploring the relationships between genes-brain-neurochemistry-behavior" (p. 648) and found that blink rate was higher in the FXS group. For this group, Roberts et al. (2005) further found that blink rate correlated with "problem behaviours and physiological arousal" (p. 647).

A change in central dopaminergic activity is supposed to be found during prolonged sleep deprivation due to "activation of the physiological mechanisms which regulate wake maintenance" (Barbato, De Padova, Paolillo, Arpaia, Russo, & Ficca, 2007, p. 151; sleep deprivation for 21 hours). Barbato et al. (2007) assume that these changes lead to increases in both sleepiness and spontaneous eye-blink rate, and may be responsible for the antidepressant effects of sleep deprivation, as well. Barbato et al. (1995) used sleep deprivation to investigate relations between EEG alpha activity and blinking behavior, since previous findings had suggested that brain areas associated with alpha activity might also be involved in regulation of spontaneous eye-blinks. Results showed that after sleep deprivation, significant correlations could be found between an increased eye-blink rate, probably due to increased central dopaminergic activity, and relative decrease of alpha power (p. 341). The authors conclude that "alpha activity and spontaneous eye blink rate could share common physiological mechanisms" (p. 341).

Regarding physiological correlates, Taylor et al. (1999) identified regions of the caudate nucleus in monkeys, namely the rostral portion of the ventromedial body of the caudate nucleus (p. 214), to have a significant impact on spontaneous eye-blink rate. Variations of dopamine levels in this brain region after treatment with dopamine agonists or antagonists correlated well with variations of spontaneous eye-blink rate.

A proposal detailing the mechanisms at work in the human brain comes from Colzato, Slagter, Spapé and Hommel (2008), who were interested in modulating effects of dopamine on the size of the attentional blink phenomenon. To investigate this research question, they draw on research stating that greater levels of dopamine are associated with larger working memory and smaller attentional blink (p. 3182), and use spontaneous eye-blink rate as an indicator for central dopaminergic function. In line with expectations, they find that participants with a higher blink rate, and thus a higher level of dopamine, show a smaller attentional blink. The authors assume that dopamine could play a role in the efficient processing of information, namely in "discriminating targets from distractors" (p. 3182), which is supposed to be important in selectively storing information in working memory. Researchers presume that this "attentional gating" (p. 3182) is resulting "from phasic increases of DA [dopamine] activity" (p. 3182), and further that higher spontaneous eye-blink rates are related to higher tonic dopamine levels. Colzato et al. (2008) speculate that a higher tonic dopamine level, as indicated by a higher blink rate, facilitates "higher and more pronounced phasic DA peaks and, thus, more efficient gating" (p. 3182). Van Opstal, De Loof, Verguts, and Cleeremans (2016) also interpret a higher blink rate as "indicating better visual detection" (p. 7). Van Opstal et al. found in their study that participants with a higher spontaneous eye-blink rate performed better in detecting stimuli during a breaking continuous flash suppression paradigm, although the blink rate was not measured during a neutral resting condition. The authors assume that his relation between higher blink rate and better detection performance could result from a higher "dopamine D2 receptor density in the striatum" (p. 7) in participants with higher spontaneous eye-blink frequency.

Van Bochove, van der Haegen, Notebaert, and Verguts (2013) used blinks as a marker in research on cognitive control. Van Bochove et al. (2013) tested predictions of a model for the Gratton effect during a flanker task. In this paradigm, a central stimulus is flanked by either congruent stimuli that suggest the same motor-response as the central stimulus (e.g., arrows pointing in the same direction), or incongruent distractor stimuli that call for a conflicting motor response (e.g., arrows pointing in the opposite direction). Usually, participants show more errors and a longer reaction time for incongruent trials; however, if an incongruent trial is followed by another incongruent trial, the reaction time in the new trial is still prolonged, but less than after congruent trials. This Gratton effect is explained with increased cognitive control that results from being confronted with the first incongruent trial. A binding model hypothesizes dopamine and norepinephrine as important components of the neuronal processes behind this effect. Based on literature on the link between spontaneous eye-blink rate and dopamine levels, van Bochove et al. used blinks as a marker for dopaminergic processes during the trials (p. 348), and assume that a "DA [dopamine] burst underlying the blink" (p. 351) contributes to binding processes. Indeed, the authors find a larger Gratton effect after trials in which participants blinked, so blinks might at least have co-occurred with greater cognitive control. Kleinsorge and Scheil (2017) found that participants with higher spontaneous eye-blink rate performed better in a task switching paradigm, presumably due to the beneficial effects of dopamine on this task. Further, the authors presume that increase or decrease of blink rate during early stages of the experiment reflects different processing strategies, influenced by different dopaminergic projections. With regard to this thesis, it remains unclear how exactly blinks relate to dopaminergic processes and mechanisms of cognitive control, but the results nevertheless show another example for a link between blink occurrences and cognitive processes.

More hints towards modulation of blink timing comes from studies on attention deficit hyperactivity disorder (ADHD), which "is also thought to involve dopamine dysfunction" (Groen, Börger, Koerts, Thome, & Tucha, 2017). Groen et al. (2017) compared blink inhibition before stimulus presentation in experimental trials, and found that ADHD diagnosed children without medication showed—with a very small effect—poorer inhibition than typically developed children or ADHD diagnosed children under medication. In this study, intervals between trials were variable and unpredictable. The authors contrast these findings to a study conducted by Fried et al. (2014), who also observed blink inhibition of ADHD patients in a trial-based experiment, but with fixed and predictable trial timing. In their study, Fried et al. found more pronounced deficits in blink timing of ADHD patients, which suggests an important role of predictable trial timing (Groen et al., 2017, p. S37). In the scope of this thesis, it can be interpreted that in ADHD patients, limited capacities in attention allocation might co-occur with less functional timing of spontaneous eye-blinks.

Not only inhibition of blinks, but also inhibition of voluntary actions has been related to dopamine function via the marker of spontaneous eye-blink rate. Colzato, Wildenberg, Wouwe, Pannebakker, and Hommel (2009) found that eye-blink rate can predict performance in a stop-signal task, where manual responses were to be omitted if a certain signal appeared, in this case represented by a change in color of an arrow. Higher blink rates, and thus higher levels of dopamine, were associated with a decreased performance in the stop-signal task. Blinks have also been used to assess dopaminergic factors for other aspects of cognitive control, namely perseveration and distractibility (Dreisbach et al., 2005). Dreisbach et al. found that participants with higher spontaneous eye-blink rates "showed increased cognitive flexibility but decreased cognitive stability" (p. 483). A follow-up study could replicate the positive correlation between cognitive flexibility and eye-blink rate, which was again used as a marker of dopamine level (Müller et al., 2007). Colzato, van Wouwe, and Hommel (2007) used spontaneous eye-blinks to investigate the role of the dopaminergic system for visuo-motor integration, and found evidence suggesting an important role of dopamine for the processing of affective stimuli and task-relevant information.

Strictly speaking, the findings presented so far merely reflect a correlation between levels of dopamine and blink rate. However, considering the influence of dopamine agonists and antagonists on blink rate, and considering altered blink rate in conditions involving dopaminergic dysfunctions, it is sound to conclude that either dopamine level itself facilitates blinking, or both dopamine level and blink occurrence share a common cause. It is not yet fully understood if eyeblinks play an active role in cognitive processes, and if yes, what their exact function is (see section 4.2.2). In addition, research on the blink-dopamine relation in most cases focuses on blink frequency, not so much on structural aspects. A study also considering change of blink rates, what could be seen as a basic structural property, dealt with the dopamine-sensitive trait of reward responsivity (Peckham & Johnson, 2016). In an effortful task with possible monetary reward, researchers found that "blink rates increased from reward anticipation to post-reward", and at least in their survey data from bipolar I disorder patients, researchers found a correlation between reward-related questionnaire measures and change in blink rate.

For the scope of this thesis, it can be concluded with some certainty that dopamine level is a factor for individual overall blink rate. As Jongkees and Colzato (2016) state in their review on blinks as a marker for dopamine processes, blink rate can be used to "reliably predict individual differences in performance on many cognitive tasks, in particular those related to reward-driven behavior and cognitive flexibility". However, this application focuses on a measure of mean frequency on an inter-individual level, while the present thesis aims at a structural measure for—ideally—both inter-individual and intra-individual differences; only this way it would be possible to discriminate phases with or without presence experience, and relate the objectively observed behavior to subjective questionnaire measures.

Unfortunately, it appears that the current body of research does not allow for a definitive answer to the relation between dopamine and blinking; however, the very recent findings of Groen et al. (2017) on blink inhibition in ADHD patients might lead the way to very interesting insights into the role of dopamine for structuring of spontaneous eye-blinks.

A large proportion of the research presented so far used experimental paradigms with a trial-based organization, which means between the well-defined trial tasks, there were explicit intervals where no action was required. This is not the case for most continuous, natural stimuli, at least not in such an explicit manner. While we have learned that comparable effects have been found for both trial-based and continuous experimental domains, we will nevertheless have another excursus and will briefly address a possible answer to the question how findings on blinking behavior can be generalized to continuous, natural stimuli: the concept of segmentation.

4.2.4 Blinking During Trials and Continuous Stimuli

As has been mentioned earlier, the research paradigms presented in this section can be grouped into two major categories: paradigms where stimuli and tasks are explicitly segmented into trials, and paradigms with continuous stimuli or tasks. Since the scope of this thesis aims at continuous and natural stimuli, we will now briefly discuss a possible link between these two extremes, and will review research suggesting that observers perceive and comprehend continuous stimuli with help of segmentation processes. Because the exact mechanisms are outside the scope of this thesis, linking these concepts to blinking behavior will largely remain speculation; nevertheless, the findings might offer a viable frame for explaining synchronization phenomena during media reception.

An approach for explaining how individuals make sense of observed content is proposed by Zacks and colleagues, who assume that "perception of event structures is biased by the influence of hierarchically organized schemata for recurring events" (Zacks, Tversky, & Iyer, 2001, p. 48). These organizations of events are supposed to be encoded "in terms of partonomic hierarchies" (p. 48), and appear to incorporate object-action units focused on "intentions and goals" (pp. 48–49). Zacks et al. argue that both information on objects and information on actions are necessary to allow for "interpretations of events as goal-directed, purposeful, [and] intentional" (p. 51).

Zacks et al. (2001) conclude from further fMRI findings that different components of such segmentation process are reflected in activity of neural networks in the neocortex, and (a) show a component of perceptual segmentation, probably part of normal event perception, (b) show sensitivity for hierarchical organization of events, (c) include areas close to the human MT and frontal eye field (FEF) structures, and (d) show distinct changes in activity preceding a conscious reporting of event boundaries (p. 653).

When observing neural processes during segmentation in another fMRI study, Speer, Swallow, and Zacks (2003) could record "strong responses to event boundaries" (p. 335) in the MT+ region, and in a frontal area near the frontal eye field. The authors conclude that "motion perception and, possibly, eye movements or shifts of attention are fundamentally related to the perception of event boundaries" (p. 344). However, the role of attention shifts, and the degree of involvement of top-down and bottom-up processes remained open questions (p. 344). For the latter aspect, a follow-up study (Zacks, 2004) suggests that low-level stimulus features like movement are important in identifying event boundaries, and that this bottom-up process is "modulated by top-down influence of

knowledge structures" (p. 979). The role of changes in movement, neural correlates of bottom-up processes, and a sensitivity for biological motion are discussed
in Zacks, Swallow, Vettel, and McAvoy (2006), and Zacks, Kumar, Abrams, and
Mehta (2009). The role of top-down processes is discussed by Reynolds, Zacks,
and Braver (2007), who suggest that self-organizing systems can use experience
from previous observations to form predictions on following events, and that
event boundaries will be introduced at instances of high errors in the prediction
of following events. These aspects are integrated into a theory of event perception, where permanent processing of perceptual input, supported by attentional
and memory processes lead to predictions for upcoming events, and an event
boundary is encoded when these predictions do not match the perceptual input
(Zacks, Speer, Swallow, Braver, & Reynolds, 2007). Segmenting processes with
appropriate event boundaries co-occur with better learning and memory performance (Zacks & Swallow, 2007), and segmentation is thought to be "related to
the updating of working memory, to the contents of long-term memory, and to
the learning of new procedures" (Kurby & Zacks, 2008, p. 72).

In an application of this theory on comprehension of text and film stimuli
(Zacks, Speer, & Reynolds, 2009), researchers found that "changes in situational
features such as characters, their locations, their interactions with objects, and
their goals are related to the segmentation of events" (p. 307). Zacks and colleagues argue that especially for reading, event models could be seen as analog to
situation models (p. 308), and that situation models are updated at event boundaries if the prediction error exceeds a critical threshold. Predictions of the theory
were tested on a short film as a continuous, natural stimulus (Zacks, Speer, Swallow, & Maley, 2010), and it was found that as in text stimuli, "situation changes
mediated the relations between event boundaries and these evoked brain responses" (p. 11). Magliano and Zacks (2011) conclude from a study with the same
short film that cinematic techniques of continuity editing serve the purpose "to
support the comprehension of meaningful events that bridge breaks in low-level
visual continuity, and even breaks in continuity of spatial and temporal location"
(p. 1489). Huff, Meitz, and Papenmeier (2014) build upon the assumption that
comprehension of audiovisual narratives is achieved by creation of situation
models; these models should include time, locations, protagonists, and actions
depicted in the mediated content. During media reception, "boundaries between
2 meaningful units" (Huff, Meitz, & Papenmeier, 2014, p. 1) may result from discontinuities in these dimensions. Huff et al. found that event models in working
memory, as a representation of such situation models, are updated incrementally
at perceived event boundaries: an increasing number of changing dimensions led
to better recall and poorer predictions of following events. Huff et al. suggest to
extend the event segmentation theory accordingly.

Explanations of the segmentation concept rely heavily on bottom-up processes, top-down processes, and construction of mental models; generally speaking, such factors are also included in the presence model by Wirth et al. (2007; see section 2.2.5 of this thesis). Wirth and colleagues see perceptual hypothesis testing as a component of presence formation: during testing of these hypotheses, existing knowledge guides perception and interpretation of media content during provision of expectation hypotheses, during gathering of information about the perceived object, and ultimately during confirmation or disproof of a perceptual hypothesis. Confirmed perceptual hypotheses can then further guide the user's perception and interpretation of media content (Wirth et al., 2007, pp. 506–507).

Both concepts, event segmentation and perceptual hypothesis testing, share similarities regarding the time scope of the respectively hypothesized processes. Segmentation, on the one hand, is defined as a continuous process, using the stream of visual information for constant evaluation of prediction errors. Testing of perceptual hypotheses, on the other hand, is defined as a process leading to confirmation or disproof of the current hypothesis, so in principle, a conclusion can be reached within the media use process. However, confirmed perceptual hypotheses are assumed to further influence processing of content, and they can still be disproved by newly emerging information, so perceptual hypotheses testing could be seen as a continuous, ongoing process, as well. Consequently, parallels could be seen between the concept of perceptual hypotheses testing on the one hand, in which constant updating of information is necessary for the confirmation or disproof of hypotheses, and, on the other hand, the ongoing construction of situation models with prediction errors and the requirement to construct new models after the occurrence of high prediction errors.

It is not perfectly clear how exactly these processes will affect blinking behavior, but the existence of ongoing processes, which involve mechanisms of attention allocation and processing of media cues, suggests that structure in blinking behavior could be influenced by both perceptual hypotheses testing and event segmentation processes.

Of course, the assumption of an influence of segmentation processes on blinking is subject to scientific discussion. For example, Wascher, Heppner, Möckel, Kobald and Getzmann (2015) propose that not only in laboratory, but also in natural settings, spontaneous eye-blinks might indicate "information segmentation" (p. 1216), whereas Nakano, Kato, Morito, Itoi, & Kitazawa (2013) draw different conclusions from their study on the role of eye-blinks during activation of the default mode network and deactivation of the dorsal attention network. Nakano et al. found in their data no neural activity typical for segmentation. Since their data was time-locked to spontaneous blinks that presumably occurred at a story's implicit breakpoints, they conclude that event boundaries in segmentation and implicit breakpoints apparently not occurred at the same time.

It becomes clear that these possible influences on blinking remain speculation at this time, and cannot be addressed in the scope of this thesis. In addition, this thesis focuses on how the structure of blinking behavior can be informative for a subject's presence experience, whereas most research on blinking and dopamine does not focus on structure, but frequencies of blinking. At least for trial-based paradigms, it would be possible to speculate on a possible link between frequency and structure: if structural characteristics in trials became more pronounced, this could manifest as an increased probability of blinks occurring at certain moments during a trial, and could thus also increase observed blink rates. If structural characteristics were lacking, blinking behavior would possibly resemble a neutral baseline condition, without a trial-dependent structuring.

Getting closer to the detailed explication of this thesis' rationale, the following subsection presents two studies from the domain of media research, in which such a deviation of blinking behavior from a resting state plays a central role.

4.2.5 Blinking During Media Use

As has been described earlier in this section, Nakano et al. (2009) observed blinking behavior in recipients of a video stimulus, and concluded that blinks were inhibited by participants in order to not interfere with perception of the stimulus. Two other research projects by Bacherle (2015) and Nomura et al. (2015) will now be presented in detail, because they address the use of blinking behavior as an objective indicator for media reception processes.

Bacherle (2015) related in his thesis several secondary measurement methods to self-report measures of transportation and narrative engagement. As secondary measures, he used real-time response ratings, secondary task reaction time, and eye-blink frequency. In one study, blink frequency correlated significantly negative with transportation, but not significantly with narrative engagement and its subscales (p. 120). In a more detailed analysis in another study of his thesis (Bacherle, 2015), several parameters derived from blink frequency were used as objective indicators. In preparation of analyses, the film stimulus was binned into 40 segments of 30 seconds each, and the participants' blinks were counted in these bins. The resulting blink rates were baseline corrected for (a) individual blink rate, which was calculated from a 60 seconds long interval prior to film start, and for (b) film blink rate, which was calculated from the blink frequencies of a control group. Mean frequency, frequency at film start, frequency at film end, number of extreme values, slope as the overall linear trend of blink rate during the observation period, and blink frequency at the moment of greatest variance were computed as indicators for blinking behavior. No significant correlations were found for any of these blink parameters with transportation, narrative engagement, or subscales of narrative engagement. The directions of some non-significant correlations were also not congruent with hypotheses. Bacherle concludes that there seems to be no linear relationship between blinking behavior and ratings of transportation and narrative engagement.

While most research addresses static factors for transportation experiences, such as education, gender, or personal tendency towards transportation, Nomura, Hino, Shimazu, Liang and Okada (2015) were interested in dynamic factors for transportation experiences during live theater performances (p. 2). As an indicator for "fluctuation between attention allocation and attention release" (p. 2), they related synchronization of audiences' spontaneous eye-blink behavior to experiences of transportation. Previous research by Nomura et al. had shown that an experienced performer of rakugo, the Japanese equivalent to western culture stand-up comedy, elicited stronger transportation experiences in audiences than a novice performer (p. 2). Further, existing research had shown that when using eye-blinks as an indicator for attentional processes, audiences watching an experienced performer's comedy showed a stronger interpersonal synchronization of spontaneous eye-blinks, even though the novice performer was interpreting the same story (p. 2). Nomura et al. then intended to use synchronization of spontaneous eye-blinks between participants as an indicator of attentional processes during the session. Based on the author's (Nomura & Okada, 2014; cited by Nomura et al., 2015, p. 2) and Nakano's research (Nakano et al., 2009; Nakano & Kitazawa, 2010; cited by Nomura et al., 2015, p. 2), they derived two assumptions. First, the synchronization of spontaneous eye-blinks should result from ongoing attentional processes in viewers, where attention is repeatedly focused on an aspect, and then released after information intake. Second, synchronization of spontaneous eye-blinks should result from an expert Rakugo performer's ability to effectively guide and bind the viewers' attention, whereby attention allocation should be accompanied by blink inhibition, and attention release should be accompanied by blink elicitation (p. 2). The authors further hypothesize that viewers' experiences of transportation are influenced by an ongoing feedback loop of information intake and processing, ensued by emotional engagement, ensued by direction of attention on the performance in preparation to absorbing further information, until information is again taken in and processed, and so on (p. 2). These stimulus-guided cycles of emotionally influenced attentional processes could then lead to synchronization of audience's blinking behavior, which could serve as an indicator for audience's transportation experiences: the more viewers' attention is directed to the stimulus, the more their natural, rather regular blinking behavior should be influenced by the stimulus. Since participants would be presented similar or identical stimuli, this stimulus-dependence should manifest as stronger interpersonal synchronization and, since the natural course of blink timing is altered repeatedly throughout the performance, as a higher variability of inter-blink intervals (p. 3).

Nomura et al. (2015) further assume that viewers use the perceived information to construct situation models of the narrative; expert viewers should be able to use existing information from their knowledge structures when constructing a situation model of the narrative, and would need to pay less attention on general narrative content. Instead, they would have greater amounts of free attentional resources to engage in details of the performance, which should facilitate formation of transportation experiences in experts right from the beginning of the performance (p. 2). To test these hypotheses, expert and novice audiences were presented two different video versions of a Rakugo performance in a 2×2 design: either a videotaped traditional style performance, or an easier to comprehend performance for beginners. Dependent variables were observed spontaneous eye-blinks, subjective ratings of transportation, and subjective ratings of humor experiences. Variability of inter-blink intervals was calculated as an attentional measure on an individual level, while mean similarity of blinking behavior between individual members of the experimental groups were used as group-level measures. Analyses results suggested that audience experience and presentation form had little contribution to transportation, and that both novice and expert recipients synchronized their blink timing, whereby novices needed more time to synchronize than experts. Self-reported intensity of transportation experiences could be predicted by self-reported humor experience and higher inter-blink interval variability.

4.3 Conclusion

The presented research findings show that there is a solid theoretical and empirical foundation for the assumption that internal processes affect spontaneous eye-blink behavior, be it due to blink inhibition or due to deliberately timed execution of blinks. Further influences on blinking behavior have been found in psychological research, such as startle responses (e.g., Filion, Dawson, & Schell, 1998; Graham, 1975; Sechenov, 1965). These influences might occur during media use, for example during jump scares in a horror movie, but are not considered in this thesis, because they are no spontaneous eye-blinks.

Blinking behavior is far from being an arbitrary process, it rather is influenced by mechanisms of attention allocation, stimulus processing, and higher cognitive processes. Without detailed explication of the involved processes, we assume as a working hypothesis that such processes with influence on blinking behavior can also be found during media use. For example, Alcañiz, Rey, Tembl, and Parkhutik (2009) structure necessary user actions in virtual reality environments into "visuospatial interaction tasks, attention tasks, and the creation and execution of a motor plan" (p. 97), and the research presented here suggests that all of these processes will likely affect blinking behavior. While this primarily addresses interactive media, a subset of such user actions should be necessary for reception of non-interactive media, as well.

It is thus possible to hypothesize that changes in blinking behavior can be found in individuals who pay close attention to a media stimulus, and who engage in processing of stimulus content. Furthermore, because blink timing has been shown to depend on current attentional and processing demands, fluctuations in the behavioral structure should not only be found with fluctuating attention on the stimulus, but also with continuous attention on the stimulus during periods of low and high processing of content. This assumption is supported by empirical evidence from media research on other media use phenomena (Bacherle, 2015; Nakano et al., 2009; Nomura et al., 2015), and we extend this reasoning—with a more thorough theoretical foundation of blinking behavior—to presence research. Presence experiences are modeled to result from both attentional and cognitive processes: First, attention allocation, and especially sustained attention allocation, is seen as a necessary precursor of presence (e.g., Wirth et al., 2007). Second, Wirth et al.'s (2007) conceptualization of presence also involves necessary cognitive processes during media use, such as construction of a spatial situation model, processes of involvement, suspension of disbelief, and testing of perceptual hypotheses. All these processes depend on continuous updating with new media information, so stimulus-dependent structures of blinking could be seen as an indicator for ongoing antecedents of presence processes; the more sustained this structuring is, the more likely it should be that the user enters—or is in—a state of presence.

Possible limitations to this idea originate from the question if the processes described earlier in the collection of psychological experiments are comparable, or even identical to the internal processes during media reception. Additionally, the blink measure's sensitivity for influence from different factors could complicate unambiguous inferences on the current reason for a change in blinking behavior. Finally, attention on the stimulus alone may not be sufficient for the emergence of presence, if this attention allocation focuses on, for example, distracting media aspects (e.g., Liebold et al., 2017)—a limitation that will be accounted for in this thesis' experimental designs as effectively as possible. These limitations will be discussed again in a later section of this thesis; in the next section, we will derive the project plan for this thesis from the presented body of research.

5 Project Outline

5.1 Recapitulation

The research question to be addressed in this thesis is whether a stimulus-dependent structure in spontaneous eye-blink behavior can be used as an indicator for spatial presence experiences. This section will lay out the rationale and methods for investigating this question, starting with a recapitulation of the theoretical background provided in the previous sections.

Presence is a concept that is still in the focus of research (Cummings & Bailenson, 2016), especially due to the recent rise of highly immersive, consumer grade virtual reality devices (section 1). Presence theories, such as the process model of the formation of spatial presence experiences by Wirth et al. (2007), conceptualize presence as a process phenomenon that occurs during media use; attentional processes, along with other cognitive processes, are attributed a central role for formation and maintenance of presence (section 2). The most common way to assess presence is by questionnaire; however, researchers have called for objective, corroborative measures for presence, and some approaches for such alternative measures have been developed and tested (section 3). Spontaneous eyeblinks are a ubiquitous behavior, and their timing is supposed to be sensible to processes of attention allocation and cognition. This alteration of blinking behavior even occurs at the cost of impairing its actual, physiological function, as can be seen, for example, in the development of dry eye symptoms during VDU work (section 4). Numerous studies have observed changes in blinking behavior, be it with focus on frequency or structure, and both in trial-based research or with continuous stimuli. While the actual neural functioning around eye-blinks, and their possible role during cognitive processing are not completely understood, yet, studies nevertheless show converging evidence for a stimulus- and task-dependence of blinking behavior across a wide range of stimuli, experimental paradigms, participant age and culture (section 4). In this thesis, we will not establish which exact processes of attention or cognition have been identified in the experiments reported in section 4, and which of these are applicable to the processing of media. For the present step in the research process, we will rather use the existing empirical evidence to assume that media users who direct their attention on the media stimulus, and engage in processing of this stimulus will exhibit structured blinking behavior. Such structure can either result from inhibition of blinks during certain periods in media use, or from elicitation of blinks timed to occur after certain media events or user actions (section 4). All perspectives presented so far—blink inhibition and blink facilitation, blinks as interference to cognitive processes and blinks as integral components of cognitive processes—can contribute to a structured blinking behavior during media use.

The presence theory used in this thesis is the model by Wirth et al. (2007); to recapitulate, the model states that users enter a state of presence if the "medium-as-PERF-hypothesis is confirmed repeatedly through processed information and is thus stabilized over time" (p. 508). To maintain the primary ego reference frame's integrity, thus making it a valid option in the perceptual hypotheses testing, it depends on "permanent updating of [...] [the] spatial mental model" with visual and other sensory cues (Wirth et al., 2007, p. 505). As long as it is accepted over the real-world frame, "mental capacities are all bound to the mediated space" (Wirth et al., 2007, p. 506). Since this process depends on continuous attention on the media stimulus and continuous processing of the perceived media information, we assume that it results in a stimulus-dependent structure in blinking behavior in media recipients or users who engage in this process.

To link blinking behavior during media use to presence, researchers could further use the concept of behavioral realism: users are supposed to be in a state of presence if their reactions correspond to reactions that would be expected for a similar real-world situation (Slater, Lotto, Arnold, & Sanchez-Vives, 2009; see section 3). Strictly speaking, two requirements can be assumed for this approach: first, the reaction to the real situation must be known precisely. In most cases, this hypothesized reaction is rather derived from existing knowledge; for example, in order to apply behavioral realism to a virtual reality pit experiment, researchers could confront participants with an identical real-world pit scenario, and compare the resulting measures of self-report, behavior, and psychophysiology. However, such reality-checks for scrutinizing experimental results are rarely performed in psychology, one of the few exceptions being a study by Liebold, Koban, and Ohler (2015), who investigated motor skill training effects of racing simulations on a real-world go-kart track. Second, the analyzed alternative measure needs to be an unambiguous indicator for the desired construct; in the case of psychophysiological measures, this approach touches on the intensely discussed problem of emotion specificity of autonomous measures (e.g., Collet, Vernet-Maury, Delhomme, & Dittmar, 1997; Levenson, 2003). Due to these reasons, most alternative measures rather need to be treated as corroborative measures, which are hard to interpret without self-report information.

However, addressing such caveats of the behavioral realism approach for the domain of eye-blinks will not be within the scope of this thesis, and would be subject to future research. Here, we will make a step towards the use of blinks as a presence indicator, and will relate structure in blinking behavior—caused by attentional and other cognitive processes—to presence experiences. We will not address if this structure corresponds to real-world behavior, as would be necessary in a strict sense of behavioral realism. We will rather assess a media-dependent structuring as an indicator for presence, since it is media content that offers the mediated situations to feel present in, and thus the information to guide structure of blinking behavior. As for virtually all corroborative presence measures, blinking would be an indirect indicator, and therefore not so much a measure for presence itself, but for processes that are presumed to occur during a state of presence. Since there is no known direct indicator for presence, even neuroimaging studies need to rely on indirect indicators that are probably accompanying presence experiences, such as activation of areas for spatial processing and navigation, emotional processing, and executive control systems (Baumgartner, Valko, Esslen, & Jäncke, 2006).

For blinking, a content-aligned structuring of blinking behavior could indicate sustained processing of the media stimulus, as would be expected during states of presence. In terms of behavioral realism, the present approach investigates another facet of behavioral congruence between experiencing of virtual environments and the supposed experiencing of a corresponding real environment; thereby, the actual structure of real-world blinking behavior is rather assumed, with a thorough examination of real-world behavior left for future research. In any case, this aim calls for a focus on structural aspects of the user-media-interaction.

For this purpose, three experiments are conducted in this thesis project, and in each experiment, observational methods are used to record the participants' blinking behavior. Externally valid media stimuli are used to observe the participant's behavior in a setting as natural as possible. This approach is in line with the ideal from human ethology to apply "direct objective non-intrusive and open-minded observation of each species' behavior in its natural environment" (Magnusson, 2016). The resulting behavioral data can then be analyzed for process features of blinking, which in turn can be related to self-report questionnaire measures of presence. Before the individual experiments are presented, we will now first address several fundamental aspects with relevance for all thesis experiments: the motivation to use features of eye-blink behavior, the subjective measure for presence used as a validation standard for the objective measures, considerations about stimulus material and manipulation of conditions, and, finally, blink measurement and analysis procedures.

5.2 Advantages of an Eye-Blink Measure

We will now review several aspects in favor of the use of blinking behavior as an alternative measurement approach for presence. Apart from blinking's sensitivity towards attentional and other cognitive processes, there are further beneficial properties of blinking that support its usefulness as an indicator for internal processes. Such properties are emphasized by Shultz, Klin, and Jones (2011), who argue that blinking has been shown to be related to "both explicit [...] and implicit [...] attentional pauses in task content" (p. 21270). They further explain that unlike other autonomic processes, blinking actually disrupts the visual channel for a short period of time, so a regulation of blink occurrences would be highly adaptive. Moreover, the inhibition of blinking might allow conclusions about the "subjective assessment of perceived stimulus salience: that is, moment-by-moment, unconscious appraisals of what is or is not important enough to warrant the inhibition of blinking" (p. 21270). Timing of blink inhibition could be seen as "a measure of not simply what a person is looking at but of how engaged that person is with what is being looked at" (p. 21270). While this does not allow the conclusion that structured blinking behavior, caused by blink inhibition in face of subjectively important stimuli, is necessarily related to presence in the sense of Wirth et al. (2007), it nevertheless encourages scientific investigation of this possible relation. This is further supported by Shultz, Klin, and Jones (2011) when they explain that blinking could be a suitable measure for assessment of "perceived stimulus salience during naturalistic, fast-paced presentations of visual content" (p. 21275). Blinking is also thought to be subject to less diverse influence factors than electrodermal or cardiovascular measures, thus allowing for more precise inferences on mental activity (p. 21275). Blinking is further thought to be superior to these measures regarding latency and refractory period, making it well suited for ecologically valid stimuli (p. 21275), and it can be measured relatively easy and unobtrusively (p. 21275). Ichikawa and Ohira (2004) note that measurement of blinking does not require an explicit response, and can thus be used non-intrusively to study both conscious and unconscious processes. Based on the research reviewed in section 4, it can further be assumed that eye-blink behavior reflects very basic cognitive processes, and shows comparable effects for participants from different age groups and cultures.

5.3 Limitations of an Eye-Blink Measure

Several additional limitations—apart from the conceptual problems we have addressed in section 3—can be found for the use of spontaneous eye-blink behavior. Due to the very high inter-individual variability, it is necessary to derive indicators that are in their conception independent of blink rate. At least on an individual level, this high variability will still lead to very different temporal resolutions of a blinking measure: less detailed information about blink timing will be gained for individuals with only rare blink occurrences. Further, it is problematic to infer on the exact reason for a change in eye-blink behavior without additional information. Because inhibition or elicitation of blinks can result from a wide variety of sources, it would be possible that structured blinking behavior is not only exhibited by participants in a state of presence. As could be shown in Liebold et al.'s (2017) study, purposefully induced breaks in presence caused detectable changes in blinking behavior, and would thus contribute to a structured blinking behavior, as well. Consequently, media events probably need to be taken into consideration when interpreting blinking behavior.

Finally, Wirth et al. (2008) criticize objective measures in general. The authors state that objective measures were frequently obtrusive, and were not unambiguous with regard to their validity; apart from that, the subjective nature of the presence concept would always call for subjective criteria (p. 75).

5.4 Questionnaire as Standard

In this thesis, blinking as a secondary, corroborative measure will be related to an established self-report measure for presence. To this end, subjective assessments of presence are collected with the German version of the SPES questionnaire (Hartmann et al., 2015), a theoretically grounded self-report measure intended for use in diverse media environments. The SPES is available in English, German, Finnish, and Portuguese, and is a refined version of the MEC-SPQ questionnaire (Vorderer et al., 2004; Wirth et al., 2008). The MEC-SPQ was developed in the same project as Wirth et al.'s (2007) process model (project Presence: Measurement, Effects, Conditions; MEC, IST-2001-37661), and has been tested in text, hypertext, film, and virtual reality media environments in 23 international studies with 1536 participants (Wirth et al., 2008). As the MEC-SPQ, the SPES questionnaire comprises five-point Likert scales for the two theorized facets of spatial presence, spatial presence self-location (SPSL) and spatial presence possible actions (SPPA) with four items each, and scales with eight items each for the media- and user-related antecedents attention (ATT), spatial situation model (SSM), involvement (INV), domain-specific interest (DSI), and visual-spatial imagery (VSI). For the thesis experiments, two additional scales were taken from the MEC-SPQ. First, a scale for suspension of disbelief (SOD), which is no longer part of the SPES questionnaire, and second, an abbreviated form of the Tellegen Absorption Scale (TAS, Tellegen & Atkinson, 1974), the MEC-SPQ Abbreviated Absorption Scale (Vorderer et al., 2004; based on the German translation of the TAS by Ritz & Dahme, 1995).

In Hartmann et al.'s (2015) validation studies with a total of 685 participants, the SPSL sub-scale showed good internal consistencies with Cronbach's alphas of $\alpha = .92$ and $\alpha = .91$. Experiments with a dual-task distraction paradigm were used to test the scale's ability to distinguish between conditions of low and high presence. In the distraction condition, participants were asked to produce five random three-digit numbers after auditory cues. The SPSL sub-scale could differentiate between conditions with an effect size of $d = 0.34$ (Hartmann et al., 2015; d calculated from descriptives). Factor analyses overall confirmed the intended factor structure. As expected, presence scores were found to correlate with the SPES questionnaire's additional scales for user traits and presence antecedents.

In their evaluation of alternative presence measures, Böcking et al. (2008) used the MEC-SPQ's scale for the self-location facet of spatial presence; here, we use the closely related SPES self-location scale. This approach is supported by previous findings suggesting that video game difficulty affects ratings of the second facet of spatial presence, possible actions: the more difficult participants perceived a game to be, the less they rated their perceived possibilities to act in the virtual environment (Brill, Ertan, Luksch, & Schwab, 2015); apparently, this is not an issue for the SPSL scale.

Wording of the SPES items was adapted to match the respective film or game media environments. Instruction texts for the questionnaire were designed following the MEC-SPQ's instructions. The questionnaire was administered as either an online questionnaire using the soscisurvey platform (Leiner, 2014; studies 1 and 3), or as a paper version (study 2). Sequences of SPES and MEC-SPQ items were randomized to prevent sequence effects. In studies 1 and 3, items were presented in random order for each participant; in study 2, the paper questionnaire was randomly handed out in one of two versions with different item order.

5.5 Stimulus Material

To evaluate the relation between structural aspects of blinking behavior and a self-report measure for spatial presence, three different types of stimuli will be used, differing on the three dimensions interactivity, continuity, and narrative. While "narrative, drama and plot in the media content" (Wirth et al., 2007, p. 510) are supposed to influence the formation of presence experiences, for example mediated by processes of involvement and attention (Wirth et al., 2007), the narrative aspect will not be considered in this thesis. Instead, we will use varying degrees of interactivity and continuity, and base the experiments on paradigms used in existing studies on blinking behavior.

5.5.1 Continuity

The aspect of continuity focuses on formal stimulus features, which are in this case cinematic stylistic means. Movies and TV shows are edited in the process of film montage, with the shot as the very basic unit; in terms of traditional filmmaking, a shot can be defined as a single, physically continuous piece of film (Monaco, 2015, p. 134; Wulff, 2012a). A scene can then be composed out of one or several shots, which have in common location, narrative, or present characters (Monaco & Bock, 2011, p. 239; Wulff, 2012b). As a more complex narrative means, a sequence can be composed out of several shots depicting a more complex action, which can span several locations, and can omit unnecessary parts of its action (Monaco, 2015, p. 181). If scenes or sequences consist of several shots, they necessarily feature cuts or transitions between the separate shots, and, on a higher level, cuts or transitions will also be found between multiple scenes or sequences. These cuts disrupt continuity of the visual stream of information; to not disrupt the cinematic experience, they are either placed unobtrusively by techniques of continuity editing (Berliner & Cohen, 2011; Magliano & Zacks, 2011), or are carefully hidden in a way that suggests the movie shows only one uninterrupted shot (Monaco, 2015, p. 134).

During reception of cinematic material, spatial situation models need to be constructed from the provided information and need to be updated either after a cut, or after continuous changes of screen content. In the sense of Wirth et al.'s (2007) model, the presented spatial cues need to be perceived, a new spatial situation model needs to be constructed, and this model needs to be accepted as the new primary-ego-reference-frame. In the sense of Liebold et al.'s (2017) assumptions, the change in screen content should elicit an orienting response and let recipients update their mental model. If the narrative is presented in a continuous shot without cuts, presentation of new spatial information, for example during a tracking shot, occurs less abrupt, and can be incorporated into the existing spatial situation model. This could be seen as a special case for the incremental updating of mental models at film event boundaries discussed by Huff, Meitz, and Papenmeier (2014). We can thus speculate that processing of both types of cinematic stimuli, segmented and continuous, is strictly speaking not identical, despite the efforts to conceal cuts by means of continuity editing. This formal aspect could possibly influence blinking behavior, because the rather abrupt changes during cuts could serve as a facilitator of blinks, similar to the end of a trial in trial-based experiments. However, existing blink research suggests that structuring of eye-blinks will also occur when using a continuous stimulus. In Nakano et al.'s (2009) study, the authors still found synchrony in participants' blinking behavior after removing blinks from analysis that occurred immediately after cuts. In Nomura et al.'s (2015) study, participants showed synchrony in blinking behavior during appreciation of continuous video recordings with a static camera position. In the study by Shultz, Klin and Jones (2011), toddlers showed patterns of blink inhibition when watching video recordings of other toddlers at play. Consequently, this thesis will test both types of film stimuli on their ability to cause structured blinking behavior. In addition, no studies were found in preparation of this thesis that deal with structure in blinking behavior towards a continuous stimulus with a smoothly moving camera, and the aforementioned studies with continuous stimuli did not investigate relations between blinking and spatial presence, but focused on other aspects of recipient experience.

5.5.2 Interactivity

In several theoretical approaches, interactivity of a media stimulus has been identified as a key factor for formation of presence, for example by Steuer (1992), Lombard and Ditton (1997), IJsselsteijn, de Ridder, Freeman, and Avons (2000), or IJsselsteijn (2002). In the latter publication, IJsselsteijn states that interactivity could be even more important than a realistically depicted environment, at least under the premise that the most interactive media environments were at this time not visually rich due to technological restrictions. Within the theoretical frame of this thesis, Wirth et al. (2007) also assume that well-implemented interactivity can benefit formation of presence, for example by supporting attention allocation on the stimulus, or because the user receives immediate feedback about her actions, thus facilitating acceptance of the medium as the primary ego reference frame (pp. 510–511). In this thesis, we will not address the exact differences between stimuli with and without requirement of motoric actions. However, since Oh, Han, Peterson and Jeong (2012) assume blinks to be an indicator for shifts in cognitive states, such as a shift from attention on the stimulus to a motor response, it can be assumed that user actions will contribute to structuring of blinking behavior in interactive media environments.

5.5.3 Stimuli for Thesis Experiments

Three experiments will be conducted with externally valid stimuli: (1) an experiment with a conventionally edited, and thus pre-segmented, non-interactive video stimulus, (2) an experiment with a continuously edited, thus not explicitly segmented, non-interactive video stimulus, and (3) an experiment with a continuous, interactive video game stimulus. The stimuli are selected to cover a broad range of media-psychological applications for a secondary presence measure. Furthermore, all experiments are based on existing studies, in which structure in blinking behavior had already been observed.

Experiment 1 uses an excerpt from a conventionally edited TV show. This stimulus is the same excerpt from a *Mr. Bean* TV show (release used as stimulus material: Birkin, Davies, & Weiland, 2014) that was used by Nakano et al. (2009); as in Nakano et al.'s study, the video stimulus is presented without audio. The stimulus can be characterized as artificially segmented, because it is edited in a conventional manner as a sequence of scenes, each consisting of a sequence of shots, with cuts and transitions in between shots and scenes. Being a video, the stimulus is non-interactive. The excerpt narrates a story, but this thesis will not take the narrative aspect into consideration.

Experiment 2 uses an excerpt from a continuously edited feature film, the Academy Award winning 2014 motion picture *Birdman or (The Unexpected Virtue of Ignorance)* (Iñárritu, 2014). The stimulus can be characterized as not being segmented artificially, because it is edited in a continuous manner to convey the impression of one continuous shot throughout the whole movie, with only few, carefully concealed transitions between shots. Being a video, the stimulus is non-interactive, as well. This makes the stimulus partly comparable to Nomura et al.'s (2009) stimulus, where they presented their participants recordings of Japanese rakugo performances. During a performance of rakugo, the comedian, or rakugoka, sits on his knees, uses only very limited props, and narrates a comic story by portraying several characters (Oshima, 1998). It can be assumed that the rakugo recordings presented by Nomura et al. featured a static camera perspective; in this respect, the material differs from the Birdman stimulus material, where the camera dynamically follows characters through the set. However, the key aspect of an uninterrupted, unsegmented stream of visual information is maintained; additionally, due to the camera's fluid movement through the sets of the Birdman movie, this stimulus is more appropriate for spatial presence research than a static comedy performance. The excerpt from the Birdman movie narrates a story, but this aspect will not be considered in this thesis.

Experiment 3 uses a Racing video game. This stimulus is similar to the video game stimulus used in a previous study of the author (Brill, 2010). As a video game, the stimulus can be characterized as continuous and interactive, because from beginning to end of the simulated race, the point of view consistently remains a first-person perspective from within the simulated car. As game mode, the experiment uses a qualifying session without other race participants, so the game sequence does not narrate an explicit story.

This selection of stimuli thus allows for evaluation of blink-related methods using representatives from the domains of (a) cinematic stimuli, as found in TV or feature films, (b) continuous video stimuli, as found in naturalistic videos, and (c) interactive digital games.

5.6 Manipulation

For the evaluation of an alternative presence measure in this study, we will compare different conditions that are supposed to elicit higher and lower presence experiences. This approach is used in existing research on the validation of presence self-report measures (e.g., Hartmann et al., 2015) or objective corroborative measures (Böcking et al., 2008; Freeman, Avons, Meddis, Pearson, & IJsselsteijn, 2000; IJsselsteijn, Ridder, Freeman, Avons, & Bouwhuis, 2001). To realize this approach, an effective manipulation of presence experiences is needed, which at the same time should not contaminate the blinking measure.

5.6.1 Manipulation of the Media Use Setting

Cummings and Bailenson (2016) provide a meta-analysis on the effectiveness of presence-relevant stimulus manipulations, and conclude that the most powerful factors are technological aspects of immersion, with "increased levels of user-tracking, the use of stereoscopic visuals, and wider fields of view" (p. 1). User tracking is not applicable for media stimuli in this thesis. Field of view is not promising in the scope of this thesis, because for a stimulus with a larger field of view, larger saccades are necessary to perceive visual information. Large saccades have been shown to co-occur with, or facilitate spontaneous blinks, and would thus contaminate the measure (Evinger et al., 1994). Presence induction by means of stereoscopic 3D stimuli is not supposed to be applicable, either, because previous study results (Brill, 2010) have shown that blink rate in participants who played a racing game with stereoscopic 3D shutter glasses was almost half the rate of participants playing in traditional 2D. Therefore, it was refrained from influencing presence by manipulating technological aspects of media presentation.

Another possibility of creating experimental conditions with different levels of presence would be to not facilitate formation of presence in one condition, but to actively hinder or disrupt formation of presence in one condition. Interference with presence experiences can be established by means of a secondary task, which is absorbing attentional resources of the user (e.g., Böcking et al., 2008; Hartmann et al., 2015). However, since previous findings have shown that such disruptions during media use reliably elicit orienting responses and blinks (Liebold, Brill, Pietschmann, Schwab, & Ohler, 2017), this approach of creating different experimental conditions is not used, either.

We can conclude that manipulations within the visual modality would most likely affect blinking behavior, and are therefore not suitable as a manipulation of presence experiences in this study. This includes factors of visual stimulus presentation reported by Cummings and Bailenson (2016), namely update rate and detail of the depicted mediated environment, which will not be implemented in these studies, either. Manipulation of audio is assumed to deliver too weak effects for this thesis (Cummings & Bailenson, 2016), and would not be possible to implement for the video-only stimulus in the first thesis experiment. We therefore try to obtain different levels of presence experiences by means of different instructions for the participants, while at the same time using identical stimulus material for both experimental groups; this way, it is possible to prevent an influence of different stimuli on blinking behavior.

5.6.2 Manipulation of Instructions

When studying narrative transportation, Green and Brock (2000) induced conditions of high and low levels of transportation by instructing participants differently. The participants should either (a) read the text as if they were to enact the narrative in a theater, or (b) pay attention to the stimulus in a regular way, or (c) screen the text for expressions too complicated on a fourth-grader level (p. 709). The latter manipulation could be interpreted as directing the media user's attention towards formal features of the medium, and thus inducing cognitive processes that hinder the emergence of transportation; however, results showed mixed effects of instruction on the dependent variables, and suggested that other influencing aspects might have overruled instructions.

Bacherle (2015) provides a collection of possible manipulations, primarily for the domain of transportation. Not all presented manipulations by instruction were successful; among these, Bacherle reports instructions to focus on formal features of a text, or cinematography and cuts of a movie (Tisinger, 2004). Bacherle further states that instructions would need to be repeated throughout the reception situation to prevent participants getting absorbed by the stimulus (p. 49). Tisinger's (2004) successful approach to reduce transportation reminded participants multiple times to attend to several tasks focusing on formal features of the stimulus movie, but at the cost of high distraction from the stimulus. However, these distractions (taking notes about badly executed cuts, number of close-up perspectives, words too complicated for 6th- to 8th-graders, and number of implausible scenes) would in our case likely contaminate structure in blinking behavior, and are also not externally valid manipulations. Bacherle successfully employed an externally valid manipulation of transportation and narrative engagement (Bacherle, 2015, p. 173) by providing participants with different information about the movie stimulus; this information mimicked a movie review and differed in as how good and gratifying the movie was described. We can see these findings as an encouragement that manipulation by instructions or by information about the stimulus can, in principle, manipulate reception phenomena. In the MEC-SPQ validation studies presented in Böcking et al. (2008), participants in one of the experimental conditions were asked to read a stimulus text with a very critical attitude; in this case, the authors suspected that reduced suspension of disbelief would hinder the participants' transition into a state of presence. We will use these findings as a starting point to develop appropriate instructions for the experiments in this thesis.

5.6.3 Manipulation in Thesis Experiments

In order to develop instructions with an impact on presence experiences, we again have a look at definitions of presence, which see overlooking of the mediated nature of a media use experience as a necessary condition for presence to emerge. Within the theoretical frame of this thesis, this crucial aspect is included in the presence concept by Wirth et al. (2007), but also in other presence theories:

- Minski (1980) predicts for the concept of telepresence that future telepresence work could be executed with highly sophisticated instruments, so the remotely operated tools become indistinguishable from the user's own hands.
- Lombard and Ditton (1997) describe presence as the perceptual illusion of non-mediation.
- Lee (2004b) sees as a feature of presence that virtual entities are treated very much like real entities.
- Garau et al. (2008) see a lack of breaks in presence—during which technology becomes apparent—as an indicator of presence.
- Slater, Lotto, Arnold, and Sanchez-Vives (2009) describe that in a state of presence, the user's senses are active like in a real-life situation.
- The International Society for Presence Research (ISPR) describes that behavior during a state of presence matches behavior in a real-world situation, and spatial presence occurs "when part or all of a person's perception fails to accurately acknowledge the role of technology that makes it appear that s/he is in a physical location and environment different from her/his actual location and environment in the physical world" (ISPR, 2009).
- Liebold, Pietschmann, and Ohler (2015) see focused attention on stimulus content as the core aspect of presence.
- Liebold et al. (2017) conclude from presented research that breaks in presence, that is transitions out of a state of presence, shift "the user's cognitive resources back to the real world" (p. 4) and direct the user's attention "at the medium as an artifact" (p. 4). Consequently, the user's cognitive resources are allocated to the media stimulus during a state of presence, and the medium is not perceived as an artifact.

We conclude that as long as attention is focused on the medium as an artificial delivery device for media content, users should not be able to perceive the content as unmediated, and consequently should not enter a state of presence. This notion parallels the concept of analytical and involved reception modes (Charlton & Borcsa, 1997; Liebes & Katz, 1986; Suckfüll, 2004; Vorderer, 1992). While Suckfüll (2004) offers the most sophisticated concept and questionnaire for reception modes, we will use Vorderer's (1992) basic conception for the purpose of this thesis; he hypothesizes that in an involved mode of reception, the recipient shows high cognitive and emotional involvement towards the media stimulus, so the mediated nature of the reception situation is neglected. In an analytical mode, on the other hand, the recipients should be distanced, uninvolved observers of media characteristics such as structure, actors, locations, or topics in the movie (Vorderer, 1992). Researchers have also suggested to understand spatial presence as a reception mode (Hartmann et al., 2005). Vorderer's (1992) approach of measuring reception modes with very short self-report measures will be used as a guideline for a manipulation check in the experiments of this thesis.

Based on this research, we intend to reduce occurrences of presence by instructing participants to closely and consciously pay attention to formal media features, so the mediated nature of the experience will always be salient. However, in order to prevent influence on blinking behavior, the instructions will not be repeated throughout the media use process, as has been suggested by Bacherle (2015). Nevertheless, the emergence of presence should be hindered without a potentially problematic manipulation of the media stimulus. The different instructions for participants are rather intended to affect the style of attention allocation on, and internal processing of the stimulus, and should influence both formation of presence and blinking behavior. Regarding the external validity of the presence-hindering instruction, the interference with internal processing of the stimulus should in theory correspond to non-laboratory instances of media use without presence, where the mediated nature of the experience is salient, as would be the case during switching to an analytical reception mode.

A problem for this approach is the common confounder between form and content in media. As Ohler (1994) states in his discourse on cognitive film psychology, there is an interdependent relationship between cinematic form and content, which he explains by applying schema-theoretical approaches to movie reception processes (p. 37). Ohler argues that knowledge of narrative content and knowledge of cinematic form features are schematically organized in a narrative form-content-correspondence-grid; as a consequence, certain cinematic form features could be understood as indicators for upcoming narrative elements, and vice versa, narrative elements could evoke expectations about upcoming cinematic stylistic means.

In the scope of this thesis, it can be questioned if two instructions to focus on either form or content will lead to distinctive patterns of attention allocation, especially for a traditionally edited film stimulus. In this worst case, both groups would, as intended, focus on either form or content, and show appropriate, stimulus-dependent structure in blinking behavior, but this structure would be very similar due to the close interdependence of form and content. However, for a rigorous evaluation of blinking behavior as an objective measure, the method must face this challenge. Additionally, this approach provides a rigorous test of the alternative measurement candidate, which should ideally be able to distinguish between attention allocated to a media stimulus in a state of presence, and attention allocated to the medium in a non-presence state.

Before detailing the experiments for this thesis, we will address in the next two subsections how eye-blink behavior will be measured, and how the resulting data will be analyzed.

5.7 Eye-Blink Measurement

We have established that eye-blinks are sensitive to internal processing that likely occurs during media use, and have seen that spontaneous eye-blink behavior possesses potentially beneficial properties as an alternative measure. However, since blinking behavior is also sensitive to external stimuli, a controlled experimental environment will be used to prevent distractions. To identify and control further interfering factors for blinking, we will now address aspects and methods of measurement, and will derive appropriate measurement procedures for the present thesis experiments.

To identify unwanted influences on blinking behavior, we rely on Cruz et al.'s (2011) overview over a large body of research on factors of spontaneous blink rate (SBR). Factors include age, with a relative stabilization of SBR after adolescence, a number of neurological and psychiatric conditions, momentary condition of the ocular surface, and mental activity. Regarding age, the samples recruited in this thesis are relatively homogenous due to the use of student samples, with participants being past their adolescence, so no interference is expected from participant age. Unlike in, for example, Siegle, Ichikawa, and Steinhauer's (2008) study, participants are not screened for psychiatric or neurological disorders, vision acuity, eye-related health problems, use of psychoactive drugs or alcohol, or other vision-related variables. Siegle et al. recruited a sample of 58 participants from a general population, and did not exclude any of their participants, so we assume that the probability of interference from such factors will be rather low. While it was not possible to use air-conditioned laboratories, room temperature and relative humidity recorded in thesis studies 2 and 3 showed that environmental conditions were in general relatively stable and comparable to, for example, Tsubota and Nakamori's study (1993), who measured their laboratory at 22.5 °C and 40% humidity. Regarding the time of day for experimental sessions, Barbato et al. (2000) found that spontaneous eye-blink rate remains relatively stable during daytime hours, as measured at 10:00, 13:30, and 17:00 hours. An increase was found for evening hours during measurements taken at 20:30

hours (p. 148), possibly because an increase in dopamine levels might counteract sleepiness during early evening hours (Barbato et al., 2000). For this thesis, no interference is expected from time of testing because all experiments were conducted during daytime hours. Bentivoglio et al. (2004) report no effects of age or corrective spectacles on blinking behavior in their study, and an effect of gender only during reading of text stimuli. This suggests that little interference can be expected from these factors. Although tear film integrity and vision acuity are supposed to be changed by wearing contact lenses (Thai, Tomlinson, & Ridder, 2002; Timberlake, Doane, & Bertera, 1992), we accept this interference because participants wearing contact lenses during experiments are most likely accustomed to the effects. Additionally, while there is evidence that blink rate is affected by the use of contact lenses (Carney & Hill, 1984), no such reports could be found for blink structure.

Since average blink frequencies have been found to vary considerably between individuals, a sufficiently long measurement period is necessary to capture a representative sample of blinking behavior, including longer inter-blink intervals (Kaminer, Powers, Horn, Hui, & Evinger, 2011, pp. 11264–11265). Research suggests that a measurement period of five minutes is sufficient for human blink rate calculation (Tada et al., 2013, p. 2; Zaman & Doughty, 1997). Although not blink frequency, but blinking structure is in the focus of this thesis, these suggestions are accounted for in the observational periods in thesis studies 2 and 3; thesis study 1 deviates from this suggestion, partly due to reasons of replication.

As for example Doughty and Naase (2006) had observed, spontaneous eyeblink rate varies significantly between individuals; related to this high variability is the question of excluding participants with extreme blink rates from analysis, which is a common approach in studies on blinking behavior. Doughty and Naase (2006) were rather interested in describing determinants of blink rate, and not so much in derivation of behavioral indices for further analyses; consequently, they only categorized participants into groups with low and high blink rates, using an empirically derived threshold of 20 blinks per minute. We thus rely on other studies for deriving a criterion for identification and exclusion of extreme outliers. Nakano et al. (2009) excluded participants with a blink rate of more than one standard deviation above or below the mean, resulting in limits of 8.2 and 41.0 blinks per minute. Nakano et al. (2010) used the same approach, what led to limits of 9 and 41 blinks per minute, respectively. In another study by Nakano et al. (2011), participants were excluded when they showed "excessive blinking" (p. 2785) or very little blinking, leading to exclusion of participants with a blink rate of 54 blinks per minute or above, and 6 blinks per minute or below. Nakano, Kato, Morito, Itoi, and Kitazawa (2013) excluded participants with more than 60 blinks per minute from analysis. Since there seems to be no established standard for acceptable limits of blink rate, we will exclude participants from analysis who deviate more than two standard deviations from the sample's mean, thus seeking a compromise between exclusion of extreme outliers, and retaining a broad behavioral range in the samples. This rather loose criterion should also allow for more generalizable conclusions from the experimental results.

Regarding the choice of an adequate measurement method for eye-blink behavior, Cruz, Garcia, Pinto, and Cechetti (2011, pp. 29–30) provide a list of several possible methods: mechanical methods, electrooculography, electromyography, video recordings analyzed by human coders or appropriate software, infrared reflectance as found in eye-tracking, and magnetic search coil techniques. Cruz et al. (2011, p. 30) judge measurement by video as a good approach if subjects should not be manipulated. Since obtrusive real-world cues can interfere with presence formation, we chose to code eye-blinks from unobtrusively recorded videos in thesis experiments 1 and 2. As Cruz et al. note, a problem for coding reliability during use of most methods is the wide range of blink amplitudes, leading to possible confusion if a recorded lid movement should be classified as a blink. For this reason, clearly observable features of lid movement were used as coding criteria in the thesis experiments: a blink was to be coded when a rapid downward and upward movement of the upper lid let the lid cover the participant's pupil at least partially. Borderline cases for coder decisions proved to be especially the lid movements during large, downward saccades; frame-by-frame reviewing of video material was necessary in these cases to determine if the upper lid exerted a larger than necessary downward movement, followed by an upward movement to an adequate position for the new gaze vector. Since we cover no theoretical background on the phenomenon of incomplete blinks, a well-known phenomenon in research on, for example, VDU work (see section 4), we will incorporate both complete and incomplete blinks into analyses; future research would need to address if the occurrence of incomplete blinks, possibly indicating a misperformance of blink suppression mechanisms, is of informative value. Because literature does not mention incomplete blinks as especially obtrusive, it could be concluded that neural visual suppression, and thus loss of visual information, is comparable to suppression found during complete blinks. In this case, even incomplete closure of the palpebral fissure would lead to complete loss of visual information, and would also vindicate to treat complete and incomplete blinks the same. Coding inaccuracies resulting from different degrees of pupil dilation during the experiment were accepted, because all experiments were conducted in darkened environments; the media stimulus represented the only source of light, and due to identical apparatus within each experiment, both average, minimum and maximum luminous emittance from the screens should be comparable within each experiment. For thesis experiment 3, eye-tracking was used as an objective and economical measurement method. Böcking et al. (2008) found eye-tracking to be an unobtrusive measurement approach; in their study, comparing conditions with and without eye-tracking showed effect sizes on presence scores from $\eta^2 = 0.00$ to 0.03. Surprisingly, eye-tracking using a chin-rest with fixed forehead was also not reported as a problematic factor in Nomura et al.'s (2015) study on transportation. We thus assume that the measurements taken with unobtrusively placed cameras (thesis study 1 and study 2) and eye-tracking glasses allowing for free movement (thesis study 3) can be considered to be unobtrusive. The limitations of this thesis project did not allow for additional, explicit testing of obtrusiveness, for example with parallel conditions without blink measurement, because necessary sample sizes would have increased considerably; this aspect remains to be addressed in future research.

5.8 Analyzing Stimulus Dependence

Determining if the structure of blinking behavior depends on the dynamic event structure of a stimulus is a key goal of this thesis. The following section will address two aspects to establish the analytical framework of this thesis: (1) a short recapitulation of why a stimulus dependence of blinking should emerge in the first place, and (2) how structural aspects of blinking behavior can be analyzed.

5.8.1 Emergence of Stimulus-Dependent Structure

In media environments, several actions of users or recipients can be required during media use; depending on the technological properties of the media environment, these necessary actions can concern attention, visuospatial interaction, or creation and execution of a motor plan (Alcañiz et al., 2009). Attention is either allocated in a controlled manner or automatically, and enables the organism to perceive and process the presented media information (Wirth et al., 2007). For presence to occur, the organism depends on a stable stream of stimuli, so information can be extracted and used for creation and updating of mental models of the mediated situation (Liebold et al., 2017; Wirth et al., 2007). We assume that such processes will cause a structured, stimulus-dependent blinking behavior, because blinks can be inhibited during intake and processing of such information, or can be executed at certain points in an information processing chain (see sections 4.2.1 and 4.2.2). Further, orienting responses occur during intake of information for presence formation (Posner, 1980; Wirth et al., 2007); recent research has proposed the significance of orienting responses for breaks in presence and updating of mental models, suggesting that blink inhibition occurs after orienting responses elicited by breaks in presence (Liebold et al., 2017).

A large body of scientific evidence has been collected on timing of spontaneous eye-blinks (see section 4.2). For example, Malmstrom, Rachofsky and Weber (1977) favored the interpretation of blinks as indicators of cognitive activity over their initial blink inhibition hypothesis. Blink timing has been described to depend on task complexity and attentional demands (Stern et al., 1984). Blinking has further been interpreted as an indicator for, or possibly a component of processes around shifts in cognitive state (Oh, Han, Peterson, & Jeong, 2012). Other researchers also see blinks as an indicator for cognitive processing, possibly triggered by finalized stimulus evaluation in tasks with and without need for motor responses (Wascher, Heppner, Möckel, Kobald, & Getzmann, 2015); these authors regard blink timing as a "reliable marker of cognitive processing speed even in no-go situations" (p. 1216). Nakano (2015) attributes blinks an active role in cognitive processing, because blinks may support switching between internal and external orienting networks. Nakano assumes that blinks might facilitate memory retrieval, and could support information processing by contributing to attention disengagement. We derive from these and other research findings presented in this thesis that the influence of cognitive processes in states of presence could lead to a stimulus-dependent structuring of spontaneous eye-blink behavior.

5.8.2 Analysis of Structured Blinking Behavior

Various approaches have been used to analyze stimulus-dependence of blinking in reception of media stimuli: *blink rate* during certain stimulus segments (Bacherle, 2015), *variability of inter-blink intervals* (Nomura et al., 2015), measures of *spike train synchrony* (Nomura et al., 2015), and *T-pattern detection* (Brill, Carolus, & Schwab, 2010, 2011; Brill, Jonsson, & Schwab, 2014). Several aspects of each method will be discussed now: the respective basic analysis rationale, existing studies employing the method, robustness of the respective method for use in different media environments, and implications for the present thesis. Another method using onset asynchrony of blink occurrences (Nakano et al., 2009) will not be discussed here due to the limitations of this thesis, but will be referred to at a later point in this thesis when adequate randomization techniques are discussed.

5.8.2.1 Blink Rate

Rationale

Researchers can use blink rate to observe stimulus- or task-dependent changes in blink frequency. To this effect, they can focus on the participant's blink rate over the whole observation period, or on the blink rate during defined intervals of the observation period, only. In any case, the measure should be especially sensitive to occurrences of extended blink inhibition or blink bursts. Early studies conclude that not so much blink rate itself, but the pattern of blink rate changes can inform researchers about an individual's internal state (Drew, 1951; Poulton & Gregory, 1952). So far, several studies have observed blink frequencies in defined intervals during media use, and have used the derived blink rate as an indicator for internal processes.

Existing Studies

Brill et al. (Brill, 2010; Brill, Carolus, & Schwab, 2011) observed spontaneous eye-blinks in users of a racing video game, and analyzed their distribution along straight and bent segments of the simulated race track. Based on Nakano et al.'s (2009) findings, it was expected that blink frequency during bent segments would be decreased, so blinks would not interfere with intake of crucial visual information. Chi-square analyses of binned frequencies showed that blinking differed significantly between the two types of segments, but contrary to hypotheses, segments with lower blink probability were located around the entries of bends, not around their apexes. It can be assumed that both need for visual information intake, and cognitive load are higher before entries, since entering a bend with appropriate speed and vector is crucial for successful passage. Different from usual calculations of blink rate, the focus in this analysis was not on the time of blink occurrence, but on the positions of blinks along the race track.

Garsoffky, Glaser, and Schwan (2012) related eye-blink frequency to ratings of transportation experiences; they hypothesized that due to increased attentional processes in a transported state, blink rate would be decreased compared to a baseline condition. They further hypothesized that in an attention facilitating condition, blink rate would be decreased more than in an attention hindering condition. To operationalize facilitation of attention, the laboratory was darkened, the stimulus was presented on a large screen, in good video quality, with stereo audio, and no distracting objects in the room. To operationalize hindering of attention on the stimulus, the video stimulus was presented on a small subsection of the large screen, in poor, noisy video quality, with a distracting overlay at the bottom of the screen, mono audio, and with distracting objects in the well-lit lab. Five-minute baselines before each experiment were used for calculation of a blinking base rate. With absorption tendency and involvement controlled, participants showed significantly higher transportation scores in the high attention condition. Baseline-corrected blink rates were significantly lower in the high attention condition, and only for the high attention condition, blink rates during film reception differed significantly from the baseline period. In the scope of this thesis, it could be criticized that manipulation of experimental conditions included interventions that might affect blinking behavior by themselves.

Bacherle (2015) derived several indicators from blink rates in 30 seconds long bins during a film stimulus, and related these indicators to self-report scores from scales for transportation, narrative engagement, and sub-components of narrative engagement (see section 3.3.2). In one study, blink frequency correlated significantly negative with transportation, but not narrative engagement or its subscales. In another study, mean frequency, frequency at film start, frequency at film end, number of extreme values, slope as the overall linear tendency of blink rate during the measurement interval, and blink frequency at the moment of greatest variance did not correlate significantly with self-report measures, and some correlations showed effects contradicting the hypotheses.

Nomura et al. (2015) found that log-transformed mean blink rate did not correlate significantly with transportation, and was no significant predictor for transportation in a multiple regression analysis.

Robustness
The indicator's applicability for diverse media stimuli can be discussed to be limited: especially for interactive stimuli, careful and individual definition of intervals would be necessary.

Implications for This Thesis
This problem of defining appropriate intervals in interactive stimuli had been circumvented in a previous study (Brill, 2010) by not analyzing when, but where in the virtual environment blinks occurred. In analogy to the analysis in time domain and frequency domain in signal processing (Broughton & Bryan, 2009, p. 72), these approaches for blink research could be labeled time domain (when does a blink occur) and spatial domain (where does a blink occur). In the aforementioned study (Brill, 2010), blink occurrences were mapped to their respective positions on the racetrack, thereby simplifying the definition of analysis intervals—bent sections vs. straight sections of the racetrack were invariant for all participants. However, such analyses do not account for the slightly different individual game experiences of different players who drive, for example, slower or faster, because this information would be part of the time domain. To counter

this challenge, bins can be defined around certain, well defined events, for example breaks in presence (Liebold et al., 2017). For the purpose of this thesis, we do not use blink rate, but focus on measures that allow for a better analysis of structure during the whole observation duration.

5.8.2.2 Blink Variability

Rationale
For the measure of blink variability, it is assumed that if blinking behavior is influenced by the stimulus, then blink intervals should be shortened or prolonged due to ongoing attention on media content, thus leading to a higher standard deviation of blink interval lengths (Nomura et al., 2015, p. 2). If a stimulus or task dependence of blinking behavior is present, then blink variability should be higher than without stimulus dependence. When not influenced by external stimuli, blink occurrences should be determined predominantly by physiological necessities. Blink variability can be observed during the whole observation period, or during defined segments of the observation period.

Existing Studies
Variability of inter-blink intervals (IBI) was examined by Nomura et al. (2015) as an indicator for transportation experiences. To this end, the standard deviation of each participant's inter-blink intervals, as an individual measure for eyeblink variability, was log-transformed and related to self-report variables. While there was no correlation of log-transformed standard deviations with questionnaire scores, the variable was found to be a significant predictor in a multiple regression analysis, and regressed on transportation experiences after controlling for perceived humor.

Robustness
Blink interval variability as a measure depends on an identical stimulus for all experimental groups. If participants are presented dynamically changing stimuli, the resulting variability will not only account for blink-timing differences caused by internal processes, but might also be the result of the different stimulus characteristics. Users of an interactive stimulus might even show a comparable structure in blinking behavior that follows the same stimulus characteristics, for example due to a very stable blink elicitation after certain events. However, the method would probably fail to portray this similar behavior towards different stimuli, because the blink-eliciting events occur with different timing, and thus lead to different inter-blink intervals.

Implications for This Thesis

The original concept makes the measure probably well suited for the video stimuli in this thesis. Due to its dependence on identical stimuli, the measure is in principle inappropriate for interactive media; however, it will nevertheless be evaluated as an easy to acquire indicator for blinking behavior in the game environment, as well.

5.8.2.3 Spike Train Synchrony

Rationale

An individual's blinking behavior during media use can be represented as a time series of blink occurrences, either as a continuous vector (e.g., with all samples coded as zero, and only samples with blink occurrences as one), or as a vector containing the time stamps of blink occurrences. When represented in this fashion, the blinking data resembles data structures used in neuroscience to describe firing behavior of neurons. In this field of research, measures have been developed to analyze stimulus dependence of such discrete event occurrences; one example is spike train synchrony, or conversely, measures for spike train dissimilarity, as used in Nomura et al.'s (2015) study. Nomura et al. used a method developed by Victor and Purpura (1997) to analyze temporal coding of neuronal impulse trains, that is coordinated firing behavior of neurons. This method is a cost-based spike train metric, meaning it estimates dissimilarity of two spike trains by finding a way to transform one spike train into another with minimal costs. For these transformations, a simple set of rules defines costs for the possible transformation steps: insertion and deletion of a spike each cause a cost of one arbitrary unit, and shifting a spike along the time axis causes costs depending on the shifted distance multiplied by a user-defined factor q. Consequently, costs increase as more spikes need to be deleted, inserted, or shifted along the time axis, thus quantifying the dissimilarity between two spike trains. Additionally, the algorithm can be tuned to be sensitive on different time scales by selecting different values for the factor q. To date, a series of different measures for spike train synchrony has been proposed (for an overview and comparison, see, e.g., Kreuz, Mormann, et al., 2007; Lyttle & Fellous, 2011; Rusu & Florian, 2014). When employed in blink research with media stimuli, the measures for spike train synchrony are expected to yield higher values of blink synchrony between participants who spend more attentional and cognitive resources on the media stimulus with similar blinking behavior, so a stimulus-dependent structure in blinking can be quantified.

Existing Studies

Nomura et al. (2015) used two cost-based measures of spike train synchrony, Victor and Purpura's D^{spike} and $D^{interval}$ (Victor & Purpura, 1997). In general applications (i.e. with a factor q greater than zero and not approximating infinity), "$D^{interval}[q]$ is sensitive to the pattern of interspike intervals, while $D^{spike}[q]$ is sensitive to absolute spike times" (Victor & Purpura, 1997, p. 131); in this case, this translates to sensitivity to changes in blink rate, and sensitivity to co-occurrence of blinks, respectively. To analyze blinking behavior in expert and novice recipients of Japanese rakugo comedy performances, the authors analyzed baseline asynchrony of $D^{interval}$ during a neutral fish tank video without explicit narrative, and found that experts had from the start higher values of synchrony. Differences in synchrony values of experts and novices in further analyses were only accepted if they exceeded this baseline threshold. Congruent with expectations, values of $D^{interval}$ tended to be lower than values of D^{spike}. The authors used the difference between the two measures to infer the degree of structuring in the respective group's blinking behavior, and conclude that experts showed higher overall structuring in blinking behavior than novices. Further, Nomura et al. binned the observation period in 12 segments to analyze the development of synchrony during the rakugo performance. To this end, Nomura et al. (2015) conducted an analysis of variances with the between-subjects factor expertise (novices vs. experts) and the within-subjects factor time (the observation period's different bins). Unlike in the regular use of an ANOVA, where data within each of the ANOVA's cells represents individual values, such as scores from a transportation questionnaire, here, the values in cells represented all possible pairs of spike train synchrony scores between participants of each group. Consequently, each cell contained $k = n * (n-1) / 2$ pairwise $D^{interval}$ scores, with n representing the number of participants in the novice or expert group. Analysis showed that experts exhibited a relatively stable structure in blinking behavior from the beginning, whereas in novices, it gradually developed during early bins of the rakugo performance.

Robustness

In the implementation presented here, spike train metrics are limited in their applicability to interactive media environments. Possibly due to the initial conceptualization of spike train metrics as a measure for neuron activity, the present use in blink analysis relies on identical stimuli for each participant. In Nomura et al.'s (2015) study, these identical stimuli were video recordings of rakugo performances; comparisons across stimuli were conducted on a group level for each of the four groups' difference in D^{spike} and $D^{interval}$. In its current use on non-interactive stimuli, dynamic changes in stimuli are not accounted for. Analyses of user behavior in, for example, interactive video games would suffer from this limitation. If a user reacted to the very same stimulus properties in the same manner like other users, but these stimulus properties occurred at a different time due to her differing interaction with the stimulus, then the method would evaluate this as a different structure of behavior.

Implications for This Thesis

Due to these issues of robustness, spike train metrics will only be used in the video stimulus settings in this thesis. With video stimuli, the method allows for a fine-grained analysis of reactions towards different events in the videos, and allows for the identification of events with salient impact on blinking behavior. For the analyses in this thesis, we will use a different measure for spike train synchrony than Nomura et al. (2015). Kreuz, Chicharro, Houghton, Andrzejak, and Mormann (2013) suggest that different measures for spike synchrony will be best suited for different scenarios, and argue that measures like $D^{interval}$ and D^{spike} have advantages due to their parameter q, which enables researchers to gain insights into, for example, the timescale of event structures. However, as Kreuz et al. (2013) argue further, it may well be possible that no optimal parameter will be found for all segments of data, for example due to a misrepresentation of segments with very different neuron firing rates. This might have consequences for the domain of blinking, were blink rates do not only differ considerably between subjects, but also within subjects over time. For the purpose of this thesis, we will follow Kreuz et al.'s reasoning and use their proposed method of *ISI distance* (Kreuz, Mormann, et al., 2007; Kreuz, Haas, Morelli, Abarbanel, & Politi, 2007). The ISI distance measure will be introduced and discussed in more detail in the description of experiment 1.

Unlike in Nomura et al.'s (2015) study, there are no experimental or quasi-experimental conditions focusing on participant expertise in the present thesis, so we won't consider baseline asynchrony as in Nomura et al.'s study.

5.8.2.4 T-pattern Detection

Rationale

T-pattern detection (Magnusson, 2000) is a statistical analysis method for the detection of recurring event patterns in event time series data, and can detect if an event B occurs after an event A within a critical interval of time more often than would be expected by chance. Regularly, the structures identified by T-pattern detection are hard to detect with the unaided eye due to the amount of noise from other event occurrences; additionally, statistical methods aiming at, for example, group differences in frequencies would not capture such structural aspects (Magnusson, 2016). The method will be described further in the description of experiment 1 (section 6.3.7.3).

Existing Studies

The T-pattern method has been applied to a multitude of research topics; for example, the latest book on T-pattern methodology edited by Magnusson, Burgoon, and Casarrubea (2016) includes studies from psychology, neuroscience, psychiatry, biology, communications, pharmacology, and sport science. Several studies have used the method in the domain of media research to identify media-dependent patterns in user behavior.

Suckfüll and Unz (2013, 2016) used T-pattern detection to relate user experience, quantified by changes in heart rate, electrodermal activity, and facial behavior to narrative structure and moments of impact of an animated short film. Using T-pattern detection, it was possible to discover reactions preceding film events, likely reflecting the viewer's anticipation, and reactions following film events, likely reflecting the viewer's reactions. This way, the narrative's effects on raising and disappointing viewer expectations could be observed.

Brill, Jonsson, and Schwab (2014) analyzed T-patterns in players of a shooter game, and aimed at relating the degree of pattern formation between game events and blink occurrences to presence scores. Contrary to predictions, results showed that players who reported high presence actually showed less patterns than players who reported low presence. A possible interpretation was that in this game, it is advantageous to show only patterns that lead to success; however, further insights into this matter are needed.

Brill, Jonsson, Magnusson, and Schwab (2016) used T-pattern detection to further explore data from Brill's (2010) racing game study. In general, participants with higher presence self-report scores showed more patterns with blinks after curve exits, compared to low presence participants. These analyses were exploratory in nature, and certain limitations apply regarding sample size and an unexpected effect of total racing time, so replication is needed to investigate the relation between structured blinking behavior and presence.

Maier, Bacherle, Adam, and Leidecker-Sandmann (2017) used content analysis and T-pattern detection to analyze how pre-electoral press releases of political parties on the one hand, and political newspaper coverage on the other hand interact in the setting of media agendas.

Robustness
Since T-pattern detection uses both media and user events, and dynamically adjusts its analysis to the time and frequency of event occurrences, it is well suited for both interactive and non-interactive stimuli.

Implications for This Thesis
The applicability to dynamic, interactive stimuli is especially important for games research, because for most interactive games, no session will be exactly like the other. T-pattern detection is an interesting candidate for the analysis of behavior in diverse media environments, including games.

In this thesis, we use T-pattern detection to identify T-patterns incorporating both media events and user events. In this case, the user events of interest are spontaneous eye-blinks. For definition of media events, we use a content-blind approach and use very basic stimulus properties that are derived from presence theories. Wirth et al. state that the primary attractor for automatic attention allocation during media use should be novel, rapid, or surprising stimulus changes (Wirth et al., 2007, p. 499). These changes elicit orienting responses, which are attributed a central role in the provision of information for presence-forming processes (Liebold et al., 2017; Wirth et al., 2007). For the traditionally edited video stimulus in experiment 1, instances of sudden changes are predominantly found at cuts in between shots, and are confounded with presentation of new spatial information. While Nakano et al.'s (2009) analyses suggest that implicit breakpoints, and not cuts, were the main contributors to blink structure, we will nevertheless test this approach, which takes into consideration often neglected, basic stimulus properties. The exact criteria and methods for identification of rapid changes in each of the experimental stimuli will be detailed during reports of the respective experiment.

5.9 Thesis Experiments

At this point, we have discussed a variety of relevant theories and empirical evidence for the different aspects of this thesis. First, the theoretical backgrounds for presence, presence measurement, and blinking have been presented, which serve as the basis for the research questions that should be answered in this thesis. Second, methodological aspects have been addressed, namely self-report measures for the assessment of presence, methods for the measurement of blinks, appropriate stimulus material, and manipulation of experimental conditions. Finally, we discussed the computation of different indices for analyzing structure in eye-blink behavior.

As has been mentioned earlier in this thesis, three experiments will be conducted in this project to relate structural aspects of blinking behavior to presence self-report, and we will now detail the experimental procedures to be used.

The guiding research question for all three experiments is if participants who report higher self-report measures of presence also show more stimulus-dependent structure in their blinking behavior. To not alter blinking behavior by manipulating sensory input, different instructions will be used instead to create conditions with high and low capabilities for elicitation of spatial presence. For analysis of stimulus dependent structure, three different indicators are derived from existing studies for quantification of structural aspects: (a) variability of inter-blink intervals (Nomura et al., 2015), (b) ISI distance as a measure for spike train synchrony (Kreuz, Mormann, et al., 2007), and (c) T-pattern detection (Magnusson, 2000). Three different media environments will be used as stimuli to cover a wide range of experimental applications: a traditionally edited video as an example for most TV and cinematic stimuli, a continuously edited video as an example for a more naturalistic video, and a video game as an example for interactive digital games. Identical or comparable media stimuli have been found to elicit structured blinking behavior in existing research.

To exactly mirror the validation approach described in Böcking et al.'s (2008) evaluation of alternative measures, it would be necessary to assess validity, sensitivity, robustness, and obtrusiveness. Because certain limitations apply to this thesis project, this approach will not be reproduced entirely. As has been mentioned earlier, robustness will not be assessed, because it would have required an additional experimental condition without alternative measurement; instead, robustness has been discussed on a theoretical basis in section 5.8.2. For Böcking et al.'s approach to assessment of validity, data for each indicator would need to be aggregated across all three experiments, data would have to be binned in SPSL tertiles, and objective indicators would then need to be correlated to these binned SPSL scores across all studies. For assessments of sensitivity, effect sizes of comparisons between high and low presence conditions of each objective measure would need to be contrasted with effect sizes of SPSL score comparisons. We will deviate from this detailed approach to assessments of validity and sensitivity. First, due to the limitations of robustness, not all alternative measures will be used in all media environments. Second, not all alternative measures in this thesis offer the proper individual values—at least in their current implementations—for validity analyses. For the present step in the research process, we will evaluate for each experiment on a group level if higher presence scores co-occur with the predicted structural aspects in blinking behavior:

1) IBI variability provides a readily computed individual value, which can be used for both group-level and individual level analyses. Its use in interactive environments is possibly limited (see section 5.8.2.2), but it will be evaluated for all settings in this study on group level and individual level.

2) ISI distance at its very core provides values for pairwise spike train synchrony, which can then be aggregated to further indicators. In this thesis, we use the most basic level, pairwise synchrony, and the most aggregated level, a group value for overall synchrony of participants in a group. Indicators from levels in between these extremes are suggested for future research in the general discussion (section 9). Due to the limited robustness (see section 5.8.2.3), ISI distance is not used for the interactive stimulus in experiment 3.

3) T-pattern detection first provides patterns found in data, and we use the number of patterns found in each participant as individual values for subsequent group analyses. However, it is not addressed in this thesis how appropriate these individual values are as an individual-level indicator: after all, participants who blink more than others can in principle also produce more patterns than others, so appropriate normalization would be necessary. Possible solutions for this issue are offered in the general discussion (section 9). For the analyses in this thesis, differences in T-patterns are interpreted on a group level, while at the same time paying attention to the number of blinks in each group.

All three thesis studies are laboratory experiments with a 2×1 between subjects design; all participants were recruited at the University of Würzburg. Since little is known about expected effect sizes with these stimuli and manipulations, sample sizes will follow the respective model studies from literature. In Nakano et al.'s (2009) study with a conventionally edited video stimulus, each of 18 participants took part in three repeated measurements experiments. Data of 14 participants were usable for analysis and were sufficient to reveal between- and within-subject effects of synchronization. However, we refer to further studies because different analysis methods and experimental designs will be employed in this thesis. In Nomura et al.'s (2015) study with a continuously edited stimulus, 72 participants were recruited in total, and data of 60 participants could be used for analysis of blinking behavior. Participants were quasi-experimentally assigned to an expert or novice group based on their familiarity with Japanese rakugo comedy, and then randomly assigned to one of two experimental conditions, resulting in a cell size of 15 in a 2x2 design. This sub-sample size proved to be sufficient for calculations of spike train metrics $D^{interval}$ and D^{spike}. In Brill's (2010) study with an interactive video game stimulus, 48 participants were recruited, and randomly assigned to stimulus presentation in 2D or stereoscopic 3D, either with or without EOG blink measurement, resulting in a cell size of 12 in a 2×2 design. In further T-pattern analysis of this data (Brill, Jonsson, Magnusson, & Schwab, 2016), the blink data of 23 participants was available, but was suspected to be not sufficient. We conclude that following the original studies, 60 participants for the two studies with video stimuli and 48 participants for the study with a video game stimulus should be sufficient, with the compromise of a slightly smaller sample for correlational analysis in study 3.

All participants provided informed consent and were aware of the recording of videos, of the voluntary nature of their participation, and conduct regarding their data. Additionally, participants could agree to future publishing of their video recordings for scientific purposes. Participants were naive to the actual purpose of the studies; no instruction regarding blinking behavior was given, because Siegle, Ichikawa, & Steinhauer (2008) stated that their instruction to blink as little as possible probably altered their participants' natural blinking behavior. Participants were asked after the sessions about their vision acuity. For the eye-tracking study in the third experiment, participants were instructed to use contact lenses, if needed. As described earlier, participants whose blink rate differed more than two standard deviations from the respective sample's mean are excluded from analyses of structured blinking behavior.

The three experiments with their setups, procedures and results are presented now, each followed by a brief discussion of the results, and implications for the following studies. A subsequent general discussion will address the theoretical implications of all experiments combined.

6 Experiment 1

The first experiment investigates if recipients of a conventionally edited video stimulus who report higher scores of spatial presence will also show a higher degree of stimulus-dependent structure in blinking behavior.

Based on the reasoning presented in section 5, two experimental conditions are created to facilitate or hinder formation of spatial presence, so it can be tested if two groups with different levels of presence show different degrees of structuring in their blinking behavior. Overlooking the mediated nature of the experience is regarded a necessary condition for the formation of presence (e.g., Wirth et al., 2007), so instructions should either support participants to overlook, or not to overlook the mediated nature. In the instructions for the first experimental group, participants are asked to concentrate on the stimulus' content, what should—just as in interested viewers in real-world situations—lead to attention allocation on the stimulus content, processing of content, and ultimately higher levels of presence. Instructions for the second experimental group ask to focus on the stimulus' form, thus making salient the mediated nature of the perceived media information; participants in this group are hypothesized to exert mental processes leading to lower levels of presence, because they need to actively pay attention to and process media form aspects.

Therefore, participants in both instructions are asked to concentrate on the stimulus, although on different aspects. As has been detailed in section 5, this approach should offer a demanding test for the measure's validity due to the interdependence of cinematic form and content (Ohler, 1994).

6.1 Manipulation Check

6.1.1 Presence Self-Report

As a manipulation check, success of the different instructions will be evaluated by comparing the group means of subjectively reported presence experiences in both groups. Participants who are instructed to pay attention to the stimulus' content (*content condition*) are hypothesized to report higher presence experiences than participants who are instructed to pay attention to the stimulus' form features (*form condition*), because the latter should less likely overlook the mediated nature of the reception situation. Further, this measure serves as the subjective benchmark for the objective indicators.

Hypothesis 1.1

> Participants in the "content" condition on average report higher presence scores than participants in the "form" condition.
>
> H_0: $\mu_{form} \geq \mu_{content}$ $\qquad\qquad$ H_1: $\mu_{form} < \mu_{content}$

6.1.2 Corroborative Items

In addition, four short items were created to assess compliance with instructions. The items address the participant's focus on content aspects, focus on technical aspects, immersion into the stimulus, and critical reflection of the stimulus. It was hypothesized that participants in the content condition report more focus on content aspects, less focus on formal aspects, higher levels of immersion, and less critical reflection than participants in the form condition.

Hypothesis 1.2

a) Participants in the "content" condition on average report to have focused more on content aspects than participants in the "form" condition.
H_0: $\mu_{form} \geq \mu_{content}$ $\qquad\qquad$ H_1: $\mu_{form} < \mu_{content}$

b) Participants in the "content" condition on average report to have focused less on form aspects than participants in the "form" condition.
H_0: $\mu_{form} \leq \mu_{content}$ $\qquad\qquad$ H_1: $\mu_{form} > \mu_{content}$

c) Participants in the "content" condition on average report to have immersed themselves more into the stimulus than participants in the "form" condition.
H_0: $\mu_{form} \geq \mu_{content}$ $\qquad\qquad$ H_1: $\mu_{form} < \mu_{content}$

d) Participants in the "content" condition on average report less critical reflection than participants in the "form" condition.
H_0: $\mu_{form} \leq \mu_{content}$ $\qquad\qquad$ H_1: $\mu_{form} > \mu_{content}$

6.2 Hypotheses

Based on the theoretical background presented in sections 2, 3, and 4, it is hypothesized that in a state of presence, attentional and cognitive processes will have a more pronounced focus on media content, and that this intense processing of media content influences timing of blinks. Consequently, participants reporting higher presence scores should show higher degrees of stimulus-dependent structure in their blinking behavior. To evaluate this relation between structure in blinking behavior and presence self-report, three methods are used to quantify structure: (a) individual variability of inter-blink intervals (IBI), operationalized by the standard deviation of each participant's IBI lengths, (b) synchrony of blink rate changes in groups, operationalized by the ISI distances of blink spike trains, and (c) occurrence of blinks after significant changes in the stream of visual information, operationalized by T-patterns involving media events and blinks.

6.2.1 IBI Variability

As described in section 5, we hypothesize that participants in a state of presence exhibit ongoing attention allocation on stimulus content, and that processes of attention allocation and processing of spatial cues lead to a stimulus-dependent structure in blinking behavior. This assumption also refers to Nomura et al.'s (2015) predictions for the influence of attentional processes on blinking behavior in a state of transportation. We therefore assume that in the content condition—which should support the formation of presence—participants will show higher inter-blink variability than participants in the presence-hindering form condition. This should hold true for both group-level analyses with t tests and individual-level analyses with correlation analysis.

Hypothesis 1.3

a) On a group level, participants in the "content" group show on average a higher IBI variability than participants in the "form" group.

H_0: $\mu_{form} \geq \mu_{content}$ $\qquad\qquad$ H_1: $\mu_{form} < \mu_{content}$

b) On an individual level, higher presence scores are correlated with higher variability of IBIs.

H_0: $r_{SPSL\text{-}IBI\_SD} \leq 0$ $\qquad\qquad$ H_1: $r_{SPSL\text{-}IBI\_SD} > 0$

6.2.2 Spike Train Synchrony

To analyze synchrony of blinking behavior within the experimental groups, we calculate two different indicators of spike train synchrony. Similar to Nomura et al.'s (2015) assumptions, it is hypothesized that blink synchrony will be higher in participants in the content group, who should also report higher presence experiences: their attention allocation and processing of spatial cues should be influenced by stimulus content to a higher degree than in the form group, leading to higher degrees of stimulus-aligned blinking. To analyze this relation, we use values of spike train synchrony from all possible pairs of participants within each group in a group level comparison with a *t* test. Different from the correlational analysis with IBI variability, no individual spike train synchrony parameters will be extracted in this thesis; deriving and testing such parameters is left for future research. A second, simulation-based approach is derived from Nakano et al. (2009) and Magnusson (2000), and compares deviation of observed blinking behavior from a hypothetical random blinking behavior. To analyze this relation, observed average spike train synchrony in real data of both groups is contrasted with repeated analyses of shuffled data. It is hypothesized that a higher degree of structure in the content group should manifest as a greater deviation from randomized data.

Hypothesis 1.4

On a group level, spike train synchrony of participants in the "content" group differs more from a random blink distribution than synchrony of participants in the "form" group.

H_0: $d_{random\text{-}form} \geq d_{random\text{-}content}$ H_1: $d_{random\text{-}form} < d_{random\text{-}content}$

Hypothesis 1.5

On a group level, participants in the "content" group show higher mean spike train synchrony than participants in the "form" group.

H_0: $d_{ISI\text{-}form} \leq d_{ISI\text{-}content}$ H_1: $d_{ISI\text{-}form} > d_{ISI\text{-}content}$

Please note that lower ISI distances indicate higher synchrony, because it is a measure of spike train dissimilarity.

6.2.3 T-Patterns

For the third indicator, T-patterns, it is again hypothesized that participants in a state of presence will show more stimulus-dependent structure in blinking behavior, because their attention allocation and processing of spatial cues is focused more on stimulus content. Because the content condition should facilitate presence formation, we expect to detect on average more T-patterns incorporating both blinks and media events in the content group.

Hypothesis 1.6

On a group level, participants in the "content" group show more T-patterns incorporating both media events and blinks than participants in the "form" group.

H_0: $\mu_{form} \geq \mu_{content}$ H_1: $\mu_{form} < \mu_{content}$

6.3 Methods

6.3.1 Stimulus

In Nakano et al.'s (2009) study, the stimulus was a 216 seconds long excerpt from the TV show episode "Mr. Bean at the dentist", preceded by a 210 seconds long baseline condition with a blank screen. The same Mr. Bean excerpt (Birkin et al., 2014) was used as stimulus in this thesis experiment. In the narrated story, Mr. Bean wakes up and finds out that he is late for an appointment. In the remainder of the story, he hurries through a series of dangerous and comical situations to still arrive at time. The excerpt used in this experiment starts with Mr. Bean leaving his house, still wearing his pajama, and getting into his car. Mr. Bean then drives through a city, while at the same time changing clothes and brushing his teeth. Mr. Bean finally arrives at his destination, pushes away a parking vehicle with his car to occupy this parking spot, uses the remaining time on the parking meter for himself, encounters a traffic warden, and then enters a dentist's house.

For each experimental condition, a video file was created to present both instructions and stimulus. First, instructions were presented as a recording of the experimenter's voice with a black screen. Three white text cues on the screen were inserted to highlight the participant's respective task, repeating key instructions from the voice over. Instructions in both experimental groups were identical except for six instances, where participants were instructed to either focus on analyzing the video's formal features, or to experience the video's content. Instructions were followed by a five second countdown, which served as a transition indicator between all segments, and a baseline condition, in which participants could relax and prepare for their task. Additionally, if future research needed baseline-corrected blink rates, there would be data to approximate individual base blink rates. The baseline differed from Nakano et al.'s operationalization: 210 seconds were found to be very long in pretests, so as a trade-off the baseline duration was reduced to 123 seconds. A white fixation cross on a black screen was used instead of a blank screen as in Nakano et al.'s study in order to minimize influence of different gazing behavior. This change was implemented because different gazing behavior might influence blink rate during baseline, for example due to large saccades in visual exploration of the lab; because reception of the experimental stimulus would be limited to the screen, the fixation cross was used to keep the participants' gaze on the screen during baseline. After the baseline, a five second countdown, together with a short reminder of the instructions, indicated the start of stimulus presentation. The Mr. Bean excerpt was available in DVD resolution, and was scaled to have the same size in the Würzburg lab setup as on a 17", 4:3 ratio screen used in Nakano et al.'s study. After the excerpt, another five second countdown indicated the end of stimulus presentation. The whole video was rendered in 1920 × 1080 pixels, with 25 frames per second, an average video bitrate of about 26,000 Mbit per second, and with 48 kHz stereo audio with an audio bitrate of about 192 kbit per second. As in Nakano et al.'s study, the Mr. Bean excerpt was presented without audio; participants were informed about that circumstance in the instruction phase.

6.3.2 Experimental Manipulation

To either hinder or facilitate formation of presence, participants were randomly assigned to one of two conditions, and were instructed to direct their attention on either form aspects, or content aspects of the stimulus video. For this purpose, two instructional texts were designed (form: 178 words; content: 169 words; see Appendix A) with identical wording, except for five instances in the text:

1) The study was allegedly conducted to find out how well suited the stimulus was for the lab's research concerning:
   a) cinematic techniques and film montage („Filmtechnik und Machart")
       or
   b) film content („Inhalt").

2) After film reception, the participants would be asked questions about their:
   a) analysis of montage („Analyse der Machart") or
   b) their experience („Erleben").
3) It was the participant's task to:
   a) focus absolutely on the video's cinematic techniques and film montage („dich voll und ganz auf die Filmtechnik und Machart des Videos zu konzentrieren") or
   b) to absolutely get oneself into the video („dich voll und ganz auf den Inhalt des Videos einzulassen").
4) The participant should:
   a) keep her thoughts in the here and now of the lab and analyze the video, so she could answer the questions on cinematic techniques („bleibe mit deinen Gedanken immer völlig hier und jetzt im Labor, um nachher die Fragen zur Filmtechnik gut beantworten zu können") or
   b) keep her thoughts within the film with Mr. Bean and let herself get carried away, so she could assess the content aspects afterwards („bleibe mit deinen Gedanken immer völlig im Film bei Mr. Bean und lass dich einfach mitreißen, um erst danach die inhaltlichen Aspekte einschätzen zu können").
5) It mattered how the participant:
   a) evaluated the formal features after his analysis („wie du die äußere Form des Videos nach deiner Analyse bewertest") or
   b) experienced video content during normal watching („wie du den Inhalt des Videos ganz normal beim Anschauen erlebst").

Supporting text cues were displayed on the screen while the instructions were read to the participants:

1) Form: Study video technique, Technique of the video, Analysis of formal features („Studie Videotechnik", „Technik des Videos", „Analyse der äußeren Form")
2) Content: Study video content, Content of the video, Normal watching („Studie Videoinhalt", „Inhalt des Videos", „ganz normal anschauen")

6.3.3 Apparatus

The experiment was conducted in a laboratory of the chair of media psychology at the Julius-Maximilians-Universität of Würzburg, Germany. The lab room contains a workspace for the experimenter, and a soundproof, acoustically optimized recording booth with internal dimensions of $300 \times 240 \times 205$ cm (Studiobox Premium, 2017; see Figure 3) for the participants. Inside the booth, a 27", 16:9, 1920×1080 pixels LCD screen (Asus VG278H) on a 72 cm high desk was used for stimulus presentation. Reviews have praised this model for its fast image presentation. The input lag, that is the sum of the internal circuitry's processing time and the screen panel's refresh time, has been measured to be as low as 6.5 ms in the screen's 120 Hz mode (Prad, 2012). Audio was presented by a 5.1 channels surround system on a medium level; level was identical for all participants. To minimize noise and heat emissions, the PC for stimulus presentation was located outside the booth, and two low-noise fans provided fresh air for the participants. Differing from Nakano et al.'s (2009) study, the video was presented without illumination of the room, so—in line with presence theories, for example by Wirth et al. (2007)—real-world cues were minimized to support formation of presence. Participants were seated on a 48 cm high chair with armrests at a distance of 90 cm from the screen.

The Noldus Media Recorder 2 (Media Recorder, 2017) software was used to record synchronized recordings of the stimulus screen and the participant's face. For recording of the stimulus screen, the stimulus presentation PC's video signal was duplicated, and recorded on the Noldus Media Recorder PC with a hardware

Figure 3. Basic laboratory setup in experiment 1.
Source: own figure.

Figure 4. Screenshot of a participant recording in experiment 1.
Source: own figure.

frame grabber. For recording of the participant, an IP pan-tilt-zoom dome camera recorded the participants in a near-infrared spectrum (see Figure 4), and sent a video stream to the Noldus Media Recorder PC.

To ensure a good and stable video quality, near-infrared LED lights unobtrusively illuminated the participant's face. The camera was located centrally, behind and above the stimulus presentation screen, and recorded with a slight downward angle over the upper edge of the stimulus presentation screen. Recordings were captured by the Noldus Media Recorder 2, and saved as XViD coded video files with 1280 × 720 pixels resolution, 30 frames per second, about 4,000 kilobits per second video bitrate, and stereo audio with about 128 kilobits per second. Based on the 30 fps frame rate, temporal resolution for identifying eye-blink apexes is 33 ms, or put differently, the identified apex occurred during the 33 ms exposure time of the respective frame, so the actual time of the blink apex hypothetically deviates from 0 ms to 33 ms from the coded timestamp. Additionally, stimulus presentation was delayed by the screen's latencies—on average 6.5 ms (Prad, 2012)—so the participants perceived the actual image slightly later, and thus reacted slightly later to the stimulus than is suggested by the recordings. In addition, measurements taken at the Technical University of Chemnitz had shown that the signal processing chain from IP-camera over frame-grabber to the final compressed video introduces varying latencies, depending on the type of camera used and CPU usage of the recording PC; upon request, the Noldus company explained to the colleagues that a latency of up to 200 ms is within the system's specifications (B. Liebold, personal communication, 14.09.2016). The total inaccuracies are not ideal, but are accepted for the intended analysis of structural features of blinking behavior.

6.3.4 Measures

6.3.4.1 Self-Report Measures

Self-report measures were collected with an online survey using the SoSci Survey platform (Leiner, 2014). Major parts of the questionnaire were the 5-point Likert scales of the SPES questionnaire (Hartmann et al., 2015), and scales for suspension of disbelief and absorption tendency taken from the MEC-SPQ (Wirth et al., 2008). Only the SPSL scale will be reported in this thesis; the additional scales were included for future analyses of, for example, the questionnaire's construct validity. Two additional 5-point Likert items were designed in reference to Vorderer's (1992) two-dimensional concept of reception modes, and two items were designed to briefly quantify the participant's focus on either content or form of the stimulus:

1) I paid attention to content aspects. („Ich habe auf inhaltliche Aspekte geachtet.")
2) I paid attention to technical aspects. („Ich habe auf technische Aspekte geachtet.")
3) I entirely immersed myself into the presented stimulus. („Ich habe mich voll und ganz in das Gezeigte hinein versetzt.")
4) I critically reflected the presented stimulus. („Ich habe das Gezeigte kritisch reflektiert.")

Four additional items were included as part of the cover story, but were not analyzed:

1) The video was fun. („Das Video war lustig.")
2) The video's quality was good. („Die Videoqualität war gut.")
3) The story was comprehensible. („Die Handlung war nachvollziehbar.")
4) The cinematic means have supported the story well. („Die filmischen Mittel haben die Handlung gut dargestellt.")

Further items asked for the participant's age, gender, course of study or profession, if the Mr. Bean excerpt was already known, if vision aids were used and if yes, of what kind, and if no, if it would have been necessary to use vision aids, how tired participants felt on a 5-point scale, as how demanding they experienced their task on a 5-point scale, if they felt disturbed or distracted by anything during reception of the video, what they assumed the purpose of the study to be, and if they had any further remarks. The questionnaire was concluded by asking for the participant's mail address for granting course credit; this input was saved separately by the questionnaire platform to ensure participant anonymity.

Order of items in the questionnaire's scales was randomized. The participants answered the questionnaire immediately after the stimulus video on the same PC to assure best recollection of the previous experience.

6.3.4.2 Observational Measures

Eye-blinks were coded in the Noldus Observer XT 11.5 (The Observer XT, 2017) software using the frontal face recordings from the Noldus Media Recorder 2. Two independent coders (coder 1: author; coder 2: JB[1]) coded eye-blinks with a precision of one video frame for the 62 participant videos; the duration of each coded segment was 6:31 minutes including baseline and five-second-countdowns. A blink was coded if a sudden movement of the upper eyelid led to an at least partial covering of the pupil. To support coding reliability, the apex of lid movement was chosen as the event of interest. The apex was defined as the frame with the highest degree of pupil occlusion. This approach is not most exact with regard to blink onset and for identifying blink-eliciting stimulus events, but provides a well-defined event for coding. The resulting inaccuracy regarding the exact moment of blink elicitation was regarded as acceptable in the scope of this thesis, because analyses focus on overall structure during media use, and not so much on blink latencies after certain media events. If the pupil had been occluded completely, the blink was to be annotated as a complete blink; if the pupil had not been occluded completely, the blink was to be annotated as an incomplete blink. Both complete and incomplete blinks were used for analyses in this thesis.

6.3.5 Participants

For the first experiment, 62 participants (age $M = 21.13$ years, $SD = 2.51$, range: 18–29, 71% female) were recruited using the internal recruitment system of the Institute Human-Computer-Media. Participants were offered course credit for their participation.

Regarding their course of study, 43 participants self-identified as students of the Medienkommunikation course, and 19 participants self-identified as students of the Mensch-Computer-Systeme course.

---

[1]   I gratefully acknowledge Johanna Bode's support in behavior coding and data preparation.

Regarding the ratings of how demanding the task was, participants rated it on average to be low demanding (M = 1.63, SD = 0.75, on a five-point scale from 1 = not demanding at all to 5 = very demanding). Participants reported medium-high estimates for their tiredness (M = 2.48, SD = 1.04, on a five-point scale from 1 = not tired at all to 5 = very tired).

Regarding the supposed purpose of the study, many participants correctly identified attention or presence as part of the study, but no participant was aware of blinking as an important variable.

Twenty-nine participants stated that they were already familiar with the stimulus. This was not seen as problematic, because previous studies have shown that structure in blinking behavior still occurs after repeated reception of a stimulus (Nakano et al., 2009; Nomura et al., 2015). Regarding vision acuity, 45 participants used no optical aids, 13 used corrective spectacles, three used soft contact lenses, and one participant stated to have used no optical aid, but needed one.

6.3.6 Procedure

Participants were welcomed by the experimenter, were introduced to the experimental setup and procedures, and declared informed consent. Participants were then seated in front of the presentation screen, and were informed that their task would be explained in the experiment's video. If there were no further questions, the experimenter left the recording booth, closed the door, and started recordings and stimulus video. After video presentation, the participants switched to the prepared online questionnaire and provided the self-report measures. Upon completion, participants were thanked and informed about the study's purpose. Participants were dismissed if there were no further questions.

6.3.7 Data Preparation and Analysis Methods

6.3.7.1 Inter-Blink Intervals

For calculation of inter-blink intervals (IBI), event logs with the coded blink and media events were exported from the Observer XT and further processed in Microsoft Excel. Only blinks were considered that occurred during the Mr. Bean segment. The timestamps of those blinks were then normalized to the onset of the Mr. Bean segment for subsequent analyses, and intervals between subsequent

blinks were computed for IBI analysis. The standard deviation of each participant's inter-blink interval durations was used as the IBI variability indicator in
further analyses.

6.3.7.2 ISI Distance

For analysis of spike train synchrony, ISI distances were computed in a Python
3.6 script using PySpike 0.5.1 (Mulansky & Kreuz, 2016), a Python implementation of algorithms for calculation of ISI distance, SPIKE distance, and SPIKE synchrony. Data preparation and plotting of PySpike results was conducted in GNU
Octave 4.0.3 (Eaton, Bateman, Hauberg, & Wehbring, 2015; Eaton & Octave
Community, 2015).

The ISI distance measure offers a parameter-free, time-resolved, multivariate
measure for spike train synchrony (Mulansky & Kreuz, 2016), and is based on
the "relative differences of the instantaneous rates of the two spike trains" (p.
184). Unlike the $D^{interval}$ algorithm, the ISI distance algorithm uses in its calculations only the timestamps of observed spikes during a given observation period,
and needs no additional parameters. The spike times are used to calculate interspike intervals in two spike trains, and lengths of current intervals are then related to each other for every moment of observation duration; the final result is
a "normalized absolute difference of these interspike intervals" (p. 187). The
measure is sensitive to co-occurring changes in blink rate, for example due to
blink inhibition occurring across participants, and should thus represent a more
robust equivalent to the measure used by Nomura et al. (2015). PySpike offers
different outputs of ISI distance results for further analyses (Mulansky & Kreuz,
2016): a scalar for an averaged total dissimilarity score of the whole data set, a
vector for an ISI profile representing the data set's average ISI distance for every
moment in time across all spike trains of the data set, and a matrix as an ISI distance matrix, containing the single pairwise ISI distances of the data set averaged
over the observation duration. In our analyses, the scalar for a real data set will
be compared to scalars calculated from randomized data sets, and the ISI distance
matrices will be used to extract pairwise ISI distances for group comparisons. The
ISI profile will be presented to illustrate development of each experimental
group's dissimilarity over time.

Recently, Satuvuori et al. (2017) proposed a series of improved measures for
spike train dissimilarity, which adapt more appropriately to multiple time scales
within a data set. This property would make the measures especially valuable for
blink research, where periods of blink inhibition alternate with blink bursts.

However, the analysis tools were not available during conduction of thesis analyses, so the use of these new measures is up to future research.

6.3.7.3 T-Pattern Detection

T-pattern detection (Magnusson, 2000) aims at revealing recurring patterns of paired event occurrences, in which an event occurs near another event more often than would be expected by chance. As Magnusson (2000) explains, the detection process is a step-by-step, level-by-level calculation of simple binomial statistics. It solely relies on the occurrences of events during the observation period, and the resulting probabilities expected for their occurrence by chance. For example, two events A and B could occur several times during the observation period. The T-pattern detection algorithm tests if B occurs after A within a certain critical interval more often than would be expected if events occurred randomly throughout the observation period. If B occurs after A sufficiently often with a timing stable enough to satisfy the critical interval requirements, then their pairwise occurrence is defined as a T-pattern. Found patterns are used as events in subsequent iterations of analysis, until no more patterns are found. This way, hierarchical, complex T-patterns can emerge from repeated simple analysis steps, and structures can be detected in large data sets. The detected patterns in observed data are then compared to the results from identical detection runs with randomized versions of the original data, so researchers can control for false-positive detection of randomly occurring patterns.

The T-pattern method has evolved considerably since its initial conception, and now offers a variety of indicators derived from the T-system (Magnusson, 2016). For the purpose of this thesis, only a very basic use of T-pattern detection is necessary. Here, it will be used to identify recurring patterns involving both user events and media events, that is a pattern with a user event either following or preceding a media event with a relatively stable timing. No higher-level T-patterns are needed to this end.

The manually coded spontaneous eye-blinks of participants are used as user events in T-pattern detection. For definition of media events, we use a content-blind approach and focus on the stream of visual information, which Nakano et al. (2009) have supposed to be the main regulator for blink inhibition. While cuts as instances of significant changes in the stimulus had been discarded by Nakano et al. as main contributors to structure in blinking behavior, we nevertheless focus on significant changes in the stimulus' visual channel due to predictions of the presence theory: in terms of Wirth et al.'s (2007) conceptualization, it can be hypothesized that at these instances, the user needs to process the newly presented spatial cues in the stimulus, needs to update the spatial situation model, and needs to confirm this spatial situation model as her primary model in order to experience presence.

For definition of media events, we first use frame differencing to identify instances of significant visual change in the Mr. Bean excerpt. Frame differencing returns the luminance change between all consecutive frames of a video, so for a video with n frames, the method returns n-1 frame differences. For computation of this measure, the video was processed by a custom Java program[2] written in Eclipse 4.5.0 (Eclipse, 2015; Rose, Paige, Kolovos, & Polack, 2008) using the OpenCV 3.0.0 library of computer vision tools (Bradski, 2000; OpenCV, 2014). Video file processing and frame difference calculation occurred in several steps. First, after the video had been loaded, a single frame was extracted. This frame consisted of 1920 × 1080 pixels, with an 8-bit RGB color value for each pixel containing a triplet of values between 0 and 255 for the intensity of the additive color components of red, green, and blue. For analysis purposes, the frame was first converted to grayscale, so each pixel was assigned only one value for luminance between 0 (black) and 255 (white). Values were converted with the grayscale conversion function included in OpenCV, which takes into account the human visual system's different sensitivities for red, green, and blue light (OpenCV team, n.d.). The grayscale function follows the ITU-R BT.601 standard (ITU, 2015) for color-space conversion in the broadcasting industry, so the luminance values are computed as a weighted average with weights of 0.299 for red color values, 0.587 for green, and 0.114 for blue. The grayscale-converted frame was then represented as a matrix with 1920 columns and 1080 rows, with the luminance value of each pixel in the respective matrix element. The sum of all matrix elements was computed as a representation of the total luminance of the frame, and the same procedure was conducted for the subsequent video frame; finally, the difference between the two matrix sums was calculated as a measure for the total change in luminance between the two consecutive frames. The process was repeated for all frames of the stimulus video, and the resulting frame differences were written to a file.

Consequently, the result of this processing was a vector representing the difference values between all consecutive frames of the Mr. Bean video (see Figure 5). This vector was further processed in GNU Octave, using the *findpeaks* function in the signal 1.3.2 signal processing package for Octave (Various authors & Miller, 2015) to identify peaks in the signal, that is instances with a high change rate in visual information. As parameters for identification of peaks, a required

---

[2]   I gratefully acknowledge Andreas Brill's support in creation of the program.

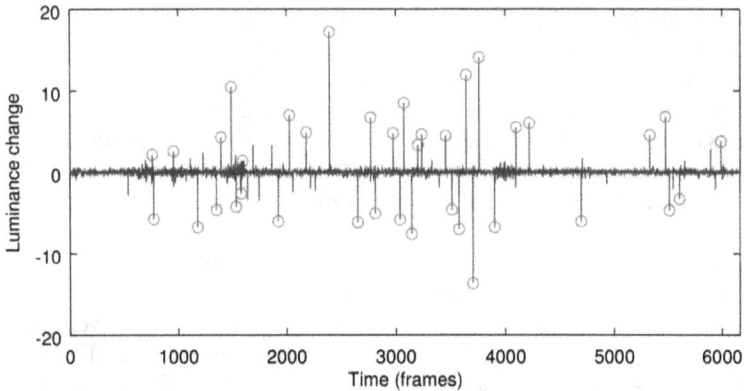

Figure 5. Luminance change and identified peaks in the stimulus of experiment 1.
Blue line: per-pixel normalized frame differences in luminance; red circles: peaks. Source: own figure.

minimum peak height of two standard deviations of the de-trended differences vector was used, with a minimum peak width of one unit, since especially the frame differences caused by cuts in the video represent very rapid changes in luminance. Further, for minimum distance between peaks, the function's default value of five units was used. Since luminance changes can lead to positive or negative frame differences, the algorithm's option for double-sided peak detection was used. The function identified 38 peaks (see Figure 5); according to visual inspection, they represented the different cuts in the video sufficiently well.

A custom Octave script was used to prepare timestamps of blink occurrences and timestamps of identified media events in the appropriate data format for T-pattern detection. Since the identified peaks and the blinks were mostly located in close proximity along the observation duration, it was decided to assign unique event labels to each of the 38 peaks, thus facilitating T-pattern detection.

6.4 Results

Data preparation was conducted in Microsoft Excel 2013; statistical calculations were conducted in Microsoft Excel 2013, JASP 0.8.0.0 (JASP Team, 2017), and SPSS 22.

6.4.1 Behavior Coding

Inter-rater reliability was evaluated with the integrated functions of the Noldus Observer XT, with a tolerance of 40 ms to account for a ±1 frame accuracy. After the first coding pass, codings of blink occurrences showed a mean percentage of agreement of 95.29% (SD = 7.42), and an average Cohen's κ of 0.81 (SD = 0.16). Independent recoding of disagreements led to perfect agreement within a 40 ms tolerance window. Two participants were excluded from analysis because they showed extreme blink rates which were more than two standard deviations above the sample's mean (see Figure 6). In total, 5,681 blinks were coded during the observation period for all 62 participants (see Figure 7).

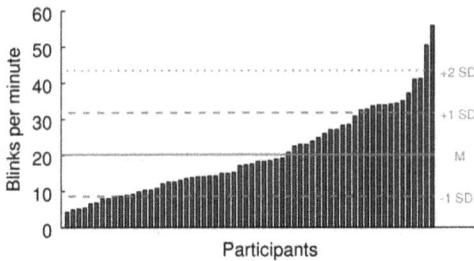

Figure 6. Individual blink rates of all participants in experiment 1.
Source: own figure.

6.4.2 Questionnaire Data

Psychometric quality of the SPSL scale was assessed using Cronbach's alpha. Reliability of the four-item SPSL presence scale was good with a Cronbach's alpha of α = .82.

6.4.3 Manipulation Check

6.4.3.1 Presence Self-Report

As a manipulation check, an independent samples t test was used to test hypothesis 1.1, according to which participants in the content group should report

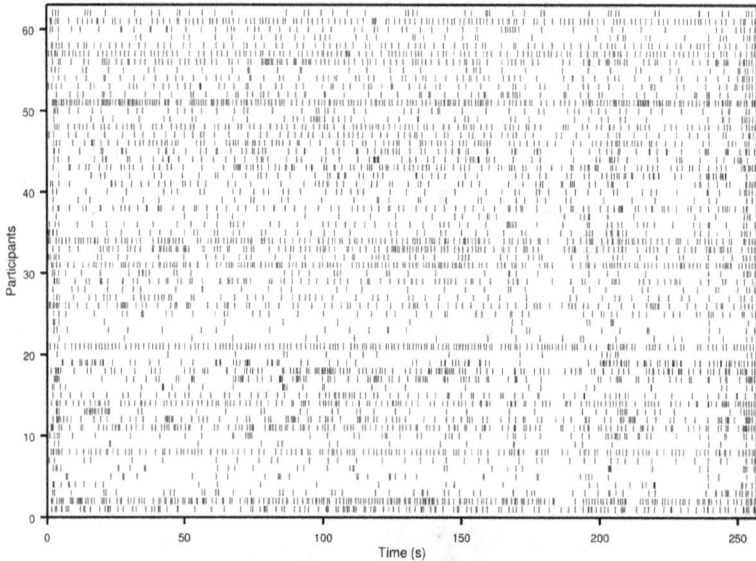

Figure 7. Raster plot of blink occurrences during the Mr. Bean excerpt in experiment 1.
Source: own figure.

higher presence scores than participants in the form group. A Levene's test indicated that variances in both groups did not differ significantly ($F(1) = 0.04$, $p =$
.845), and a Shapiro-Wilk test indicated that the normality requirement was borderline satisfied (content: $W = 0.94$, $p = 0.080$; form: $W = 0.95$, $p = 0.201$), so the
requirements for a t test were met. The t test showed no significant group-differ-
ence in SPSL scores ($t(58) = -0.25$, $p = 0.599$, $d = -0.07$; see Table 1 for analysis
results of experiment 1). Hypothesis 1.1 is rejected, and the manipulation of presence was not successful.

6.4.3.2 Corroborative Items

For the four short items designed to corroborate the manipulation check, it was
expected in hypothesis 1.2 that (a) participants in the form condition would report in comparison less attention on content aspects, (b) more attention on form
aspects, (c) less immersion into the depicted environment, and (d) more critical
reflection of the perceived stimulus. The results of t tests, or U tests, where t test
requirements were not met, show that participants in the form condition (a) did

not differ significantly from the content condition in their attention on content aspects ($U = 499.50$, $p = .213$, $d = 0.21$), (b) paid significantly more attention to technical aspects ($U = 100.00$, $p = .001$, $d = -1.86$), (c) immersed themselves significantly less into the mediated environment ($U = 567.50$, $p = .032$, $d = 0.45$), and (d) reflected the perceived stimulus significantly more critical ($U = 329.00$, $p = .034$, $d = -0.48$). Hypothesis 1.2 (a) is rejected, and hypothesis 1.2 (b), (c), and (d) are accepted. The results show that apart from the comparable degree of attention on the video's content, the groups showed the predicted differences.

6.4.4 Behavioral Data

6.4.4.1 Hypothesis 1.3

For hypothesis 1.3 (a), a group-level analysis tested if mean IBI variability in the "content" group was higher than in the "form" group.

Inspection of IBI standard deviations showed that their distribution was heavily skewed towards smaller values. A Levene's test indicated that variances in both groups differed significantly ($F(1) = 17.44$, $p < .001$), and a Shapiro-Wilk test indicated that the assumption of normality was not satisfied (content: $W = 0.89$, $p = .004$; form: $W = 0.82$, $p < .001$). The requirements for a t test are thus not met. Nomura et al. (2015) also found a log-normal distribution of IBI standard deviations, so scores were log-transformed prior to analysis; we use the same approach and log-transform the IBI standard deviations. Examination of log-transformed values shows that the requirements for a t test are now met: according to a Levene's test, variances do not differ significantly ($F(1) = 0.00016$, $p = .990$), and according to a Shapiro-Wilk test, the tested values do not deviate significantly from normal distribution (content: $W = 0.97$, $p = .652$; form: $W = 0.96$, $p = 0.297$). An independent samples t test on log-transformed standard deviations of interval durations shows that mean IBI variability in the content condition is not significantly higher than in the form condition ($t(58) = 0.45$, $p = .327$, $d = 0.12$). Hypothesis 1.3 (a) is rejected.

For hypothesis 1.3 (b), analysis on an individual level tested if individual IBI standard deviations correlated positively with individual presence scores. The results show no significant Pearson correlation between SPSL scores and log-transformed IBI standard deviations ($r = 0.08$, $p = .535$; see Figure 8). Hypothesis 1.3 (b) is rejected.

Table 1

Descriptives and test results for subjective and objective measures in experiment 1

	Form		Content		t	df	U	p	95% CI	d
	n	M (SD)	n	M (SD)						
			Corroborative items							
Content focus	30	4.17 (0.83)	30	4.33 (0.76)			499.50	.213	[-0.00003, ∞]	0.21
Form focus	30	4.43 (0.50)	30	2.77 (1.17)			100.00	<.001	[∞, -1]	-1.86
Immersion	30	3.57 (0.90)	30	3.97 (0.89)			567.50	.032	[0.00003, ∞]	0.45
Critical reflection	30	3.47 (1.31)	30	2.83 (1.32)			329.00	.034	[-∞, -0.000008]	-0.48
			Presence self-report							
SPSL	30	2.63 (0.87)	30	2.58 (0.84)	-0.25	58		.599	[-0.42, ∞]	-0.07
			Inter-blink interval variability							
IBI_SD_log	30	0.43 (0.36)	30	0.47 (0.36)	0.45	58		.327	[-0.11, ∞]	0.12
			Spike train synchrony							
ISI distance	435	0.50 (0.10)	435	0.59 (0.14)			132318.00	1.000	[-∞, 0.11]	0.78
			T-patterns							
T-pattern occurrences	30	10.17 (2.51)	30	3.57 (2.10)			17.50	1.000	[-8.00, ∞]	-2.86

Notes. All tests are one-tailed, with direction of effects according to hypothesis.

6.4.4.2 Hypothesis 1.4

For testing of hypothesis 1.4, it should be evaluated if blinking behavior of participants in the content condition differed more from a hypothetical random blinking behavior than in the form condition. To this end, calculations of average ISI distances were combined with randomizations programmed in Python and statistical analyses in JASP.

To quantify the degree of structuring within both groups, we contrast the mean ISI distance within each group with mean ISI distances from analyses of randomized versions of the group's blink data. This distance between real and randomized blinking behavior provides another measure for the degree of structuring within groups. To operationalize randomization, we use the approach by Nakano et al. (2009), who analyzed eye-blink synchronization within and between participants. In their study, real values were compared to randomized versions of the data. The randomization was realized as a shuffling of inter-blink intervals. Unlike in a randomization with random re-placement of blinks, the shuffling of intervals made sure that the distribution of IBI lengths remained the same, but an eventual fine-grained structure in blinking behavior was removed (Nakano et al., 2009). This randomization approach is especially beneficial for blinking behavior, because a randomization with random rearrangement of

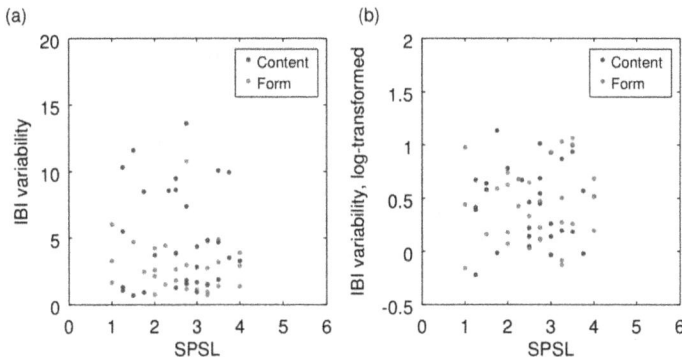

Figure 8. Scatter plots of presence self-report scores and IBI variability in experiment 1. Figure (a) shows original IBI standard deviations, figure (b) shows log-transformed IBI standard deviations. Source: own figure.

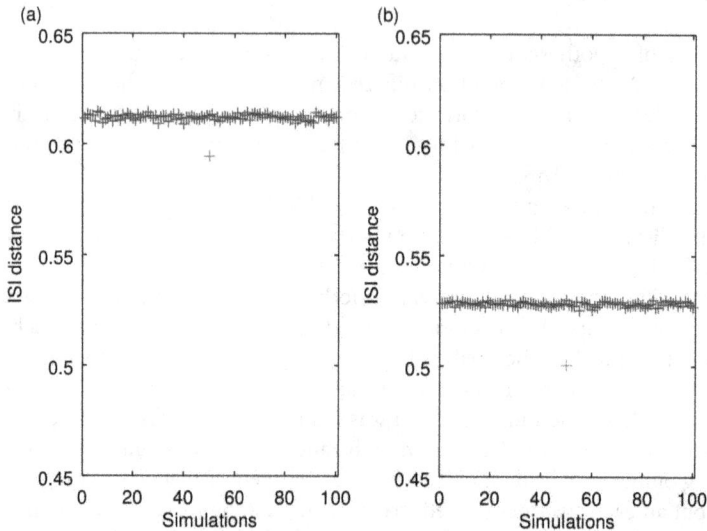

Figure 9. Average ISI distances of real and randomized blinking behavior in experiment 1. Results for (a) content group and (b) form group. Red crosses: real data; blue crosses: randomized data. Note: lower ISI distances indicate higher similarity. Source: own figure.

blinks could create very artificial inter-blink intervals, with blinks located unnaturally close together, or far apart. For the present study, 100 runs of randomization and recalculation of ISI distances were programmed in Python.

It was hypothesized that mean ISI distance in the "content" group would differ more from randomized data than in the "form" group. Results (see Figure 9 and Table 2) show that contrary to hypothesis, the "form" group differed more from randomized data both in terms of absolute values ($d_{random-form}$ = 0.0277; $d_{random-content}$ = 0.0177), and in terms of standard deviations of randomized data. For the latter, the absolute difference values were divided by the standard deviations of the randomized ISI distances. Again, the form group shows higher degrees of behavioral structure in their spontaneous eye-blink behavior (form: 29.08 SD; content: 14.97 SD). Hypothesis 1.4 is rejected.

6.4.4.3 Hypothesis 1.5

Hypothesis 1.5 assumed that participants in the "content" group show higher blinking synchrony than participants in the "form" group, because their blinking

Table 2

Results for ISI randomizations in experiment 1

	Real	Random		Difference random-real	
		M	SD	Absolute	in SD
Content	0.59448	0.61220	0.00118	0.01772	14.97271
Form	0.50039	0.52811	0.00095	0.02772	29.08097

Notes. Lower ISI distances indicate higher similarity.

should be subject to stronger influences by processing of stimulus content. Following Nomura et al.'s (2015) approach, pairwise synchrony values between all members of each group were used for analysis. To this end, pairwise ISI distances were computed for each group in PySpike, processed in Octave, and the resulting data used for group comparison in JASP (see Figure 10 for each group's average ISI profile, and Figure 11 for each group's matrix with pairwise average ISI distances).

During check of t test requirements, a Levene's test showed that variances within the pair-wise ISI distances in both groups differed significantly ($F(1) = 68.92, p < .001$), and that the normality assumption could not be accepted (content: $W = 0.97, p < .001$; form: $W = 0.97, p < .001$). The requirements for a Student's t test were not satisfied. A non-parametric alternative was not chosen, because the Mann-Whitney U test has been shown to deliver distorted results under certain circumstances: if the t test or U test are superior seems to depend on the given pattern of sample sizes and variances (Zimmerman, 1987); with both homogeneity of variances and normality assumptions violated, the U test is less robust than Student's t test, and Welch's t test offers calculations which are superior over both tests (Zimmerman, 1998). Further, it has been suggested that even minor inequalities in the groups' variances can inflate Type 1 error in U tests with large sample sizes (Zimmerman, 2000, 2003). Welch's t test has been suggested as the method of choice under satisfied normality assumptions (Gibbons & Chakraborti, 1991; Ruxton, 2006). While normality could not be assumed in this case, Welch's t test is used as the best alternative, because according to the central limit theorem, the large sample size should compensate this limitation. A one-

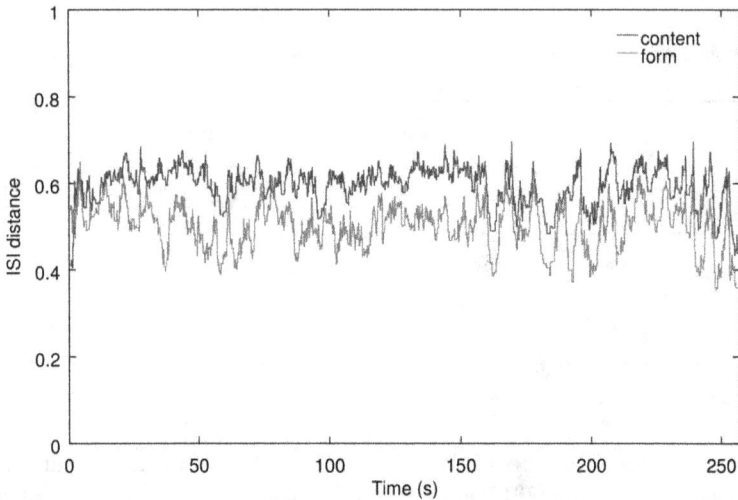

Figure 10. ISI profiles of blinking behavior in experimental groups in experiment 1.
Note: lower ISI distances indicate higher similarity. Source: own figure.

tailed Welch's t test indicated that pairwise ISI distances in the content group were not significantly smaller than in the form group ($t(789.4) = 11.57, p = 1.000$, $d = 0.78$). On the contrary, descriptives showed that ISI distances were lower in the form group (content: $M = 0.59, SD = 0.14$; form: $M = 0.50, SD = 0.10$; see table 1). Based on this pattern of descriptives, a one-tailed Welch's t test as a follow-up check showed that this difference was statistically significant ($t(789.4) = 11.57, p < .001, d = 0.78$, 95% CI = [0.08, ∞]). Hypothesis 1.5 was rejected.

6.4.4.4 Hypothesis 1.6

As a third measure for quantification of structure in blinking behavior, T-pattern detection was used to reveal greater-than-chance occurrences of blinks before or after certain media events.

It was hypothesized that on a group level, participants in the "content" group show more T-patterns incorporating both media events—in this case instances of significant changes in visual information—and blinks than participants in the

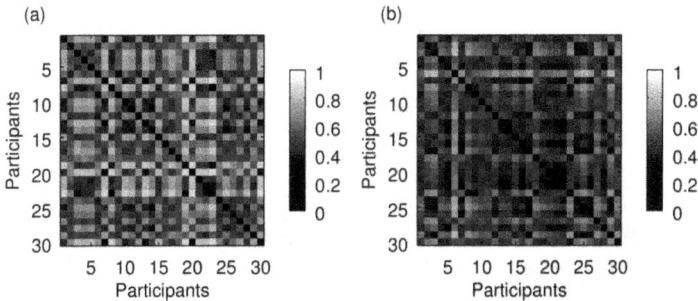

Figure 11. Matrices with pairwise ISI distances of blink occurrences in experiment 1.
Results for (a) content group and (b) form group. Please note that lower ISI distances indicate
higher synchrony and that ISI matrices are symmetric. Source: own figure.

"form" condition, thus reflecting their hypothesized greater structuring of blinking behavior, which should reflect their more intense processing of stimulus content.

In principle, it would be possible that higher event frequencies in one group could lead as an artefact to more detected T-patterns in this group, what will be discussed again in sections 8.4.4.2 and 9.2.4. However, no tests were performed on this issue because participants were assigned randomly to experimental conditions, and no systematic influence on event counts was assumed.

T-pattern analysis was conducted in Theme 6 (Theme, 2017). Raw data was imported into separate Theme projects for each experimental group, because a function to split analysis along an independent variable was not available in the Theme version at hand. In each project, the raw data of participants was concatenated into one sample; this approach supports the detection algorithm in identifying event relations that occur only rarely, but in multiple participants, and effectively creates one long observation period with all individual observation periods in sequence. Theme's default values were used as search parameters for T-pattern detection, with a level of significance of $\alpha = .005$ for the critical interval, a required minimum of 3 occurrences for patterns, and a maximum level of 1. T-pattern detection in randomized data was conducted in 40 runs of shuffled and rotated data, because Nakano et al. (2009) reported 40 runs to be sufficient for their randomization approach.

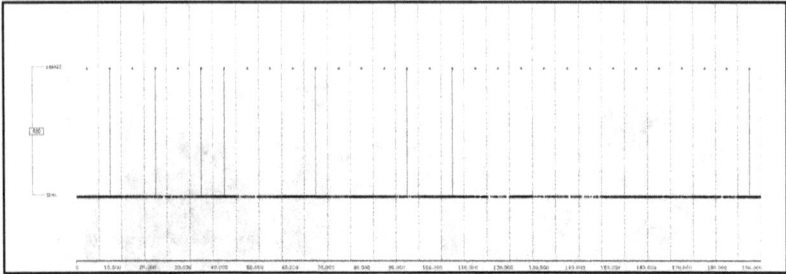

Figure 12. Example for a T-pattern detected in experiment 1.
Segments between dotted blue lines: participants' individual observations. Dots in upper row: occurrence of the 23rd peak in frame differences. Dots in lower row: blink occurrences. Connecting lines between rows: occurrences of identified T-patterns. Eight participants blinked with greater-than-chance timing after the 23rd peak in frame differences. Source: own figure.

Resulting T-patterns were reduced to patterns containing blinks as an element; patterns containing only media events were discarded, because they would only reflect the stimulus structure, but not recipient behavior. The filtered results contained for the content group 11 unique T-patterns, which in total occurred 107 times; 16 different T-patterns were found in the form group, with 305 total occurrences. Considerably less patterns of length 2 were detected in randomized data (see Table 3; see Figure 12 for an example T-pattern); patterns detected in the real data can thus be assumed to be valid detections.

Table 3

Frequencies of detected T-patterns in real data and randomized data in experiment 1

	Real		Randomized				Difference in SD	
			Shuffle		Rotation			
	Unique	Total	M	SD	M	SD	Shuffle	Rotation
Content	11	107	3.73	1.83	4.50	1.59	3.99	4.10
Form	16	305	3.87	2.12	7.33	1.85	5.73	4.70

The number of patterns found in each participant were used as individual values for a group comparison. A check of t test requirements showed that variances in both groups did not differ significantly ($F(1) = 2.07, p = .155$), but normality assumption was partly violated (content: $W = 0.96, p = .376$; form: $W = 0.93, p = .046$). The requirements for a t test were not satisfied, so a Mann-Whitney U-test was used instead to compare T-pattern occurrences in both groups. A one-tailed U-test revealed that individual numbers of T-patterns were not higher than in the form group ($U = 17.50, p = 1.000, d = -2.86$). A follow-up U test testing for the opposite direction of the hypothesized effect showed that contrary to expectation, significantly more T-patterns were found in the form group ($U = 17.50, p < .001, d = -2.86$). Hypothesis 1.6 is rejected.

6.5 Discussion

In this thesis experiment, two conditions had been created by means of different instructions: participants were randomly assigned to instructions asking for either a judgement of the stimulus video's content, or the video's formal features. It was hypothesized that participants who focus on media form will not be able to overlook the mediated nature of the experience, and will thus enter states of presence less frequently.

The success of this manipulation was tested by comparing the four corroborative manipulation check items and presence self-report scores from both groups. The manipulation check shows contradictory evidence. Three of the four items which assessed the participants' tendency to focus on form or content showed significant group differences in the hypothesized direction: participants who were instructed to focus on form aspects stated to have paid significantly more attention on technical aspects, to have reflected the video significantly more critically, and to have immersed themselves significantly less into the mediated environment; no significant difference was found between groups for the participants' focus on video content. Since no definition of form or content was given in the instructions, it is possible that participants in the form condition implicitly assumed that paying attention to "content" was included in their task. While the results for these items suggest that the manipulation was in most parts successful, the effects on self-report presence scores were not in line with hypotheses: no significant difference between groups was found in analysis of the SPSL scores. When assuming that all self-report measures were valid, then this result is hard to explain within the boundaries of presence theories: participants who were well aware of the video being a technological artefact should not enter a state of presence. The manipulation of presence must be regarded as not successful, and because the SPSL questionnaire was intended to serve as a validation standard for the objective measures, this result questions the further analysis of objective indicators.

Nevertheless, because behavioral differences may have existed, but did possibly not translate to different self-report scores, objective variables were still analyzed. It was tested if the three measures for structured blinking behavior could distinguish between both groups. For the measure of eye-blink variability, individual predictions were tested, as well.

Analyses show no significant group differences in IBI variability, and no significant correlation between IBI variability and SPSL self-report scores. The indicator did not distinguish between groups, what is in itself no problem so far, because the presence manipulation was not successful.

However, the remaining two objective indicators show different results. First, the averaged ISI distance scores indicate that blinking behavior in the form group led to lower spike train dissimilarity scores, so participants in the form group showed more similar blink rate changes than participants in the content group. Random simulation analyses further show that it was the form group whose average ISI distance of real data deviated more from ISI distances calculated from randomized data, both in terms of absolute values and in units of random ISI distance's standard deviations. All three results suggest that the form group showed a more similar structure in blinking behavior. Comparison of pairwise ISI distances in the two groups again shows that contrary to hypothesis, the form group shows a more similar structure in their blinking behavior.

Finally, the results for T-pattern detection are in line with results from ISI distance analyses: contrary to hypothesis, more T-patterns containing both media events and user events could be found in the form group. Interestingly, comparisons of T-patterns detected in real and randomized data showed that as in ISI distance analyses, the deviation from randomized data was greater in the form group.

In this light of considerably converging findings from ISI distance and T-pattern analysis, it can be questioned if IBI variability assesses the same structural aspects as the other objective indicators. In any case, the lack of an appropriate manipulation of presence makes interpretation of results difficult within the boundaries of the presence concept. Two explanatory approaches can be used to interpret the results. First, regarding manipulation of conditions, it could be speculated that instructions for the content group might have been counterproductive. The content group's alleged task was to focus on content and provide their evaluation afterwards, what might have interfered with their formation of presence. In this case, the content group's presence experiences would have been reduced by the same amount as the form group's presence, what could have led to the comparable presence scores in both groups. Second, regarding structured blinking behavior, the form group's increased focus on not only formal, but also content aspects of the stimulus—they reported to have focused on content as much as the content group, but scored higher on form-focus and critical reflection—has most likely caused more attentional processes and more structure in blinking behavior. Alternatively, it could be speculated that the evaluation of the video's content led to less similar structures in blinking behavior because the evaluation of content—in this case including humor—offers more degrees of freedom, or a larger interpretative space, for cognitive processes than a focus on clearly observable formal features of the video.

Aside from the unpredicted outcome of the experimental manipulation, it should be noted as an interim conclusion that two of the three objective indicators found converging evidence for stimulus-dependent structure in blinking behavior. Moreover, these two indicators find significant differences in the degree of structuring between two experimental groups, which were presented the exact same stimulus video. The two groups were merely instructed to pay attention to different aspects of the stimulus, and process these aspects in different ways. While the differences between groups were not in line with expectations, we nevertheless interpret that there seems to be differential influence of internal processing on objectively observable blinking behavior.

Returning to the scope of this thesis, we have detailed in section 5 that directing attention on formal features is a behavior that will most likely also occur in a real-world scenario, for example during breaks in presence (also see Liebold et al., 2017). Thus, the ability to distinguish between attention allocation on the medium within and outside of a state of presence would be a beneficial property of an objective indicator. We will therefore continue to pursue our approach, but will modify the manipulation of conditions in thesis experiment 2 to prevent a possible interference with formation of presence in the content group.

7 Experiment 2

The first experiment addressed the research question if there is a relation between stimulus-dependent structure in blinking behavior and self-report measures of spatial presence in recipients of a conventionally edited video stimulus. For the second study, we use the same measures to assess again if participants who report higher levels of presence also show higher structuring in spontaneous eye-blink behavior. Different from experiment one, the stimulus is not explicitly segmented by conventional editing, but gives the impression of a continuous camera recording. Because manipulation of conditions was not successful in experiment one, instructions for the experimental group with focus on stimulus content were modified, as well.

As in study one, two experimental conditions were created to facilitate or hinder formation of spatial presence, and to test if according differences in objectively observable blinking behavior can be found with three structure-focused methods. Different instructions were used again as experimental manipulations for two groups, but with different wording. Participants were either instructed to focus on the stimulus' form, thus making salient the mediated nature of the perceived media information, or to watch the movie as they would normally do in a cinema. The first experimental condition should still hinder formation of presence, because it should be harder for participants to overlook the mediated nature of the perceived media information when focusing on media form aspects. The modified second instruction, on the other hand, was intended to reduce the artificiality of the laboratory situation, and thus reduce a possible distraction from stimulus content that could be caused by a task that specifically asks for attention on media content aspects.

7.1 Manipulation Check

7.1.1 Presence Self-Report

The success of this manipulation was again analyzed by comparing the group means of subjectively reported presence experiences in both groups:

Hypothesis 2.1

> Participants in the "content" condition on average report higher presence scores than participants in the "form" condition.
>
> H_0: $\mu_{form} \geq \mu_{content}$ $\qquad\qquad\qquad$ H_1: $\mu_{form} < \mu_{content}$

7.1.2 Corroborative Items

As in study 1, four short items were used to ask for compliance with instructions. The items addressed the participant's focus on content aspects, focus on technical aspects, immersion into the stimulus, and critical reflection of the stimulus. It was expected that participants in the "content" condition report more focus on content aspects, less focus on formal aspects, higher levels of immersion, and less critical reflection than participants in the "form" condition.

Hypothesis 2.2

> a) Participants in the "content" condition on average report to have focused more on content aspects than participants in the "form" condition.
>
> H_0: $\mu_{form} \geq \mu_{content}$ $\qquad\qquad\qquad$ H_1: $\mu_{form} < \mu_{content}$
>
> b) Participants in the "content" condition on average report to have focused less on form aspects than participants in the "form" condition.
>
> H_0: $\mu_{form} \leq \mu_{content}$ $\qquad\qquad\qquad$ H_1: $\mu_{form} > \mu_{content}$
>
> c) Participants in the "content" condition on average report to have immersed themselves more into the stimulus than participants in the "form" condition.
>
> H_0: $\mu_{form} \geq \mu_{content}$ $\qquad\qquad\qquad$ H_1: $\mu_{form} < \mu_{content}$
>
> d) Participants in the "content" condition on average report less critical reflection than participants in the "form" condition.
>
> H_0: $\mu_{form} \leq \mu_{content}$ $\qquad\qquad\qquad$ H_1: $\mu_{form} > \mu_{content}$

7.2 Hypotheses

Based on the same reasoning as in experiment 1 (see section 6.2), three methods are used again to quantify structure in blinking behavior and relate it to presence self-report scores: individual variability of inter-blink intervals (IBI), operationalized by the standard deviation of IBI lengths, synchrony of blink rate changes in groups, operationalized by the ISI distance of blinking spike trains, and co-occurrences of blinks with instances of significant changes in the stream of visual information, operationalized by T-patterns with media events and blinks.

7.2.1 IBI Variability

Hypothesis 2.3

a) On a group level, participants in the "content" group show on average a higher IBI variability than participants in the "form" group.

H_0: $\mu_{form} \geq \mu_{content}$ $\quad\quad\quad\quad\quad\quad$ H_1: $\mu_{form} < \mu_{content}$

b) On an individual level, higher presence scores are correlated with higher variability of IBIs.

H_0: $r_{SPSL-IBI\_SD} \leq 0$ $\quad\quad\quad\quad\quad\quad$ H_1: $r_{SPSL-IBI\_SD} > 0$

7.2.2 Spike Train Synchrony

Hypothesis 2.4

On a group level, spike train synchrony of participants in the "content" group differs more from a random blink distribution than synchrony of participants in the "form" group.

H_0: $d_{random-form} \geq d_{random-content}$ $\quad\quad\quad$ H_1: $d_{random-form} < d_{random-content}$

Hypothesis 2.5

On a group level, participants in the "content" group show higher mean spike train synchrony than participants in the "form" group.

H_0: $d_{ISI-form} \leq d_{ISI-content}$ $\quad\quad\quad\quad\quad$ H_1: $d_{ISI-form} > d_{ISI-content}$

Please note that lower ISI distances indicate higher synchrony, because it is a measure of spike train dissimilarity.

7.2.3 T-Patterns

Hypothesis 2.6

> On a group level, participants in the "content" group show more T-patterns incorporating both media events and blinks than participants in the "form" group.
>
> H_0: $\mu_{form} \geq \mu_{content}$ $\qquad\qquad$ H_1: $\mu_{form} < \mu_{content}$

7.3 Methods

7.3.1 Stimulus

In Nomura et al.'s (2015) study, the stimuli were 53:40 minutes and 50:20 minutes long recordings of rakugo performances, preceded by a baseline condition of unspecified duration with a fish tank video. For this thesis experiment, we chose an excerpt from the movie *Birdman or (The Unexpected Virtue of Ignorance)* (Iñárritu, 2014) as a cinematic stimulus. The movie is shot and edited without visible cuts or transitions, but lets the camera follow the characters through sets in what is edited to appear like one continuous shot. In this thesis, the same video file was used for both experimental conditions, and presented both a baseline condition and the Birdman excerpt. For presentation in a cinema-like laboratory setting, the quality requirements for the stimulus were higher than in the previous study. The Birdman excerpt was available in Blu-ray quality, so the video was rendered in 1920 × 1080 pixels, with 23.976 frames per second, using h.264 compression with an average video bitrate of about 40,000 kilobits per second, and 48 kHz 5.1 channels audio with about 320 kilobits per second. Instructions were not included in the stimulus video, but were read to participants by the experimenter prior to video start. The video began with a five second countdown, which also served as a transition indicator between the following stimulus segments, and a baseline condition. Because participants of the previous study reported eyestrain due to the high contrast fixation cross, the baseline condition in this experiment was a recording of a large fish tank (Rawlinson, 2009). The fish tank video showed guests of the Okinawa Churaumi Aquarium in front of a big basin with numerous fish; the video was one of few found fish tank videos that met quality requirements for this study. The source clip was available in a 1920 × 1080 resolution, with 30 frames per second, and an average video bitrate of about 4,500 kilobits per second. The baseline video was presented for 1:55

minutes without audio. After the baseline, a five second countdown indicated the start of the experiment. The Birdman excerpt showed the first 20:23 minutes of the Birdman movie. After the excerpt, a five second countdown concluded stimulus presentation.

7.3.2 Experimental Manipulation

To either hinder or facilitate formation of presence, participants were randomly assigned to one of two conditions, and were instructed to either direct their attention on form aspects of the video or content aspects of the stimulus video.

Instructions were presented orally by the experimenter (form: 72 words; content: 72 words; see Appendix B) with identical wording, except for three instances in the text:

1) The researchers were allegedly interested in:
   a) appreciation of cinematic techniques („Wahrnehmung von Filmtechnik") or
   b) appreciation of films („Wahrnehmung von Filmen").
2) The participants were asked to:
   a) pay attention to the cinematic techniques as closely as possible („möglichst genau auf die Filmtechnik achte[n]") or
   b) watch the movie as they would do in the cinema („einfach nur anschauen […], wie ihr das im Kino auch machen würdet").
3) After the movie, participants would be asked about:
   a) their analysis of cinematic techniques („Analyse der Machart") or
   b) their experience („Erleben").

These instructions were intended to still motivate participants in the form group to pay attention to form aspects, but also prevent participants in the content group from employing a too analytical approach to the movie's content. The announced question about their personal experience during the film was seen as uncritical, because this is a standard procedure in laboratory media research.

7.3.3 Apparatus

The experiment was conducted in a joint laboratory of the chair of Media Psychology and the department of Media and Business Communication at the Julius-Maximilians-Universität of Würzburg, Germany. The lab room is built in

Figure 13. Basic setup of the laboratory in experiment 2.
Source: own figure.

style of a cinema, with a large 150" projection screen, black acoustic curtains around the room, acoustic ceiling panels, and two ascending rows of cinema chairs. A separate room is used for operating stimulus presentation and observation hardware. Stimuli are projected on the screen by a 4K projector (Sony VPL-VW1000) in a resolution of 4096 × 2160 pixels, scaled up from 1920 × 1080 pixels source material. Audio was presented by a 7.2 channels surround system (six Pioneer S-71B satellites, one S-71C center speaker, two S-71W subwoofers; AV receiver: Pioneer SC-LX85) on a medium level, with identical level for all participants; the audio system was calibrated for a center seating position using the AV receiver's built-in MCACC calibration tool. The video was presented without illumination of the room, so real-world cues, which could distract from the media stimulus, were minimized. Participants were seated in cinema chairs at a distance of 430 cm from the screen (see Figure 13).

The Noldus Media Recorder 2 software was used to obtain synchronized recordings of the stimulus screen and the participants' faces. For recordings of participants, up to two IP pan-tilt-zoom dome cameras recorded up to five participants, and sent a video stream to the Noldus Media Recorder PC. The faces of one to two participants were recorded on each video; during two sessions, three participants were recorded on one video. For synchronization purposes, the stimulus screen was recorded by an additional PTZ camera. The cameras were placed unobtrusively, and were recording in a near-infrared spectrum with unobtrusive near-infrared illumination.

Temperature and relative humidity were recorded prior to each session with a combined digital thermometer and hygrometer (TFA Dostmann Comfort Control 30.5011; manufacturer specified thermal resolution: 0.1 K, temperature accuracy: ±1 °C, humidity accuracy: ±4% between 35% and 75% relative humidity; TFA Dostmann, n.d.).

7.3.4 Measures

7.3.4.1 Self-Report Measures

Self-report measures used the same scales as in study 1, but questionnaires were handed out as a printed survey in this experiment. The questionnaire comprised 5-point Likert scales of the SPES questionnaire (Hartmann et al., 2015), the former MEC-SPQ scales for suspension of disbelief and absorption tendency (Wirth et al., 2008), and additional items. The same 5-point Likert items derived from Vorderer's (1992) two-dimensional concept of reception modes were used as a check for compliance with instructions:

- I paid attention to content aspects. („Ich habe auf inhaltliche Aspekte geachtet.")
- I paid attention to technical aspects. („Ich habe auf technische Aspekte geachtet.")
- I entirely immersed myself into the presented stimulus. („Ich habe mich voll und ganz in das Gezeigte hinein versetzt.")
- I critically reflected the presented stimulus. („Ich habe das Gezeigte kritisch reflektiert.")

Four additional items were included as part of the cover story, but were not analyzed:

- The video was fun. („Das Video war lustig.")
- The video's quality was good. („Die Videoqualität war gut.")
- The story was comprehensible. („Die Handlung war nachvollziehbar.")
- The cinematic means have supported the story well. („Die filmischen Mittel haben die Handlung gut dargestellt.")

Further items asked for the participant's age, gender, course of study or profession, if the Birdman excerpt was already known, if vision aids were used and if yes, of what kind, if no vision aids were used, if they would have been necessary, how tired participants felt on a 5-point scale, as how demanding they experienced their task on a 5-point scale, if they experienced any distractions during reception of the video clip, what they assumed the purpose of the study to be, and if they had any further remarks. The participant's mail address for granting course credit was asked for on a separate list to ensure participant anonymity.

The questionnaire was provided in two versions with different, randomized order of items to avoid sequence effects. Participants answered the questionnaire immediately after the stimulus video ended, while still being seated in the cinema chairs to ensure best recollection of the previous experience.

7.3.4.2 Observational Measures

Participants were recorded with a near-infrared pan-tilt-zoom dome camera, located either above the stimulus presentation screen and recording with a downward angle, or located at the side of the stimulus presentation screen, recording a half profile from slightly below eye-level. The videos were saved as XViD coded files in a resolution of 1280 × 720 pixels, with a bit rate of about 3,000 kilobits per second, at a frame rate of 30 frames per second, and without audio (see Figure 14). The same restrictions apply to recording precision as in experiment 1: Based on the frame rate of 30 frames per second, temporal resolution for identifying eye-blink apexes was 33 ms, and the video recording pipeline could introduce latencies of up to 200 ms. As in experiment 1, we accept these inaccuracies for the intended analysis of structural features.

To achieve an automatic, computer-assisted coding of spontaneous eye-blinks, a customized version of the Fraunhofer IIS FaceDetect tool was used, which is based on Fraunhofer's SHORE library for recognition of facial features, which include the degree of eye closure (FaceDetect, 2016; Kueblbeck & Ernst, 2006; technology licensed by Fraunhofer IIS[3]). Blinks should be deduced as spikes in the time series data of automatically obtained, frame-by-frame codings of participants' eye closure. In preparation of this step, video recordings of participants were recoded on a Linux system using the FFmpeg library (FFmpeg, 2016): videos were cropped to the location of each participant's face, with a sufficient margin to compensate for participant movement. Pre-tests had shown that the reduced computational costs during face detection in the SHORE library justified the effort for this additional recoding step. To minimize rendering time, prevent introduction of further compression artefacts, and retain the original temporal resolution of participant videos, the "copy stream" option in FFmpeg was used. The resulting videos of participant faces were then analyzed on the same Linux system with the customized FaceDetect tool. While the procedure worked in general, face recognition proved to be not robust enough towards participant movement: detection performance was not sufficient due to suboptimal recording angles of the cameras, so faces or eyes could not always be detected reliably depending on facial features, illumination, and head position.

---

[3]   I gratefully acknowledge the support by Dr.-Ing. Jens-Uwe Garbas and Nicolas Stenz from the Intelligent Systems Group, Electronic Imaging Department, Fraunhofer Institute for Integrated Circuits IIS, in Erlangen, Germany.

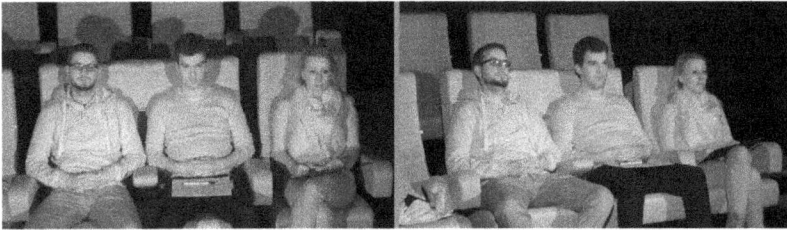

Figure 14. Screenshots of a participant recording in experiment 2.
Source: own figure.

Due to this limitation, spontaneous eye-blinks were coded manually. Eye-blinks were coded from the Noldus Media Recorder 2 files in Noldus Observer XT 11.5. Two coders independently coded eye-blinks with one video frame accuracy for the 53 participant videos, with each 22:32 minutes duration including baseline. Coder one (author) coded the entire material, coder two (MH[4]) coded a random 10% subsample of the material. To define these subsamples, the start timecodes of coding intervals for each participant were determined using randomly generated numbers from Microsoft Excel; the end timecodes of coding intervals were necessarily defined by the desired 10% of the whole stimulus duration. A blink was coded if a sudden movement of the upper eyelid led to an at least partial covering of the pupil. To enhance coding precision, the apex of lid movement as a well-defined state during each blink was coded, so again, the coding delivered the time stamp of the frame with greatest pupil occlusion. The resulting inaccuracy regarding the exact moment of blink elicitation was regarded as acceptable for the intended analysis of behavioral structure. If pupil occlusion was complete, the blink was to be annotated as a complete blink; if pupil occlusion was not complete, the blink was to be annotated as an incomplete blink. However, both types of blinks were used for analysis.

7.3.5 Participants

For the second thesis experiment, 61 participants (age $M = 22.39$ years, $SD = 2.73$; range: 19–33 years; 63.9% female) were recruited using the institute's internal recruitment system and by recruitment on campus[5]. Participants were offered

---

[4] I gratefully acknowledge Marina Hofmann's support in behavior coding.
[5] I gratefully acknowledge the support in on-campus recruitment by Dr. Astrid Carolus, Ricardo Münch, Catharina Schmidt, and Florian Schneider.

course credit for their participation if they were studying either Medienkommu-nikation or Mensch-Computer-Systeme courses. Because participants of thesis study 1 had been debriefed about the purpose of the experiment, it was made sure that no participant of the second experiment had already participated in the first experiment.

Regarding their course of study, 38 participants studied Medienkommu-nikation, 7 participants studied Mensch-Computer-Systeme, and 16 participants stated other or no occupations.

Regarding the ratings of how demanding the task was, participants rated it on average to be low demanding ($M = 1.46$, $SD = 0.65$, on a five-point scale from 1 = not demanding at all to 5 = very demanding). Participants gave a medium-level estimate for their tiredness ($M = 2.57$, $SD = 0.94$ on a five-point scale from 1 = not tired at all to 5 = very tired).

Regarding the suspected purpose of the study, many participants correctly supposed attention or presence to be part of the study; two participants supposed blinking behavior as a variable of interest, but were included in analysis.

Twenty participants (32.8%) stated that they were already familiar with the stimulus. As in experiment 1, this was not considered to be a problem because repeated reception of a stimulus does apparently not suppress the emergence of stimulus-dependent structure in blinking behavior (Nakano et al., 2009; Nomura et al., 2015).

Regarding vision acuity, 37 participants used no optical aids, 13 used correc-tive spectacles, and 11 used soft contact lenses; no participant stated to be in need of an optical aid, but had not used one.

7.3.6 Procedure

Participants were welcomed by the experimenter, were introduced to the exper-imental setup and procedures, and declared informed consent. Participants were then seated in front of the presentation screen, and were informed orally about their task in the experiment. If there were no further questions, the experimenter went to the separate control room and started recordings and stimulus video. After the video presentation was finished, the experimenter stopped recordings and asked the participants to answer the questionnaire. Upon completion, the experimenter disclosed the experiment's purpose. Participants were thanked and dismissed if there were no further questions.

7.3.7 Data Preparation

Analysis methods and data preparation were largely the same as in experiment 1 (see section 6.3.7 for a detailed description of data preparation in experiment 1), so we now focus primarily on differences in data preparation.

7.3.7.1 Inter-Blink Intervals

As in experiment 1, event logs with the manually coded blink and media events were exported from the Observer XT. In Microsoft Excel, data was reduced to blinks during presentation of the film excerpt, timestamps were normalized to onset of the Birdman movie, and inter-blink intervals were computed.

7.3.7.2 ISI Distance

As in study 1, ISI distances were computed with PySpike using a custom Python program. GNU Octave and JASP were used for data preparation and statistical analysis, respectively.

7.3.7.3 T-Pattern Detection

As in study 1, T-pattern detection was used as the third measure to analyze structure in blinking behavior. For definition of media events, we again use a content-blind approach to identify instances of significant changes in the stream of visual information. Tools from OpenCV are again used in a custom Java program[6] for stimulus analysis; however, since the Birdman stimulus differs from the Mr. Bean excerpt in its cinematic form, a different computational approach is used for event definition. While the Mr. Bean stimulus was edited conventionally, the Birdman stimulus was produced to present its content in apparently one continuous shot; consequently, significant changes in visual information are not introduced with a cut, but rather by movement of camera or objects in space. To account for this focus on movement, we do not use frame differencing, but rely on optical flow (e.g., Burton & Radford, 1978) to quantify the degree of change in the visual channel. OpenCV offers different algorithms for computation of

---

[6]   I gratefully acknowledge Andreas Brill's support in creation of the software and for the implementation of multi-threaded processing.

optical flow; we use the implementation suggested by Farnebäck (2003) as a com-
putationally intensive, but precise measure for optical flow. The method offers a
robust algorithm for motion estimation between two frames. Computations consist of the two key steps of first approximating "each neighborhood of both
frames by quadratic polynomials" (p. 363), and then estimating "displacement
fields from the polynomial expansion coefficients" (p. 363). For computation of
the optical flow measure, the custom Java program was used to load the video
and extract a single frame with 1920 × 1080 pixels and 8-bit RGB color values for
each pixel. The procedure was repeated for the next frame in the video, and both
frames were passed to the Farnebäck algorithm, which computed the amount of
optical flow from the first to the second frame. The process was repeated for all
consecutive frames of the stimulus video, and values for optical flow were exported to a file.

The resulting vector of optical flow values was further processed in GNU Octave, and the *findpeaks* function from the Octave signal processing package was
used again to define media events of interest. To increase performance of peak

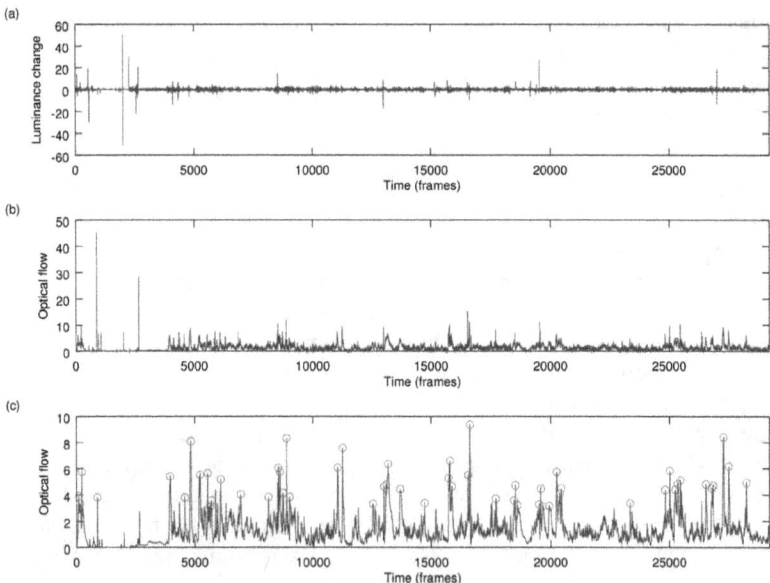

Figure 15. Luminance change, optical flow, and identified peaks in the stimulus of experiment 2.
Figures show (a) per-pixel normalized frame differences in luminance, (b) per-pixel normalized
changes in optical flow, and (c) per-pixel normalized changes in optical flow smoothed with a
moving average filter; red circles indicate detected peaks. Source: own figure.

detection, the noisy raw signal (see Figure 15 a) was smoothed using a moving average filter with a window size of twelve frames, what corresponds to about 0.5 seconds in the video (see Figure 15 b). As parameters for identification of peaks, a required minimum peak height of two standard deviations of the detrended, smoothed optical flow vector was used, with a minimum peak width of 1 unit. The parameter for minimum distance between peaks was fine-tuned to 48 frames, corresponding to about two seconds in the video, to best represent the signal's maxima identified in visual inspection. The function identified 55 peaks in the Birdman video (see Figure 15 c). A custom Octave script was used to prepare timestamps of blink occurrences and timestamps of identified media events in the appropriate data format for analysis in the Theme software. The identified peaks were again numbered consecutively for a clearer T-pattern detection.

7.4 Results

Statistical calculations were conducted in Excel 2013, JASP, and SPSS 22.

In total, 29 experimental sessions were conducted (content: $n = 13$; $M = 2.31$ participants, $SD = 1.32$; form: $n = 16$; $M = 1.94$ participants, $SD = 1.12$).

The experimental condition was chosen randomly for each session, except for the last sessions, where conditions were selected to achieve equal group sizes. Depending on recruitment, group sizes differed for the sessions, but no significant difference was found for average group sizes between experimental conditions ($U = 120.00$, $p = .471$, $d = 0.31$).

Environmental conditions were relatively stable, with an average temperature of 20.26 °C ($SD = 0.27$; range: 19.50–20.90) and an average relative humidity of 39.79% ($SD = 1.82$; range: 38.20–44.00); no significant difference was found between experimental groups (temperature: $U = 101.50$, $p = .929$, $d = -0.29$; humidity: $U = 91.50$, $p = .595$, $d = -0.50$).

7.4.1 Behavior Coding

Inter-rater reliability was calculated with the integrated functions of the Observer XT, and due to the lower quality of participant recordings, a tolerance of 170 ms was allowed to account for an accuracy of five frames.

Several participants had to be excluded from blink analysis. During debriefing, one participant had reported abnormal blinking behavior due to a foreign object in her eye. Four participants failed to comply with instructions, and either talked to each other during the experiment, or showed very high motoric activity during the experiment. Two participants were excluded prior to blink coding, because they showed from the beginning a very high blink frequency of more than 60 blinks per second.

Concordance between coders one and two was calculated for the random 10% subsample, and resulted in a mean percentage of agreement of 92.72% ($SD = 8.64$, range: 64.30–100). Despite high agreement, Kappa statistics were extremely low ($M = 0.15$, $SD = 0.39$, range: -0.2–1), a paradox that can occur under certain conditions (Feinstein & Cicchetti, 1990). We therefore rely on the percentage of agreement and accept blink codings because inspections of disagreements showed that the reduction agreement mainly resulted from not coding blinks during downward saccades in participants with a low blink frequency.

After the exclusion of participants prior to coding, 53 participants remained, who showed during baseline, pauses, and stimulus presentation a total of 24,361 blinks. During stimulus presentation, the 53 participants showed an average blink rate of 20.88 blinks per minute ($SD = 11.07$; see Figure 16), and 22,546 blink occurrences in total (see Figure 17). Four participants were excluded from further analyses due to a very high blink rate, which was more than two standard deviations above the sample's mean (see Figure 16). The two participants excluded prior to coding due to extremely high blink rates were not included in the calculation of this exclusion criterion.

7.4.2 Questionnaire Data

Psychometric quality of the four-item SPSL presence scale was assessed using Cronbach's alpha. The scale's internal consistency was very good with a Cronbach's alpha of $\alpha = .93$.

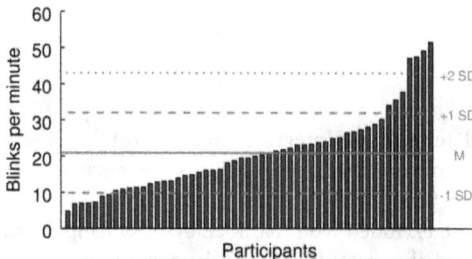

Figure 16. Individual blink rates of all participants in experiment 2.
Source: own figure.

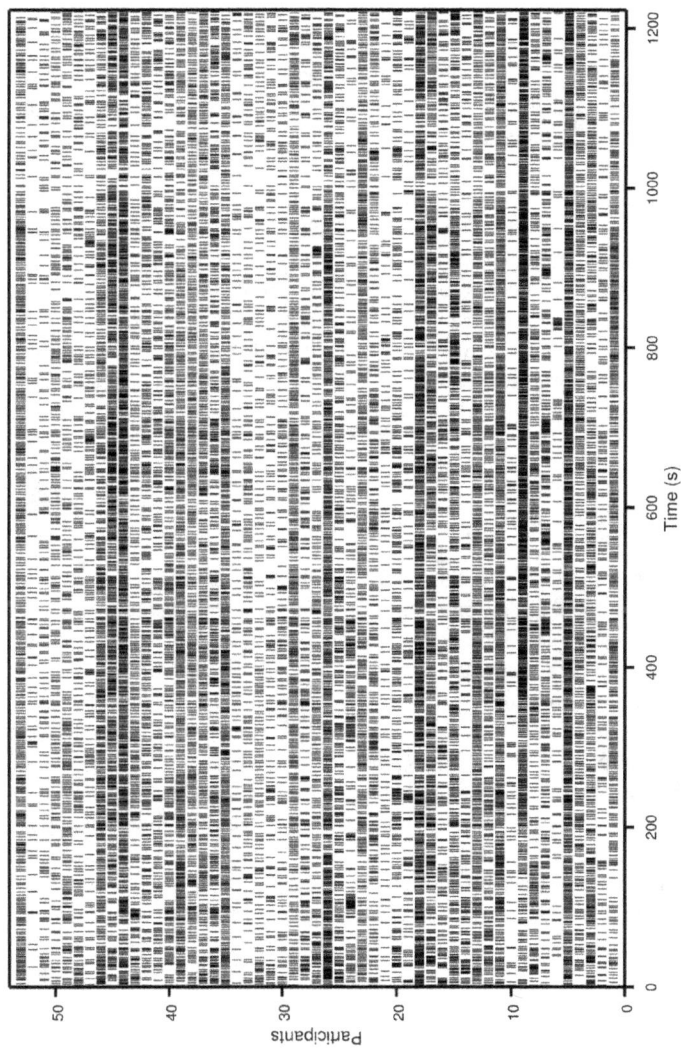

Figure 17. Raster plot of blink occurrences during the Birdman excerpt in experiment 2.
Source: own figure.

7.4.3 Manipulation Check

7.4.3.1 Presence Self-Report

As a manipulation check, an independent samples t test was used to test hypothesis 2.1, which assumed that participants in the content group showed higher SPSL scores than participants in the form group. A Levene's test indicated that variances in both groups did not differ significantly ($F(1) = 0.08$, $p = .774$). A Shapiro-Wilk test indicated that the normality requirement was satisfied (content: $W = 0.97$, $p = 0.703$; form: $W = 0.93$, $p = 0.098$). The one-tailed t test showed that SPSL scores in the content group were not significantly higher than SPSL scores in the form group ($t(47) = -1.69$, $p = 0.951$, $d = -0.48$). Contrary to expectation, participants in the form group reported higher SPSL scores (content: $M = 3.27$, $SD = 0.95$; form: $M = 3.72$, $SD = 0.92$). A follow-up one-tailed t test showed that this effect in the opposite direction of hypothesis was statistically significant ($t(47) = -1.69$, $p = 0.049$, $d = -0.48$; see Table 4 for analysis results of experiment 2). Hypothesis 2.1 was rejected.

7.4.3.2 Corroborative Items

For the four short manipulation check items, hypothesis 2.2 again assumed that participants in the form condition would (a) report in comparison lower attention on content aspects, (b) higher attention on form aspects, (c) less immersion into the depicted environment, and (d) more critical reflection of the perceived stimulus. Because the normality requirements for t tests were not met, one-tailed Mann-Whitney U tests were conducted and showed that participants in the form condition did not pay significantly less attention to content aspects ($U = 339.50$, $p = .198$, $d = 0.32$), reported significantly higher attention on technical aspects ($U = 153.50$, $p = .001$, $d = -0.30$), did not immerse themselves into the mediated environment to a significantly lesser degree ($U = 283.00$, $p = .647$, $d = 0.17$), and did not reflect the perceived stimulus more critically ($U = 344.50$, $p = .827$, $d = 0.34$). These results show that participants in the form group had on average a stronger focus on technical aspects than participants in the content group, but showed no significant difference for the other variables. Consequently, hypothesis 2.2 (b) was accepted, and hypotheses 2.2 (a), (c) and (d) were rejected.

7.4.4 Behavioral Data

7.4.4.1 Hypothesis 2.3

For hypothesis 2.3 (a), a group-level analysis tested if mean IBI variability in the "content" group was higher than in the "form" group.

Inspection of IBI standard deviations shows that they are again skewed towards smaller values. A Levene's test indicated that variances in both groups did not differ significantly ($F(1) = 2.30, p < .136$), but a Shapiro-Wilk test indicated that the normality assumption was not satisfied for one group (content: $W = 0.95$, $p = .222$; form: $W = 0.78, p < .001$). The requirements for a t test are thus not met. As in Nomura et al.'s (2015) study and in experiment 1 of this thesis, standard deviations of IBIs were log-transformed. Examination of log-transformed IBIs shows that the requirements for a t test are still not met: according to a Levene's test, variances do not differ significantly ($F(1) = 0.79, p = .379$), but according to a Shapiro-Wilk test, values did in part still deviate significantly from normal distribution (content: $W = 0.97, p = .681$; form: $W = 0.92, p = 0.041$). A Mann-Whitney U test was used to compare log-transformed IBI standard deviations; results show that IBI standard deviation was not significantly larger in the content group ($U = 344.00, p = .194, d = 0.20$). Hypothesis 2.3 (a) was rejected.

For hypothesis 2.3 (b), the relation between IBI variability and presence scores was analyzed on an individual level. To this end, the observed individual

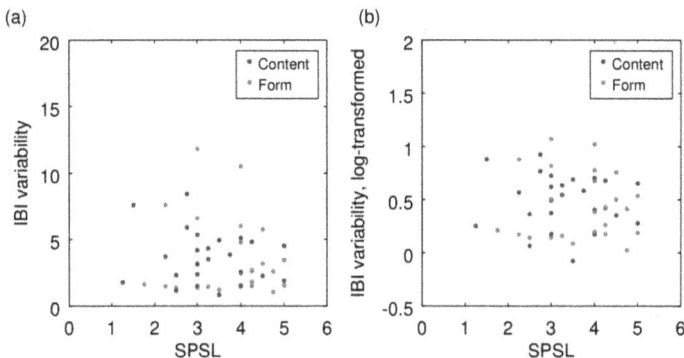

Figure 18. Scatter plots of presence self-report scores and IBI variability in experiment 2. Figure (a) shows original IBI standard deviations, figure (b) shows log-transformed IBI standard deviations. Source: own figure.

Table 4

Descriptives and test results for subjective and objective measures in experiment 2

	Form		Content							
	n	M (SD)	n	M (SD)	t	df	U	p	95% CI	d
				Corroborative items						
Content focus	25	3.60 (2.74)	24	4.25 (0.79)			339.50	.198	[-0.00004, ∞]	0.32
Form focus	25	3.68 (2.73)	24	3.04 (1.23)			153.50	.001	[-∞, -1.00]	-0.30
Immersion	25	3.60 (2.75)	24	3.96 (0.91)			283.00	.647	[-0.00002, ∞]	0.17
Critical reflection	25	2.48 (2.60)	24	3.17 (1.20)			344.50	.827	[-∞, 1.00]	0.34
				Presence self-report						
SPSL	25	3.72 (0.92)	24	3.27 (0.95)	-1.69[a]	47		.951	[-0.90, ∞]	-0.48
				Inter-blink interval variability						
IBI_SD_log	25	0.44 (0.31)	24	0.49 (0.26)			344.00	.194	[-0 08, ∞]	0.20
				Spike train synchrony						
ISI distance	300	0.55 (0.12)	276	0.53 (0.08)	-2.03[b]	532.1		.022	[-∞, -0.003]	-0.17
				T-patterns						
T-pattern occurrences	25	21.64 (4.76)	24	24.17 (5.72)	1.68[a]	47		.050	[0.01, ∞]	0.48

Notes. All tests are one-tailed, with direction of effects according to hypothesis. [a]Student's *t* test; [b]Welch's *t* test.

IBI standard deviations were log-transformed and then correlated to individual SPSL scores (see Figure 18). Analysis results show that a Pearson correlation coefficient was not significant (r = -0.07, p = .626). Hypothesis 2.3 (b) was rejected.

7.4.4.2 Hypothesis 2.4

Hypothesis 2.4 addressed the degree of stimulus-dependent structure in each group's blinking behavior by comparing actual structure to structure found in randomized versions of the data. It was assumed that the content group would show a greater deviation from a hypothetical random behavior, because participants in this group should be invested more in processing of stimulus content. As in study 1, the degree of structuring within both groups was assessed by comparing the average ISI distance within each group's real data with mean average ISI distances from repeated analyses of randomized behavioral data. As in study 1, a custom Python program was used to calculate ISI distances with PySpike and for data randomization. Real blink data was again randomized in 100 simulation runs by shuffling inter-blink intervals (see Figure 19).

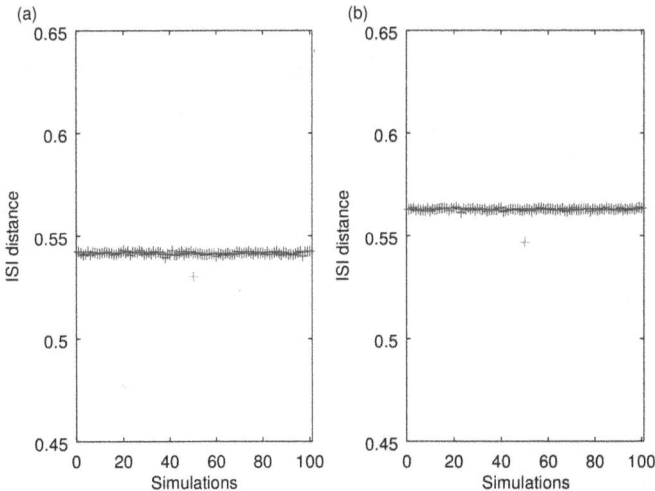

Figure 19. Average ISI distances of real and randomized blinking behavior in experiment 2. Results for (a) content group and (b) form group. Red crosses: real data; blue crosses: randomized data. Lower ISI distances indicate higher similarity. Axis limits are identical to Figure 10 with simulation analysis in experiment 1. Source: own figure.

Results showed that contrary to hypothesis, the "form" group differed more from randomized data (see Table 5). In terms of absolute values, average ISI distance in the form group differed slightly more from randomized data than the average ISI distance in the content group ($d_{random-form} = 0.0162$; $d_{random-content} = 0.0113$). To express this deviation in terms of standard deviations of ISI distances found in randomized data, the absolute difference values were divided by the standard deviations of the randomized data's ISI distances. Contrary to hypothesis, the form group showed a greater deviation from a random behavior (form: 32.6834 SD; content: 17.2621 SD). Hypothesis 2.4 is rejected.

7.4.4.3 Hypothesis 2.5

For the comparison of spike train synchrony between groups, it was again hypothesized that synchrony in the group with content instruction would be higher than in the group with form instruction. Since ISI distance is a measure of dissimilarity, lower ISI distance values were expected for the content group. Pairwise ISI distances were computed for each group in PySpike, processed in Octave, and the resulting data used for statistical group comparisons in JASP (see Figure 20 for each group's average ISI profile, and Figure 21 for each group's matrix with pairwise average ISI distances).

Check of t test requirements showed that variances within the pair-wise ISI distances in both groups differed significantly ($F(1) = 51.54$, $p < .001$), and the normality assumption could not be accepted (content: $W = 0.96$, $p < .001$; form: $W = 0.95$, $p < .001$). The requirements for a Student's t test were not satisfied. However, as in analysis of hypothesis 1.5, no Mann-Whitney U test was performed, because the U test had been suggested to be less appropriate for such

Table 5

Results for ISI randomizations in experiment 2

	Real	Random		Difference random-real	
		M	SD	Absolute	in SD
Content	0.53019	0.54153	0.00066	0.01134	17.26210
Form	0.54674	0.56293	0.00050	0.01618	32.68338

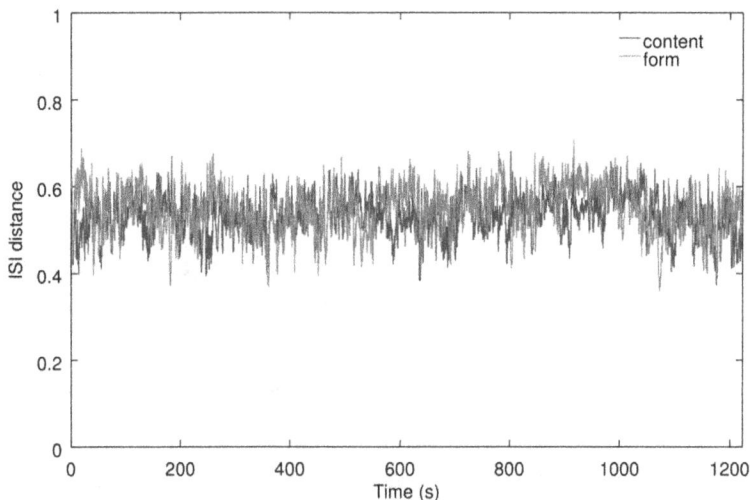

Figure 20. ISI profile of blink synchrony for content and form groups.
Note: Lower values indicate higher synchrony. Source: own figure.

violations of assumptions with the given sample size (Zimmerman, 1987, 1998, 2000, 2003). Instead, Welch's *t* test was used again due to the large sample size (Gibbons & Chakraborti, 1991; Ruxton, 2006).

A one-tailed Welch's *t* test showed that pairwise ISI distances in the content group were, with a small effect size, significantly lower than in the form group

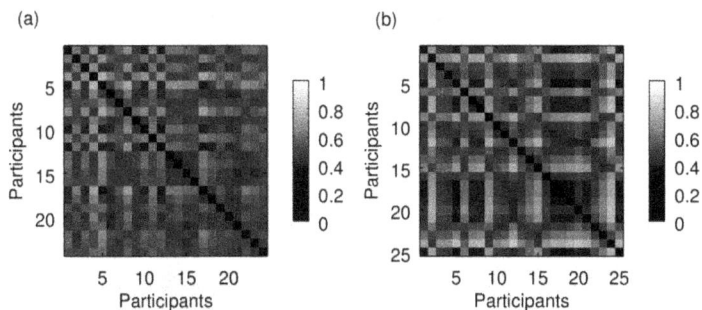

Figure 21. ISI distance matrices for (a) content and (b) form groups in experiment 2. Source: own figure.

$(t(532.2) = -2.03, p = .022, d = -0.17, 95\%$ CI $= [-\infty, -0.003]$; content: $M = 0.53$, $SD = 0.08$; form: $M = 0.55$, $SD = 0.12$; see table 4). Because ISI distance is calculated as a measure for spike train dissimilarity, this means that participants in the content group showed higher synchrony in their blinking behavior. Hypothesis 2.5 is accepted.

7.4.4.4 Hypothesis 2.6

For T-pattern analysis, it was again hypothesized that participants in the "content" group show on average more T-patterns with media events and blinks than participants in the "form" condition, thus reflecting a greater stimulus-dependent structuring of blinking behavior.

T-pattern analysis was conducted in Theme 6. Raw data was again imported into separate Theme projects for each experimental group, and for each analysis, data was concatenated into one artificial observation period. The search parameters for T-pattern detection were the same as in experiment 1, with a significance level for the critical interval of $\alpha = .005$, a required minimum of 3 occurrences, and a maximum level of 1; T-pattern detection in randomized data was conducted in 40 runs of shuffled and rotated data. Resulting T-patterns were reduced to patterns containing blinks as one component, so patterns representing the stimulus structure alone were discarded.

The filtered results contained for the content group 43 different T-patterns, which in total occurred 580 times; for the form group, 42 different T-patterns were found, which in total occurred 541 times (see Figure 22 for an example T-

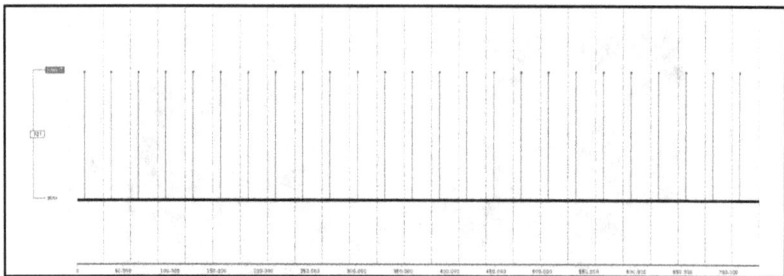

Figure 22. Example for a T-pattern detected in experiment 2.
Segments between dotted blue lines: participants' individual observations. Dots in upper row: occurrence of the 17th peak in frame differences. Dots in lower row: blink occurrences. Connecting lines between rows: occurrences of identified T-patterns. All participants in the form group blinked with greater-than-chance timing after the 17th peak in optical flow. Source: own figure.

Table 6

Numbers of detected T-patterns in real data and randomized data in experiment 2

	Real		Randomized				Difference in SD	
			Shuffle		Rotation			
	Unique	Total	M	SD	M	SD	Shuffle	Rotation
Content	43	580	13.06	3.53	17.43	3.76	8.47	6.80
Form	42	541	10.83	3.09	15.86	3.35	10.10	7.81

Pattern). Considerably less patterns of length 2 were detected in randomized data (see Table 6); the patterns detected in real data can thus be assumed to be valid.

The number of patterns found in each participant was used as individual data for a group comparison. Check of t test requirements shows that variances in both groups did not differ significantly ($F(1) = 1.47$, $p = .231$), and normality could be assumed (content: $W = 0.93$, $p = .121$; form: $W = 0.97$, $p = .564$). The requirements for a t test were thus satisfied. A one-tailed t test indicated that participants in the content group showed significantly more T-patterns with blinks and media events than the form group ($t(47) = 1.68$, $p = .050$, $d = 0.48$; see Table 4). Hypothesis 2.6 is accepted.

7.5 Discussion

The second thesis experiment followed the same approach as the first experiment. Again, participants were randomly assigned to one of two experimental conditions with identical stimulus, but different instructions prior to stimulus presentation. Some aspects of the instructions from experiment 1 were modified. The instruction designed to hinder presence experiences was similar to experiment 1, and asked participants for an analysis of cinematic techniques, so the participants' awareness for the mediated nature of the reception should be increased. The instruction designed to facilitate presence experiences was designed with less demand character, and rather aimed at inducing a normal reception situation as would be expected for a regular cinema attendance. The same objective indicators as in experiment 1 were used to test if the intended different levels of presence experiences mirrored as different levels of structure in spontaneous eye-blink behavior.

Presence self-report scores and the four corroborative items were used as a manipulation check. The intended effect on presence self-report could not be found in analysis. On the contrary, participants in the form group reported on average significantly higher presence scores, despite their presence hindering instruction. The four corroborative items show a different pattern than in experiment 1, and significant group differences in the hypothesized direction were only found for focus on formal features of the stimulus. For the remaining three items, non-significant tendencies of means in both groups showed the predicted directions in the content focus item and on immersion into the stimulus, but not for critical reflection. It could be possible that the by tendency higher mean for critical reflection in the content group is a result of thorough processing of serious content elements in the Birdman narrative, such as sexual harassment in the show business. In sum, the manipulation of conditions was not successful, if not counterproductive. Again, these findings are difficult to explain within the boundaries of established presence theories, especially since the modified instructions for the content group were intended to reduce possible interferences of the content-focused task with presence formation. It could be speculated that the reception situation in the darkened cinema laboratory interfered with the form group's task, because it might have been too long in duration, and too overwhelming in presentation as to sustain an analytical point of view during the whole stimulus presentation. However, in this case participants in the form group should report equal or only slightly less pronounced presence experiences, but rather not almost half a standard deviation higher presence scores. The higher reported presence scores in the form group are problematic, because again participants in the form group reported to have paid significantly more attention to stimulus form features. Nevertheless, as in experiment 1, we still analyzed the objective indicators for a more complete picture of the reception processes.

Analyses of inter-blink interval variability again showed no significant results for group comparisons or individual calculations.

Analyses of ISI distances in the two experimental groups showed mixed results. Contrary to expectation, the random simulations showed that the form group's difference between averaged ISI distance in real and randomized data was considerably larger than the differences found in the content group's data, so the form group differed more from a random behavior. The examination of ISI distances in the two groups, on the other hand, showed the expected results: the content group's averaged ISI distance was lower than in the form group.

Analysis of group differences in pairwise ISI distances showed that this difference was significant: the content group exhibited a structurally more similar blinking behavior than the form group.

For T-pattern detection, a different approach was used for definition of media events in this experiment. Instead of frame differences in luminance, which were used for the conventionally edited stimulus in experiment 1, peaks in optical flow were used to identify significant visual changes in the continuous stimulus without consideration of stimulus content. In line with hypothesis, results of a T-pattern analysis of the blink and optical flow data revealed significantly more T-patterns in the content group. Thus, T-pattern detection again revealed considerable amounts of structure in blinking behavior, and again the results converged with results from the ISI distance analysis.

Because several relevant aspects differed between experiments 1 and 2, it can only be speculated why analyses in experiment 2 found more structure in blinking behavior of the content group, while in experiment 1, more structure was found in the form group. Three differences between the two experiments should be discussed with regard to possible explanations for these results. First, the stimuli differed in several aspects of form and content. Apart from different duration, narrative, and presentation, the continuous stimulus in the second experiment offered less explicit cues for an analysis of formal features, because the movie was not divided into separate shots. A participant who pays attention to formal features would thus need to continuously scan the stimulus for relevant aspects, whereas each cut would offer the chance to pay attention to the new camera position, type of shot, framing, frame composition, and so on. If participants in a group reacted to these abrupt stimulus changes after cuts, a similar timing in their processing could lead to structural similarities in their blinking behavior. This seems to be the most promising speculation to explain the discovered results. Second, definition of media events was different for T-pattern analyses in experiments 1 and 2, but this aspect seems to have less explanatory value: after all, the entirely stimulus-blind ISI analysis showed comparable results, regardless of the type of media event used in T-pattern detection. Third, instructions for the content group were changed for experiment 2. Because it was suspected that the instruction in experiment 1 to focus on content aspects could have hindered presence formation, the strong focus on content had been removed from the content group's instruction in experiment 2. However, another unexpected finding complicated interpretation of the results: the higher presence scores reported by the form group.

The change in instructions for the content group was intended to improve induction of the intended levels of presence by facilitating presence formation in the content group, and hindering presence formation in the form group. However, the opposite occurred: the form group reported significantly higher presence self-report scores than the content group, despite a significantly higher reported focus on formal aspects of the stimulus. Without the intended differences in presence, it would be complicated to relate behavioral structure in blinking to presence experiences, because it could be questioned if the higher questionnaire scores actually reflect higher presence experiences.

At the very least, it is safe to conclude that the converging findings from two objective indicators were consistently in disagreement with subjective self-reports: in experiment 1, both groups reported comparable levels of presence scores, but the form group was found to be more synchronous in their blinking behavior; in experiment 2, the content group was found to be more synchronous in their blinking, but it was the form group who reported higher presence scores. In an interim conclusion, it can be noted that despite the quite different experimental settings, (a) participants in the form condition reported in both experiments equal or higher presence experiences than participants in the content group, what apparently contradicts predictions by presence theories; further, that (b) two different objective indicators detected stimulus-dependent structure in blinking behavior during media reception, and (c) this objectively quantified structure differed between groups of participants who received the very same stimulus, but supposedly engaged in different processing of the stimulus.

The converging results of detected structure were found despite several differences between experiments 1 and 2: a different laboratory with different stimulus presentation, a stimulus differing in both content and formal features, individual testing versus a group setting, and different instructions for participants. However, the manipulation by different instructions did not yield the desired results for the second time; moreover, under the assumption that all questionnaire measures provided valid information, the results were even contradicting established theorizing on presence: individuals should not experience higher levels of presence when they focus on the medium as a technological delivery device for media content (e.g., Liebold et al., 2017; Wirth et al., 2007). In addition, if our assumed causes for the different results in experiments 1 and 2 were correct and the stimulus' cinematic structure actually was a stronger guide for blinking behavior than the video's content, then this would be further evidence against the use of an instructional manipulation. We therefore refrain from another implementation of presence manipulation by instruction, and will create groups with high and low presence experiences by other means. Experiment 3 will now address blinking behavior during use of yet another stimulus, and investigate the application of two objective indicators in an interactive media setting.

8 Experiment 3

The third thesis experiment investigated the relation between stimulus-dependent structure in blinking behavior and self-report measures of spatial presence in users of a video game. Several aspects differed from the previous thesis experiments, due to both conceptual reasons and the results of experiments 1 and 2. First, due to the experiment's conceptualization, the stimulus was continuous, and—different from the studies before—interactive. Due to this interactivity, not all objective measures under assessment in this thesis offer equally adequate indicators for blink structure in an interactive media environment, so only inter-blink interval variability and T-pattern detection were used for analysis. Both were used to compute indicators for structured blinking behavior, which were then related to presence self-report scores. As a different method for data collection, eye-tracking was used instead of manual coding procedures to economically identify eye-blinks in this experiment.

Results of experiments 1 and 2 had shown that different instructions did not result in the intended changes in presence experiences. Because alternative manipulations, especially manipulations of stimulus presentation, might affect blinking behavior (see section 5.6), no experimental manipulation was used to create groups with different levels of presence. Instead, a quasi-experimental approach was used and the sample was divided into participants with lower or higher presence scores by means of a median split, very similar to splitting the sample into tertiles as described in Böcking et al.'s (2008) project.

For the purpose of this thesis, we analyzed a part of this experiment, namely the relation between spatial presence self-report and blinking behavior during a time trial race. For future analyses of the developing structure in blinking behavior during active and passive periods, the experiment also included training periods and passive viewing of videos showing a computer-controlled driver on the race track, which will not be considered here.

8.1 Quasi-Experimental Groups

To assess the different measures' ability to differentiate between users with low and high presence self-report scores, two groups with different levels of presence experiences should be compared. However, as the manipulation checks in thesis experiments one and two had shown, instructing participants to dedicate their attention to either form or content media aspects was not appropriate to induce the intended different levels of presence in recipients of videos. We thus refrained from using different instructions for the creation of different levels of presence in this study. In the author's former racing game experiment (Brill, 2010), the game was presented in either a traditional way or in stereoscopic 3D to create different levels of presence, but results had shown that this manipulation influenced blink rate, so we will resort to a traditional presentation of the game. To be nevertheless able to compare groups with low and high levels of presence in this thesis experiment, all participants were presented an identical stimulus, and quasi-experimental conditions were created post-hoc by means of a median split. Participant number was used as a secondary sorting criterion for participants with identical SPSL values. Analogous to the manipulation checks in the previous studies, a statistical group comparison checked if presence scores in the low presence group were significantly lower than in the high presence group.

8.2 Hypotheses

In experiment 3, not all methods were used to evaluate the relation between structures in blinking behavior and presence self-report: the most suitable method, T-pattern detection, was used to quantify occurrences of blinks near instances of significant changes in visual information in the medium. While variability of inter-blink intervals (IBI), operationalized by the standard deviation of IBI lengths, is possibly not ideal for interactive stimuli (see section 5.8.2.2), it was nevertheless evaluated as an easy to compute measure. The very sensitive ISI-distance measure is, at least in the way it was applied in this thesis, probably not adequate for analyses with interactive, varying stimuli (see section 5.8.2.3), and was not evaluated in this experiment.

8.2.1 IBI Variability

The hypotheses for IBI variability during use of the interactive stimulus were the same as in experiments 1 and 2, and were based on the assumption that attention allocation on and processing of spatial cues in the stimulus affects timing of blink occurrences: users who are indifferent towards the stimulus should exhibit a more regular blinking behavior, whereas allocation and release of attention on stimulus details should prolong and shorten inter-blink intervals (e.g., Liebold et al., 2017; Nomura et al., 2015), thus increasing IBI variability.

Hypothesis 3.1

a) On a group level, participants in the "high presence" group show on average a higher IBI variability than participants in the "low presence" group.

H_0: $\mu_{low\text{-}presence} \geq \mu_{high\text{-}presence}$ H_1: $\mu_{low\text{-}presence} < \mu_{high\text{-}presence}$

b) On an individual level, higher presence scores are correlated with higher variability of IBIs.

H_0: $r_{SPSL\text{-}IBI\_SD} \leq 0$ H_1: $r_{SPSL\text{-}IBI\_SD} > 0$

8.2.2 T-Patterns

A similar rationale is used to derive the hypothesis for T-pattern detection, which is used to search for greater-than-chance temporal relations between blinks and media events. Media events will be defined as instances with high change rates in the visual domain, which should be moments of interest for attentional and other cognitive processes related to construction and updating of mental models (Liebold et al., 2017; Wirth et al., 2007). Attention on and processing of spatial cues should then lead to stimulus-dependent, structured blinking behavior (e.g., Liebold et al., 2017; Nakano et al., 2009; Nomura et al., 2015). This structure should result in increased numbers of T-patterns, if blink timing of participants is influenced by the stimulus.

Hypothesis 3.2

On a group level, participants in the "high presence" group show more T-patterns incorporating both media events and blinks than participants in the "low presence" group.

H_0: $\mu_{low\text{-}presence} \geq \mu_{high\text{-}presence}$ H_1: $\mu_{low\text{-}presence} < \mu_{high\text{-}presence}$

8.3 Methods

8.3.1 Stimulus

In the author's previous study (Brill, 2010), the racing game *Need for Speed: Shift* (2009) was used. Since technological advancements made the visual appearance of Need for Speed obsolete, the more recent racing simulation *Project CARS*

(2015) was used as stimulus; the game has been praised by critics for its above-average simulation accuracy and advanced visuals, and holds a Metacritic score of 83 out of 100 (Metacritic, 2015). As in the previous racing study, the simple Silverstone National race track was used for a time trial race without opponent drivers. The track can be divided into four curved sections and four straight sections (see Figure 23).

Pretests determined an easy to control car (Audi R10) for the simulation to also allow beginners a good racing experience. Each time trial race begins with two short establishing shots depicting the car at its start position; then the camera switches to a first-person perspective for the remainder of the race (see Figure 24). As an aid for beginners, a racing line was displayed as an overlay of colored arrows to help users find the optimal path for their simulated car, and thus reduce distractions from accidents.

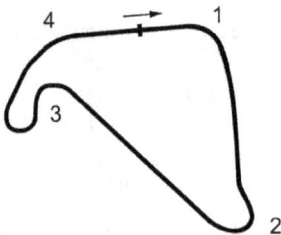

Figure 23. Schematic figure of the race track used in experiment 3.
Source: own figure.

8.3.2 Apparatus

The experiment was conducted in the gaming laboratory of the chair of Media Psychology at the Julius-Maximilians-Universität of Würzburg, Germany. The lab room was the same as in experiment 1, with a desk for the experimenter and a soundproof, acoustically optimized recording booth. Participants played the game in the booth on a 27", 16:9, 1920 × 1080 pixels LCD screen on a 72 cm high desk. Audio was presented by a 5.1 channels surround system on a medium level, with identical level for all participants. The gaming PC was set up outside the booth to prevent distracting noise and heat emissions. Two low-noise fans provided fresh air for the participants. There was no illumination in the booth for the duration of the experiment; in line with presence theories, real-world cues

Figure 24. Schematic drawing of the player's perspective in the game Project CARS.
Source: own figure.

were minimized to support formation of presence. Participants were seated on a 48 cm high chair with armrests, 90 cm from the screen. Participants controlled the game with an Xbox One controller. An unobtrusively placed PTZ, near-infrared dome camera behind and slightly above the screen was used for backup recordings of participants.

The Noldus Media Recorder 2 was used to obtain synchronized recordings of the stimulus screen and the participant's face. For recording of the stimulus screen, the stimulus presentation PC's video signal was duplicated, and recorded on the Noldus Media Recorder PC with a hardware frame grabber. For recording of the participant, the near-infrared video stream was passed to the Noldus Media Recorder, as well. Additionally, the screen was captured in native resolution on the gaming PC with the Nvidia ShadowPlay tool, a resource efficient tool for graphics-card assisted screen capturing; while it produced larger files than the Media Recorder, the encoding technology allowed a higher video quality without compromising processing of the backup participant recordings. In a pretest, a ShadowPlay recording with an overlay of current frames per second showed that the minimum frame rate during a typical race lap was 65 frames per second, thus making sure that the PC hardware allowed for a fluent stimulus presentation; due to the PC setup with only one graphics card, the problem of micro-stuttering, which can occur in multi-GPU setups (PC Games Hardware, 2008), was supposed to be not present. Because subjective perceptions in the pretest also indicated no stutter, no in-depth frame time analysis was conducted.

SMI Eye-tracking Glasses[7] (Eye tracking glasses, 2016) were used to record ocular behavior. The glasses are a light-weight device for tracking movements of both eyes at a rate of 60 Hz. The glasses' frame contains integrated IR illumination, one camera for each eye, and a front-facing camera for recordings of the participant's field of view. The glasses were connected to a laptop running the SMI Experiment Suite 360° software (Experiment Suite 360°, 2016) with iView X 2 for recording and BeGaze 2 for analysis of data.

Before start of each session, temperature and relative humidity inside the recording booth were read from a combined digital thermometer and hygrometer (TFA Dostmann Comfort Control 30.5011; manufacturer specified thermal resolution: 0.1 K, temperature accuracy: ±1° C, humidity accuracy: ±4% between 35% and 75% relative humidity).

8.3.3 Measures

8.3.3.1 Self-Report Measures

In general, self-report measures were the same scales as in the previous studies, and were presented as a SoSci Survey online questionnaire (Leiner, 2014). The survey assessed the 5-point Likert scales of the SPES questionnaire (Hartmann et al., 2015), and scales for suspension of disbelief and absorption tendency from the MEC-SPQ (Wirth et al., 2008). Only the SPSL scale was used for analyses and is reported in this thesis. No additional items for a manipulation check were necessary.

Further items asked for the participant's age; gender; course of study or profession; if the Project CARS video game was already known; the participant's preferences for PC video games in general, console video games in general, PC racing simulations, and console racing simulations; the participant's average gaming time per week; if vision aids were used; if yes, of what kind; if no, if it would have been necessary; how tired participants felt on a 5-point scale; as how demanding they experienced their task on a 5-point scale; if they found something disturbing during reception of the video clip; what they assume the supposed purpose of the study to be; and if they had any further remarks. The questionnaire was concluded by asking for the participant's mail address for the

---

[7] I thank Prof. Dr. Jörn Hurtienne, Dr. Tobias Grundgeiger, and Frank Seyfarth for provision of the eye-tracking hardware and software.

purpose of course credit; this input was saved separately by the questionnaire platform to ensure anonymity.

Order of SPES and MEC-SPQ items was randomized. The participants answered the questionnaire immediately after the stimulus video on the same PC to support recollection of the previous experience.

8.3.3.2 Observational Measures

Observational measures included eye-tracking, recordings of the participant's field of view from the eye-tracker's camera, ShadowPlay screen captures of the video game screen, and telemetry of the simulated car. Media recorder screen captures and dome camera recordings of the participants were recorded as backups.

The near-infrared backup recordings of participants were captured with the Noldus Media Recorder 2, and saved as XViD coded video files in 1280 × 720 pixel resolution, with 30 frames per second, about 5,000 kilobits per second video bitrate, and stereo audio with about 128 kilobits per second. The screen capture backup was also captured with the Noldus Media Recorder 2 in 1920 × 1080 pixel resolution, with 29 frames per second, at a bit rate of about 4,600 kilobits per second, and 128 kilobits per second stereo audio.

Content of the gaming screen was captured with the Nvidia ShadowPlay tool in native 1920 × 1080 pixel resolution, with a desired frame rate of 30 frames per second, at a bit rate of about 26,000 kilobits per second, with 192 kilobits per second stereo audio. Final screen recordings showed slight deviations in frame rate, possibly due to a variable frame rate encoding algorithm.

The participants' ocular movements were recorded at a rate of 60 Hz with SMI eye-tracking glasses and the SMI iView X 2 software. Prior to experiment begin, the eye-tracker was calibrated with the eye-tracking suite's one-point calibration procedure at a viewing distance corresponding to the distance during gaming. The eye-tracking glasses recorded one video for each eye, and additionally a real-world, 24 frames per second video from the participant's point of view, including the computer screen.

Race data and telemetry of the simulated car were recorded with the community-provided *Project Cars Telemetry* tool (2016). Telemetry data was used to extract individual race times, which were counter-checked in video recordings, and to assess driving performance. The telemetry data also offers the simulated car's yaw rate, which should correspond well with horizontal optical flow. However, it was decided to code optical flow from screen captures, because different sections of the race track—with closer or far away elements such as buildings—could produce different optical flow, even at the same yaw rate.

8.3.4 Participants

For the third thesis experiment, 48 male participants (age M = 22.42 years, SD = 2.66; range: 19–30) were recruited using the institute's internal recruiting system. Because a pre-screening of PC or console video game expertise was not possible, the limitation to male participants was intended to provide a sample with as homogenous racing skills as possible. While this decision was primarily made on the basis of experiences with the institute's student population, there also is empirical evidence to justify this limitation: Phan, Jardina, Hoyle, and Chaparro (2012) found that the PC platform was predominantly used by male gamers; more recently, and after conduction of the thesis experiments, Yee (2017) reported findings from a survey indicating that only 6% of racing game users are female.

Participants were offered course credit for their participation if they were studying either Medienkommunikation or Mensch-Computer-Systeme courses.

Regarding their course of study, 25 participants studied Medienkommunikation, 20 participants studied Mensch-Computer-Systeme or Human-Computer-Interaction, and 3 participants stated other courses of study.

Regarding the ratings of how demanding the task was, participants rated it on average to be medium demanding (M = 2.63, SD = 0.94, on a five-point scale from 1 = not demanding at all to 5 = very demanding). Participants gave medium-level estimates for their tiredness (M = 2.54, SD = 1.11, on a five-point scale from 1 = not tired at all to 5 = very tired).

Regarding the supposed purpose of the study, several participants correctly supposed attention or presence to be of interest in the experiment; one participant stated that he supposed blinking behavior to be a relevant variable. This suggests that participants were virtually naive to the experiment's purpose.

Regarding familiarity with the type of stimulus used in this study, participants could rate different facets of their media use habits on a scale from 1 = very rarely to 5 = very frequently. Participants rated their use of games on the PC platform in general with an average of 2.92 (SD = 1.50), games on a console platform in general on average 2.60 (SD = 1.35), racing simulations in particular on the PC platform on average 1.54 (SD = 0.90), and racing simulations in particular on a console platform on average 1.88 (SD = 1.04).

Regarding vision acuity, 41 participants used no optical aids, 1 used corrective spectacles, and 6 used soft contact lenses; no participant stated to be in need of an optical aid, but not having used one.

8.3.5 Procedure

In each experimental session, participants were welcomed and provided informed consent about the experimental procedures and data collection. They were then asked to have a seat in the recording booth, and were assisted in putting on the eye-tracking glasses, followed by eye-tracker calibration. Participants were then informed about the different steps of the experiment. As the first step, participants observed a video of a computer-controlled car, driving smoothly over the Silverstone National course. Participants were then introduced to the game controls, and were asked to drive six laps for training purposes. After the training, the recording of the computer driver was presented once more. Finally, participants were asked to drive a six-laps-qualifying session, and were instructed to drive as fast as they could without leaving the racetrack, or crashing the simulated car. These steps were intended to help participants—and especially unexperienced players—get gradually accustomed to the game and the racetrack; in addition, the collected data can serve future hypotheses testing about the development of blinking structure in relation to the emerging spatial knowledge during this training. During all four steps, eye-tracking data was collected, and after each step, participants answered SPES scales for state variables during media use. Upon completion of the last questionnaire, participants were informed about the purpose of the study, thanked and dismissed[8].

8.3.6 Data Preparation

8.3.6.1 Eye-Blink Coding

Eye-blinks were identified from eye-tracking data using the detection algorithms provided in the BeGaze 2 software. Blink timestamps were then offset-corrected

---

[8] I gratefully acknowledge the support by Maximilian von Andrian-Werburg in conduction of experiment sessions.

in relation to the onset of green lights at race start in the real-world point-of-view recordings of the eye-tracking glasses[9].

8.3.6.2 Video Coding

As in experiments 1 and 2, a content-blind approach was used for defining media events and for analysis of data: media events are defined exclusively on the base of basic formal features, regardless of what had been presented in media content. This is a challenge especially for the interactive stimulus, because individual game experiences can differ considerably, for example due to the player's skills and resulting collisions or swinging off in the simulation. For the purpose of this thesis, we accept these limitations because the focus is on significant changes in visual information and its role in creation and updating of mental models.

Similar to the approach for the continuous video stimulus in experiment 2, optical flow is used to identify instances with a high change rate in the visual domain. In the racing simulation used here, the simulated car is moved along a simulated race track, and this movement causes an illusion of optical flow, conveying the player's speed and direction in the virtual environment. The Nvidia ShadowPlay screen captures were analyzed using the implementation of Farnebäck's (2013) algorithm in OpenCV to quantify optical flow perceived by participants at any moment during the race. We again argue that moments of interest are instances with significant change in visual information, because an updating and re-testing of spatial situation models should be necessary at these instances. The highest amount of new visual information should be presented after the simulated car is steered in a new direction. Optical flow is used to determine this change of information caused by steering of the car, and change in spatial cues should be depicted best by using the horizontal component of optical flow (labeled "x" in Figure 25). To extract the direction and magnitude of total horizontal movement from the screen capture videos, the Farnebäck algorithm from OpenCV is again used in a custom Java program[10] for stimulus analysis. Video files of the Nvidia ShadowPlay screen captures were loaded into the program frame by frame, frames were converted to matrices with luminance values, and the Farnebäck algorithm returned a measure for optical flow between two consecutive frames. The flow measure consisted of two matrices equally sized as the input video's resolution, containing the x- or y-components of optical flow

---

[9]   I gratefully acknowledge the support by Johanna Bode and Maximilian von Andrian-Werburg in data preparation.

[10]   I gratefully acknowledge Andreas Brill's support in creation of the software and for the implementation of multi-threaded processing.

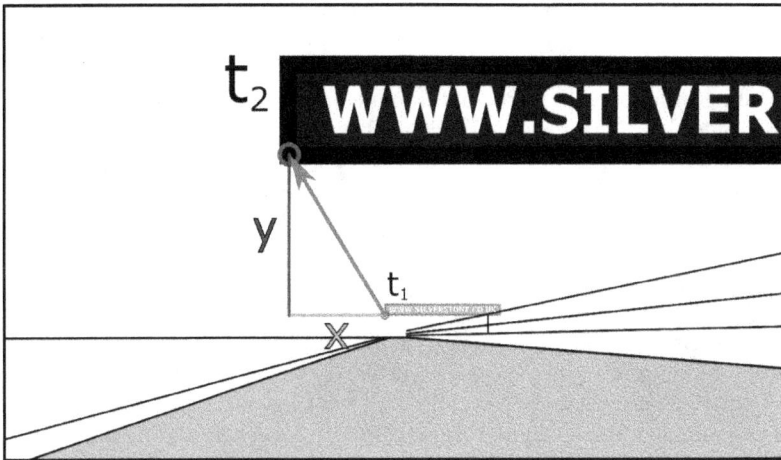

Figure 25. Illustration of optical flow in experiment 3.
As the simulated car is driving, a point in the game environment changes its position on the screen between time t_1 and t_2 (red circles). The diagonal vector describing this offset (red arrow) can be deconstructed into x- and y-components (green and blue lines). Source: own figure.

computed for the respective pixels (see Figure 25). As analysis of Project CARS screen recordings has shown, the player's point of view is by default centered on the horizontal axis, so the vanishing point for movement is located in the middle of the screen. Because there is no simulated head movement, we can compute the sum of optical flow x-vectors to infer the direction and magnitude of the simulated car's yawing movement. If the car drives straight ahead, all x-vectors on the left and right screen sides cancel out, and the result for total horizontal flow is zero. If the car is steered to the right, the simulated environment is shifted to the left, and the resulting sum of leftward optical flow is represented as a negative value; on the opposite, when the car is steered to the left, the result is a total horizontal flow to the right, represented as a positive value. The procedure was repeated for all consecutive frames, and the resulting optical flow vectors were stored in a file. The procedure was repeated for each participant's screen recording. While the screen captures were encoded with about 30 frames per second, the actual game output on the stimulus screen was higher, and thus offered a smoother stimulus presentation. Nevertheless, the rate of 30 Hz is sufficient for our analysis, and resembles the frame rates of the video stimuli in experiments 1 and 2.

Hence, the results of video processing were vectors representing the difference values in optical flow between all consecutive frames of the individual screen captures. These vectors were further processed in GNU Octave. For convenience of interpretation, all flow values were divided by the number of pixels in a frame. Inspection of data showed a large amount of high frequency noise, presumably resulting from the very short control inputs from the digital gamepad buttons (see Figure 26 a). To remove noise and to obtain a clearer representation of visual input during the race, all vectors were filtered with a 0.1 Hz, second order Butterworth low-pass filter. The filter was applied forwards and backwards to prevent introduction of a delay into the signal due to filter response issues (see Figure 26 b).

Onset of green lights at race start and crossing of finish line at race end were used to trim flow vectors to the individual race durations. The findpeaks function from the Octave signal processing package was used to identify maxima in optical flow. To detect flow peaks in these particular signals, a required minimum peak height of 0.5 standard deviations of the detrended flow vector proved to be useful, with a minimum peak width of 1 unit, and a required minimum distance of 60 frames. Double-sided peak detection was used because total horizontal optical flow can produce both positive and negative values. The analysis routine was repeated for all participants, and the identified peaks' positions were translated from frame number to milliseconds from race start; because the ShadowPlay recordings were apparently coded with a variable frame rate, each screen recording's individual average frame rate was used in the conversion process in order to minimize introduction of inaccuracies. The identified individual peaks (see Figure 26 b) were then merged with the offset-corrected timestamps for individual blink occurrences in a custom Octave script, and saved in a data format appropriate for the analysis with Theme. Peaks were not numbered in this study because they do not necessarily represent identical media events (e.g., apex of the first bent section) for all participants.

8.3.6.3 Coding Precision

Several sources for inaccuracies were introduced during recording, coding, and synchronizing of the different data streams. While reduction in coding precision was accepted for the purpose of this thesis, the contributors to error margins should nevertheless be discussed briefly. With eye-tracking at 60 Hz, blinks could be identified with greater precision than by means of manual coding from the 30 fps videos in experiments 1 and 2. However, several inaccuracies were introduced

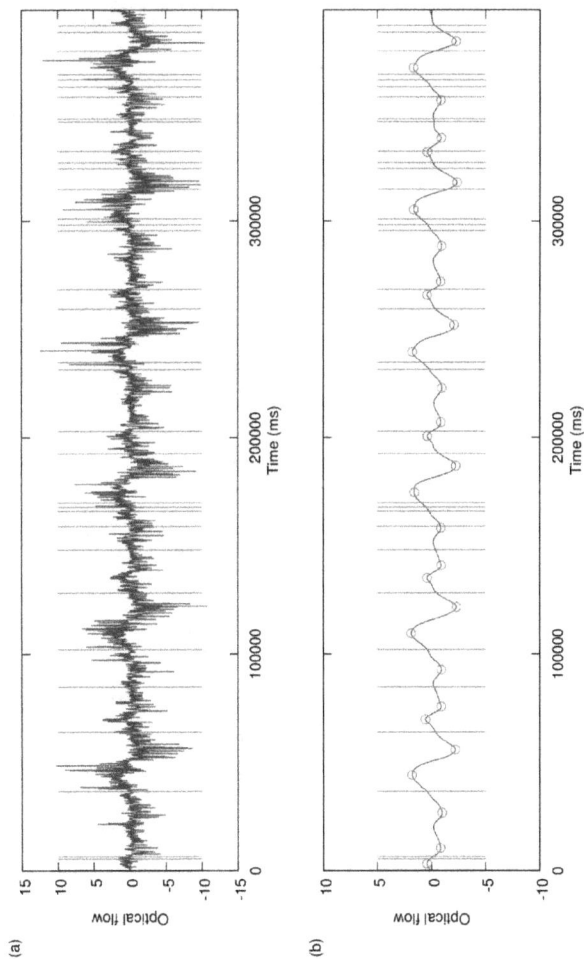

Figure 26. Example for per-pixel normalized optical flow and blinks in experiment 3.
Figure (a) shows raw data for optical flow of one participant, figure (b) shows the same signal smoothed with a 0.1 Hz low-pass filter. Blue lines: optical flow; red vertical lines: blinks; red circles: identified peaks. Source: own figure.

during the synchronization process. First, the 30 fps ShadowPlay screen captures were apparently recorded with a variable frame rate, what might introduce minor inaccuracies. Green lights at race start in these videos were used as a synchronization signal for eye-tracking data: using the eye-tracking glasses' real-world recordings at 24 Hz, all blink timestamps were normalized to race start, whereby the real race start occurred during an interval that was defined by a 30 ms window for the respective frame in the ShadowPlay video, which was then captured in the about 42 ms exposure time of the eye-tracking glasses' front camera; no information is available about delays introduced by the eye-tracking system's video recording pipeline. However, these inaccuracies were again accepted for the analysis of spontaneous eye-blinks, which typically occurred at a rate of less than 1 Hz, and with the intended analyses presumably not depending on millisecond-accuracy.

8.4 Results

Statistical calculations were conducted in Excel 2013, JASP 0.8.0.0, and SPSS 22.

Overall, environmental conditions in the laboratory were relatively stable for the 48 different sessions. Average relative humidity was 34.04% ($SD = 1.73$, range: 30.90–38.40); temperatures inside the recording booth varied slightly more and were on average 23.30 °C ($SD = 1.19$, range: 20.80–27.70).

8.4.1 Behavior Coding

8.4.1.1 Eye-Blink Behavior

One participant was excluded from analyses because his blink rate exceeded the sample's mean by more than two standard deviations (see Figure 27). Data of nine participants was unusable for the combined analyses due to technical failures or synchronization issues.

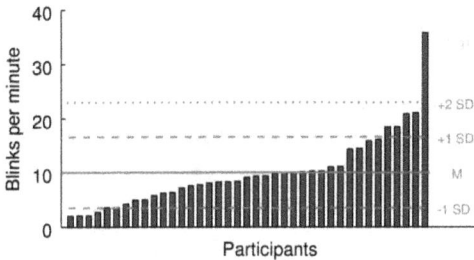

Figure 27. Individual blink rates of all participants in experiment 3.
Source: own figure.

8.4.1.2 Racing Performance

Inspection of telemetry data shows that the average time to complete the six laps of time trial was 407.46 seconds for all participants, 411.43 seconds for the low-presence group, and 403.50 seconds for the high presence group (see Table 7).

8.4.2 Questionnaire Data

For the four-item SPSL presence scale, analysis shows a very good reliability with a Cronbach's alpha of $\alpha = .91$.

8.4.3 Manipulation Check

As a manipulation check, presence scores of the two quasi-experimental groups (low presence: $n = 19$, $M = 2.80$, $SD = 0.79$; high presence: $n = 19$, $M = 4.16$, $SD = 0.42$) were compared. Since the requirements for a t test (equality of variances, Levene's test: $F(1) = 8.22$, $p = .007$; normality, Shapiro-Wilk Test: low presence: $W = 0.92$, $p = 0.124$; high presence: $W = 0.85$, $p = 0.008$) were not met, a Mann-Whitney U test was used to compare group means. Results show that the high-presence group reported significantly higher SPSL scores ($U = 9.00$, $p < .001$, $d = -2.14$, 95% CI = $[-\infty, -0.75]$). The quasi-experimental manipulation was successful.

Table 7

Race times of participants in experiment 3

		Total race time				Number of perfect laps			
SPSL	N	M	SD	Min	Max	M	SD	Min	Max
Low	19	411.43	28.45	390.82	514.13	4.68	1.13	2	6
High	19	403.50	16.75	382.53	449.37	5.21	1.00	3	6
Total	38	407.46	23.68	382.53	514.13	4.95	1.10	2	6

Notes. Perfect laps are defined as laps without collision, skidding, or leaving the track.

8.4.4 Behavioral Data

8.4.4.1 IBI Variability

For hypothesis 3.1 (a), a group-level analysis should test if participants in the low presence group showed lower inter-blink interval variability than participants in the high presence group. Because IBI standard deviations were heavily skewed, the values were log-transformed prior to analysis. Assumption checks for a t test showed no significant difference of variances between groups (Levene's test: $F(1)$ = 0.04, p = .842), but a violation of the normality assumption (low presence: W = 0.96, p = .625; high presence: W = 0.87, p = .015). A Mann-Whitney U test was performed to compare group means, but showed no significant group difference (U = 185.00, p = .557. d = -0.13). Hypothesis 3.1 (a) was rejected.

For hypothesis 3.1 (b), correlation analysis was used to test on an individual level if higher presence scores were related to higher variability of IBIs. Results showed no significant correlation (r = -.04, p = 0.596; see Figure 28). Hypothesis 3.1 (b) was rejected.

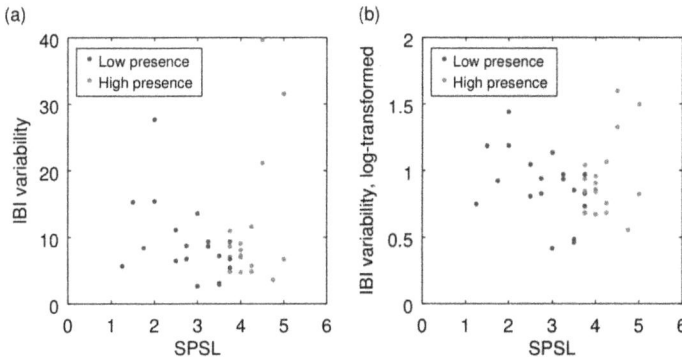

Figure 28. Scatter plots of presence self-report scores and IBI variability in experiment 3. Figure (a) shows original IBI standard deviations, figure (b) shows log-transformed IBI standard deviations. Source: own figure.

8.4.4.2 T-Patterns

T-pattern detection was used to search for greater-than-chance co-occurrences of blinks and significant formal media events. It was hypothesized that on a group level, participants in the high-presence group would show more T-patterns incorporating both media events and blinks than participants in the low-presence group, thus reflecting their higher degree of stimulus-dependent structure in blinking behavior.

Because participants were not assigned randomly to the quasi-experimental conditions, it was first tested if event frequencies differed significantly between groups; for example, a confounded imbalance of blink rates could possibly influence the numbers of detected T-patterns in the two groups. Assumption checks for an independent samples t test showed several violations of test requirements. While both measure did not differ significantly in their variances (blinks: Levene's test $F(1) = 1.86$, $p = .181$; peaks: $F(1) = 1.89$, $p = .178$), a Shapiro-Wilk test showed significant deviations from normal distribution (blinks: for low presence $W = 0.89$, $p = .035$, for high presence $W = 0.95$, $p = .355$; peaks: for low presence $W = 0.65$, $p < .001$, for high presence $W = 0.76$, $p < .001$). Instead of a t test, a Mann-Whitney U test was performed, and showed no significant differences in event counts between groups (blinks: $U = 182.50$, $p = .965$, $d = 0.15$; peaks: $U = 231.00$, $p = .131$, $d = 0.47$; see Table 8).

Table 8

Event counts for T-pattern analysis in experiment 3

Variable	SPSL	N	M	SD	U	p	d	95% CI
Blinks	Low	19	66.32	39.63	182.50	.965	0.15	[-17.83, 28.57]
	High	19	60.95	30.27				
Peaks	Low	19	32.47	3.49	231.00	.131	0.47	[-0.00006, 2.00]
	High	19	31.21	1.59				

T-pattern analysis was conducted in Theme 6 (Theme, 2017). Raw data for each participant was imported into a Theme project and analyzed individually with a level of significance for the critical interval of $\alpha = 0.005$, with at least three pattern occurrences required, with detection of bursts at a significance level of $\alpha = .005$, and a maximum pattern level of one. For randomization purposes, 40 runs of shuffling and rotation were used. Since the pattern level was capped at level one and only two event types were included in analysis, three types of patterns could be detected: patterns containing blinks only, peaks only, or both peaks and blinks in any order. Because the participants' blinking behavior in interaction with the stimulus was in the focus of interest, the analysis results were filtered to contain only patterns with both peaks and blinks.

Results of T-pattern detection show that 95 occurrences of patterns with both blinks and peaks had been detected in participants in the high-presence group, whereas 34 pattern occurrences were found in participants in the low-presence group. However, these patterns were produced by only 8 participants in each group, and the difference between patterns detected in real and randomized data was considerably smaller than in the previous studies (see Table 9; see Figure 29). This limitation needs to be considered when discussing the detected patterns' validity.

Individual T-pattern counts of the 38 participants were analyzed for group differences between the low-presence and the high-presence group. Participants in the low-presence group showed on average 1.80 T-patterns (SD = 2.42); participants in the high-presence group showed on average 5.00 T-patterns (SD =

Table 9

T-pattern detection results for real and randomized data in experiment 3

| | Real | | | Randomized | | | | Difference in SD | |
| | | | | Shuffle | | Rotation | | | |
SPSL	Total	M	SD	M	SD	M	SD	Shuffle	Rotation
Low	34	1.80	2.42	0.64	0.17	0.89	0.27	0.79	0.47
High	95	5.00	11.40	0.49	0.12	0.90	0.27	1.68	1.10

Notes. Results differ from calculations in the Theme software, because here, only participants with identified T-patterns were included.

11.40). A Levene's test showed that variances differed significantly between groups (F(1) = 4.10, p = .050).

A Shapiro-Wilk test showed that normality could not be assumed for both groups (low presence: $W = 0.74$, $p < .001$; high presence: $W = 0.49$, $p < .001$). Because the requirements for a t test were not met, a Mann-Whitney U test was used to assess whether high-presence participants showed more T-patterns with

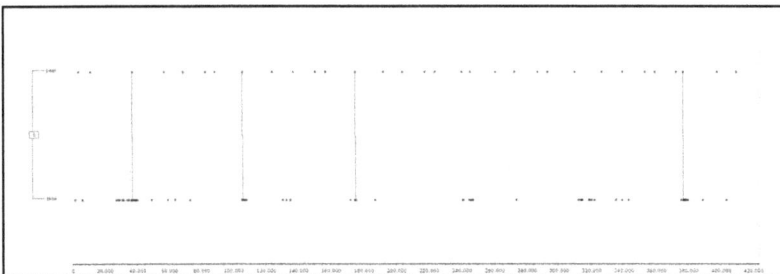

Figure 29. Example for a T-pattern detected in experiment 3.
During the race, the participant executed an eye-blink (lower row of event markers) four times after a peak in optical flow (upper row of event markers) with greater-than-chance timing; these four T-pattern occurrences are indicated by the vertical lines. Also note the clustering of eye-blinks during the six-laps race. Source: own figure.

both media events and user actions than low presence participants. According to the test results, T-patterns did not differ significantly between groups ($U = 167.50, p = .342, d = .39$).

8.5 Discussion

The third experiment in the present thesis investigated relations between stimulus-dependent structure in spontaneous eye-blink behavior and presence self-report measures during use of an interactive, dynamic media stimulus. Interactivity was the key difference between this and the earlier thesis experiments, and did not only raise challenges in data collection, preparation and synchronization, but also for data analysis. Only two methods were used to derive objective indicators for quantification of stimulus-dependent structure in blinking: inter-blink variability as an estimator for the overall influence of attentional processes on normal, more regular blinking behavior, and T-pattern detection for identification of recurring, significant temporal relations between media events and user events. The third method used in this thesis, ISI distance as a measure for spike train dissimilarity, was not used in this experiment due to methodological constraints; these constraints in principle also applied to IBI variability. Both objective measures captured behavior during the extended duration of the race. This longer, relatively natural observation of gaming behavior comes at the expense of varying game experiences in participants, resulting from, for example, different racing performance due to different skill levels. These caveats are not addressed in this thesis, even though the objective measures could possibly be more sensitive than the questionnaire to events such as interruptions of the gaming experience.

Another aspect differing from the previous studies concerned creation of experimental conditions: because manipulation of presence experiences by instruction did not show the intended effects, all participants took part in an identical experiment, and the sample was later split along their presence self-report median. While this approach might not treat participants adequately who reported medium levels of presence, it nevertheless resulted in two groups with significantly different presence scores.

The results for inter-blink interval variability showed no significant differences between high- and low-presence groups, and no significant correlation with presence self-report.

Results of T-pattern detection showed different mean pattern occurrences in both groups in descriptive analysis, with more patterns for the high-presence group; however, both groups showed a very high variability in pattern formation, and inferential statistics show that the difference between groups is not statistically significant. While this might at first glance be merely an issue of test power, comparison of T-patterns found in real and randomized data show considerably less deviation from randomized data results, what indicates that behavioral structure is actually less dependent on the chosen media events than in the previous experiments. The media events were derived from the theoretical background on presence: peaks in the visual channel were supposed to represent media events during which an existing mental model would need to be discarded or updated with new information, in this case to provide a spatial situation model of the upcoming race track segment, so the car's course could be planned. The findings suggest that these media were no appropriate triggers for blinking. Two alternative explanations are possible. First, participants might already have constructed a sufficiently detailed mental model of the track; after all, participants had been passively observing two laps on the track, and drove themselves six laps during the training phase before they started the race. This could be clarified by additional free or cued recall of the race track course or of track details, and by analyzing the development of structure in blinking behavior over the experiment session. Second, since visual inspection of blink occurrences suggested a certain degree of structuring, it seems likely that eye-blink timing was influenced by other events that were not included in analysis. The defined media events were maxima in filtered optical flow signals to best reflect the course of the race track. The purpose of filtering was to eliminate high-frequency noise, especially due to abrupt control inputs on the rather sensitive gamepad, so these local peaks were not present in the data set. If blinks had been coupled to, for example, the player's motor actions, then these filtered-out events would been of high relevance. Furthermore, maxima in the smoothed signal most likely occurred near curve apexes, where the simulated car's yaw rate reached its maximum. Earlier results using position of blink occurrences along the race track (Brill, 2010) suggested that curve apexes were not essential for blink structure in this particular game setting, likely because the critical period for processing of spatial cues and planning of car trajectory is located before curve entries; the present results could support this conclusion with evidence from the actual visual input that was perceived by the players. However, it is not clear if this assumption can be generalized to other, more difficult game settings with different cars or race tracks. In addition, future studies would need to consider blinking behavior in real-world situations to assess the measure's appropriateness in the sense of behavioral realism. At least for professional Formula 1 drivers, curve apexes seem to play a more significant role in real-world racing. After an eye-tracking session on a race track featured by a motor sports network (Sky Sports F1, 2016), professional Formula

1 driver Nico Hülkenberg explained to a motor sports journalist that apexes are fixated on during the passage of a curve, followed by fixation on the next apex, and so on.

Few definite conclusions can be drawn from experiment 3 due to the lack of conclusive findings. For the third time in this thesis, the measure of inter-blink interval variability delivered no valuable results. As was predicted, the few patterns found in T-pattern analysis occurred more frequently in the high presence group, but this difference was not statistically significant, and found T-patterns differed little from randomized data analysis. The experiment's results can nevertheless be informative for future research. Future T-pattern analysis could incorporate more events in the visual channel, positional information of the simulated car, and user inputs along with blinking behavior to provide a more complete picture of the gaming experience. Comparisons with real-world blinking behavior in a motor sports context could serve as an external validation for the measures of the attentional processes at work during playing. Regarding methodology, further indicators could be derived and tested on an individual level. For example, Magnus Magnusson suggested in an informal discussion that individual deviations between T-pattern counts in real and randomized data could serve as an indicator for structuring of behavior. The same approach could be used for the ISI distance measure, where dissimilarity between an individual's real blinking behavior and randomized versions thereof could indicate the degree of structure. The ISI measure would also offer a comparison between real data and randomized data during the whole observation period, so researchers could identify periods during media use where a participant's blinking behavior is similar to a random process from other periods where the degree of structure increases. A final application for randomization methods would concern optical flow during eye-blink occurrences. When looking at Figure 26, it is possible to speculate if blinks occur predominantly during strictly monotonically increasing or decreasing segments of the optical flow signal, but less likely at the peaks. While previous analyses determined if blinks occurred during straight or bent segments of the race track, it could now be calculated during which segments of the optical flow signal blinks occur predominantly. Moreover, calculation of slopes during real blink occurrences could then be compared with slopes found for randomized blink occurrences, which would offer another individual-level estimator for stimulus-dependent structure in blinking behavior.

9 General Discussion

9.1 Recapitulation

The present thesis aimed at advancing presence research by evaluating aspects of spontaneous eye-blink, namely objective indicators for a stimulus-dependent behavioral structure, as a possible alternative measurement method for presence. To achieve this aim, a solid theoretical foundation has been established for the presence concept (section 2), for both subjective and objective presence measurement approaches (section 3), and for causes and determinants of spontaneous eye-blink behavior (section 4). Several factors with influence on blink timing have been reported (section 4), and we have used this collection of theories and empirical evidence to substantiate a relation between structured blinking behavior and formation of presence experiences. This relation is in line with assumed relations between blinking behavior and other reception processes, such as transportation in Nomura et al. (2015) or transportation and narrative engagement in Bacherle (2015). Beyond these existing assumptions, the relation suggested here provides more detailed explanations of the assumed mechanisms by referring to findings on attentional and other cognitive processes from blink research and presence research.

Three different methods for quantifying structural aspects in blinking behavior were chosen from existing research, and were used to relate indicators for structured behavior to presence self-report. The first measure under evaluation, variability of inter-blink intervals, is based on the assumption that processing of ongoing media content during media use introduces irregularities into the natural course of spontaneous eye-blink behavior (Nomura et al., 2015). The second measure, ISI distance as an indicator for spike train dissimilarity (Kreuz, Mormann, et al., 2007), was also derived from Nomura et al.'s (2015) study. It reflects the synchrony in blink rate changes between participants who are perceiving the same stimulus and was used in the thesis' two video stimulus studies. As for IBI variability, the reasoning for this measure assumes that ongoing processing of media content leads to alterations of spontaneous eye-blink behavior; participants who are in this way influenced by the same media stimulus should show more synchrony in their blink timing than participants who are not influenced by the stimulus. As the third method, T-pattern detection was used in all three studies (e.g., Brill, Jonsson, Magnusson, & Schwab, 2016; Suckfüll & Unz, 2016). This method identifies repeated co-occurrences of events with a relatively stable temporal organization (Magnusson, 2000). In this case, we use a content-blind approach for definition of media events and search for patterns incorporating both the user's blinks and instances with a high rate of visual information change in the medium.

To test the applicability in diverse media environments, three different media stimuli were used in the thesis experiments: a conventionally edited, and thus pre-segmented, non-interactive video stimulus, a continuously edited, and thus not pre-segmented, non-interactive video stimulus, and a continuous, interactive game stimulus. Unlike specifically constructed stimulus material, as was in part used in the series of experiments presented by Böcking et al. (2008), these media environments had less carefully controlled immersive capabilities, and differed in several form and content features. However, existing studies had shown that these, or at least similar, media environments were able to elicit a stimulus-dependent structure in blinking behavior, and were thus deemed appropriate for the investigation of blink structure in this thesis.

We will now review the results from all three thesis experiments and derive implications for methods and theories of presence research. In the methodological conclusions, the combined findings are interpreted in a broader context, and future improvements of the alternative measurement methods are derived. In the theoretical conclusions, the experiments' results are reviewed with respect to their implications for presence research, and it is discussed how the methods used in this thesis could serve to advance our understanding of presence.

9.2 Methodological Conclusions

The evaluation of methods will address the manipulation of presence experiences by instruction and the three methods used for deriving objective indicators for stimulus-dependent structure in blinking behavior: inter-blink interval variability, spike train synchrony, and T-pattern detection. The discussion of these three methods will each conclude with suggestions for future refinements of the measures.

9.2.1 Manipulation of Presence Experiences

In this thesis, experimental conditions with different levels of presence were to be created by means of different instructions: participants were asked to either focus on content aspects or on form aspects of the stimulus. This manipulation was derived from the theoretical background on presence and from empirical evidence. The instructions were intended to modulate presence formation in an externally valid way, while at the same time avoiding contamination of spontaneous eye-blink behavior by, for example, orienting responses towards real-world stimuli. Success of manipulations was assessed in a manipulation check with an established presence self-report measure, and additional short items asked for compliance with the respective instruction.

In experiment 1, participants were instructed to either pay close attention to formal or content aspects of the stimulus, and it was announced that they would be asked for judgements of the respective aspects after reception of the video. Results of the short items suggest that instructions were understood and followed in general; however, no significant difference was found for presence self-report scores. This complicated interpretation of behavioral results and also raised the suspicion that instructions for the content group, which should have facilitated presence experiences, might actually have hindered the formation of presence: if the instruction had led participants to focus on video content in an analytical manner, then presence formation could have been impeded.

Because the experimental manipulation in experiment 1 failed to induce different levels of presence experiences, the content group's instructions were modified in experiment 2: participants in the content condition were instructed to watch the movie just as they would do in a cinema, and report their subjective experience afterwards, which is a standard procedure in media research. Participants in the form condition were still asked to pay attention to the movie's formal features in an analytical way, and to provide their judgement after reception of the video. Compared to experiment 1, group differences in the four short items were considerably reduced, and variation within groups was higher. However, participants in the form group still reported significantly higher focus on technical stimulus aspects than participants in the content group. Presence self-reports showed—contrary to hypothesis—that participants in the form condition reported higher presence scores than participants in the content condition. Together with the reported higher focus on formal features of the medium, this finding contradicts established presence theories: participants should not be able to enter states of presence more readily if they are perfectly aware of the mediated nature of their viewing experience. Further, this contradiction is a significant problem for the rationale of this thesis: after all, the established presence questionnaire should serve as a benchmark for the new objective presence measures—however, with arising questions about the questionnaire's validity in this particular setting, the intended rationale could not be followed.

Due to the unexpected effects of instructions in experiments 1 and 2, the instructional approach was not used in experiment 3. Instead, a median split was used to successfully create quasi-experimental conditions with low and high presence experiences.

With the given results pattern, we can arrive at the methodological conclusion that manipulation of presence experiences by instruction is problematic, at least in the way it was realized in this thesis. While the instructions to focus on form or content were thoroughly based on predictions by presence theories, the desired effects on presence were not only absent, they were, at least in part, even in contradiction to theory. It could be argued that the instruction to focus on formal aspects did not deliver the intended results because it had not been understood; after all, instructions were kept as general as possible, because they should fit the diverse media environments in all three experiments. However, virtually all participants were recruited from media-related university courses that include media production aspects in their curricula, so a more detailed instruction about formal aspects was probably not necessary. A different possible effect of instructions will be discussed in subsection 9.2.3, when we discuss that not only the overall degree of stimulus-dependent structure should be informative, but also on what aspects of the stimulus this structure depends—after all, it would be possible that the different instructions supported formation of both form-dependent and content-dependent structure in blinking, with different proportions of both in the two experimental groups. However, such more detailed observations of blinking behavior will be subject to future research.

The instructional approach could be beneficial for future studies that do not rely on the very sensitive blink measure. For example, participants could be explicitly instructed to pay attention to cuts or camera perspectives. For studies on blinking behavior, it may be more worthwhile to use our approach from experiment 3, let presence emerge naturally, and then test hypotheses on presence factors either with post-hoc created groups, or ideally by considering the participants' presence self-reports individually.

9.2.2 Inter-Blink Interval Variability

The measure of inter-blink interval (IBI) variability uses the straight-forward indicator of individual IBI length standard deviations. In line with Nomura et al.'s (2015) approach, it was hypothesized that participants in the high presence condition show higher variability of inter-blink intervals, because their blink timing should be subject to influence by more intense internal processing of the stimulus. Groups with presumably low and high presence experiences were created by manipulation in studies 1 and 2, and by median split in study 3. As in Nomura et

al.'s study, the IBI standard deviations were log-transformed prior to analysis because they showed a log-normal distribution. Analyses were conducted on group
level by comparing IBI standard deviations between low and high presence
groups, and on an individual level by correlating individual standard deviations
to presence self-report scores. No significant results were found in any experiment, neither in group differences, nor on an individual level. While the measure's inadequacy would be comprehensible in an interactive media setting,
where differing event sequences and event timing across participants pose an additional source of variability, the lack of significant relations in all three media
environments questions the measure's appropriateness. The small effect sizes in
all experiments (experiment 1: $d = 0.12$, $r = .08$; experiment 2: $d = 0.20$, $r = -.07$;
experiment 3: $d = -0.13$, $r = -.04$) suggest that the lack of significant results is not
just a problem of test power, and even more so because sample sizes were chosen
after Nomura et al.'s experiment, where at least some results could be found with
this measure. With regard to the unsuccessful manipulation of presence in experiments 1 and 2, it could be argued that the measure's failure to detect structural differences in blinking is not an issue because there just were no appropriate
differences in structure to detect. However, the other two objective measures under observation agreed in detecting structural differences, and IBI variability further detected no differences in the median-split conditions in experiment 3.
Apart from that, blink interval variability as a process measure would have limited informative value for describing the dynamic unfolding of stimulus events;
to analyze such dynamics, it would be necessary to bin the observation period
into meaningful intervals, and compare variability between these bins. However,
when referring to suggested minimum durations for appropriate measurement
of blink rates (see Kaminer, Powers, Horn, Hui, & Evinger, 2011, pp. 11264–
11265), it could be argued that smaller bins would make estimates of blink interval variability less reliable, as well; participants with very low eye-blink rates
might not even blink in a given interval, at all. In addition, it would be necessary
to investigate if resulting variability scores are independent of individual blink
rates, and if some form of normalization to individual blink rate would be necessary. Additional open questions concern if valuable information is lost during
log-transformation, and if there maybe exist non-linear relations between IBI
variability and presence self-report, which would not be captured by linear correlation measures. For example, the relation between IBI variability and SPSL
scores in experiment 3 apparently shows a curvilinear relation, which was not
tested for in this thesis (see Figure 28).

In conclusion, the collected evidence suggests that inter-blink interval variability in its current from seems to be no appropriate indicator for internal processes occurring during presence formation.

9.2.3 Spike Train Synchrony

Spike train synchrony, operationalized as the spike train dissimilarity measure ISI distance (Kreuz, Mormann, et al., 2007), has been used to quantify co-occurring changes in blink rate within groups. Two indices have been derived for group level analysis: first, as in Nomura et al.'s (2015) study, pairwise ISI distances between group members have been used to compare average synchrony within each experimental group; second, following Nakano et al.'s (2009) and Magnusson's (2000) randomization approaches, each group's real ISI distance was compared to ISI distances computed from randomized versions of the real data. The ISI distance measures were used in experiments 1 and 2, where each experimental group was presented identical video stimuli. The method was not used in experiment 3, because the differences in blinking behavior resulting from the different stimulus dynamics could not have been distinguished from differences in blinking behavior caused by internal processes. It was hypothesized that participants in the high presence groups would show higher synchrony within groups, because they would engage more in processing of content and spatial media cues, and this processing should influence blink execution with a stimulus-dependent timing. Analyses in experiments 1 and 2 showed mixed results.

In experiment 1, participants in the form group showed higher degrees of similarity in their blinking behavior, which was consistently found for both the within-group synchrony indicator and for randomization analyses. The ISI distance results were in line with results from T-pattern detection, so, contrary to hypothesis, the form group apparently showed higher synchrony in blinking behavior. Moreover, both groups did not differ significantly in their presence self-reports, so it could not be concluded if higher stimulus-dependent structure was related to higher presence experiences.

With a different stimulus and different instructions for the content group in experiment 2, findings from the ISI distance and T-pattern methods were again in agreement. In this experiment, the convergent findings of ISI distance and T-pattern indicators showed higher degrees of stimulus-dependent blinking structure in the content group. However, it could again not be concluded if greater stimulus-dependent structure was indicative for presence experiences, because participants in the form group unexpectedly reported significantly higher presence scores, despite their self-reported, significantly higher focus on formal stimulus features. This finding contradicts predictions of presence theories, because these participants focused on the medium as an artefact; possible explanations for this finding will be discussed in section 9.3. The result of simulation analysis was in disagreement with the result of the ISI distance group comparison: as in experiment 1, the form group showed a higher deviation from the hypothetical random blinking behavior. This suggests that both ISI-distance-based indicators do not necessarily depict the same aspects of behavioral structure, and theoretical reconsiderations about the randomization approach are needed for future research.

A possible explanation for the higher degree of structuring in participants instructed to focus on form features in experiment 1 could be that in processing of these features, cognitive processes might have been more restricted than in the content group, so structure imposed on blinking behavior was more restricted, as well. Put differently, one might argue that the cognitive range for processing of form features is limited, whereas processing of content might allow for more diverse interpretations and processes. This might hold true especially for processing of humoristic stimuli; for example, participants in study 1 reported rather divided appreciations of the Mr. Bean humor. To test these assumptions, participants could be further separated into groups with homogenous humor preferences, and then again be compared regarding their structure in blinking behavior. In addition, dispersion measures for group data of presence, manipulation check items, and blink indices could be used not only as a requirement check for group comparison measures, but also as informative group characteristics in themselves, so it could be tested if a broader range of cognitive processes results in a broader range of blinking behavior, and thus less structural similarity.

With regard to its methodological properties, three limitations can be identified for the ISI distance measures used in this thesis. First, as has already been discussed during this method's introduction in section 5.8, the current conceptualization relies on identical stimuli for all observed participants: differences in the participants' synchrony can then be attributed directly to different processing of the very same stimulus. However, as soon as the dynamic structure of stimulus events is not fixed, as for example in interactive video games, variance is introduced into the measure that does not result from different reactions towards the stimulus, and thus reduces the degree of synchrony in an undesired manner. To circumvent this issue, the method could be modified to apply the randomization approach used in this thesis not only on a group level, but also on an individual level. In such analyses, the individual spike trains of blink occurrences would be randomized repeatedly, and average ISI distances between real and random data could be calculated. Effectively, each participant would be compared to randomized version of her own data, instead of comparing group synchrony to that found in randomized group behavior. The resulting individual ISI distance indicators could inform about overall individual deviation from a hypothetical random blinking behavior, and by using the ISI profile, information could also be gained about periods with lower or higher deviations from the simulated random behavior. This could allow for identification of significant media events even in interactive media, or could corroborate group-level ISI profiles in non-interactive media. The second limitation concerns the nature of the identified structure in blinking behavior. When applied in the way it was done in this thesis, then the method only detects if a stimulus-dependent structure is present in general, but offers no further information on what might have caused this structure. For example, it would be possible that participants in the two experimental groups had shown comparable degrees of structuring in their blinking behavior, but in one group, this structure resulted from attention allocation on content aspects of the stimulus, and in another group, this structure resulted from attention allocation on form aspects of the stimulus. Such differences would not be visible for the analysis approach applied in this thesis. To circumvent this issue, pairwise comparisons could be made not only within each experimental group, but between all participants in the sample[11]. This way, it would be possible to determine if the structuring exhibited within each group is the same, or actually shows different characteristics. In addition, participants could be clustered according to their similarity, and convergence with clustering in other measures, such as presence self-report, could be tested. Clustering functions, and also routines for the analysis of synchrony as a response to external stimuli, are already included in certain implementations of the ISI distance algorithm (Kreuz, Mulansky, & Bozanic, 2015).

Regarding its use as a process measure, ISI distance appears to be well suited for analyzing the dynamic unfolding of events along the temporal dimension. The degree of synchrony between participants is calculated for each moment in time, and different aggregation of data (see Kreuz, Mormann, et al., 2007) allows for analyses of different aspects of behavior: the overall level of structure between experimental conditions can be compared along the temporal dimension, or average values of individual- or group-ISI-distances can be compared for the whole observation duration or intervals thereof. Together with the suggested enhancements, the method would allow future research the identification of media events with remarkable impact on user behavior. Future research should also use the recently presented, refined A-ISI distance algorithms (Satuvuori et al., 2017), and could use the A-SPIKE distance measure to not only consider co-occurring changes in blink rate, but also co-occurrences of blink elicitation.

---

[11] I thank René Weber and Ron Tamborini for their helpful comments on this matter during an informal discussion at an earlier stage of the thesis project.

9.2.4 T-Pattern Detection

For the evaluation of T-pattern detection, user events and media events were necessary for analysis. User events were readily available as coded eye-blink occurrences. Media events were defined using content-blind identification of instances with a high change rate in the visual channel, where great amounts of new visual information need to be attended to, taken in, and processed. For the first study, significant changes in luminance between frames was used; because the stimulus was a conventionally edited video, these events largely equaled cuts between different shots in the video. For the second study, a stimulus with apparently one continuous shot was used, so no cuts were visible in the video. Instead, the video content was presented by fluid camera movements between and within locations. We assumed that frame-to-frame optical flow would capture these movements better than frame differencing, so instances with high changes in optical flow were used as media events in T-pattern analysis. For the third study, high changes in the visual input's horizontal optical flow during an interactive car racing simulation were used as media events, because they should best represent the change in visual information on the simulated race track. In all studies, it was not further investigated what content was presented at the defined moments; in a content-blind approach, it was rather assumed that these instances of high visual change are moments during media use when new visual information is presented to the user. The presence theory by Wirth et al. (2007) argues that in order to sustain a state of presence, the user first needs to perceive such new visual information, including spatial cues about the simulated environment, about potential actors, their positions and actions. Then, the user needs to process this information in order to update her spatial situation model, and finally test and accept this model in the process of perceptual hypotheses testing. We argued that attentional and other cognitive processes during this continuous, complex process of presence formation would influence blinking behavior, so users who engage more in processing of stimulus information in a state of presence would show more stimulus-dependent structure in their blinking behavior. Consequently, more patterns incorporating both media and user events were expected for these participants.

For analysis of structure in media events and user events, a very basic T-pattern analysis was conducted. The Theme software was used to search for T-patterns with a level not higher than one, which represented only greater-than-chance occurrences of either one media event, followed within a critical interval by one user event, or one user event, followed within a critical interval by one media event. Occurrences of such patterns were then compared between experimental groups. In experiment 1, results of T-pattern analysis converged with results from spike train synchrony analysis. However, the results were contrary to expectations, and T-Pattern results showed that behavioral structure in blinking of the form group, and not the content group, depended more on cuts in the video. Considering the form group's instruction to focus on formal aspects of the video, this likely reflects a higher degree of attention allocation to video form features. Because the presence manipulation with instructions to focus on form or content features was not successful, these behavioral results could not be related conclusively to presence self-report. In experiment 2, with peaks in optical flow representing media events of interest, analyses showed that T-pattern results were again in agreement with results from the ISI distance method: as was hypothesized, more T-patterns were found in the content group. However, the manipulation of conditions was not successful and participants in the content group even reported lower presence scores than participants in the form condition, so the results are difficult to interpret with regard to presence. The results of experiment 3 showed the weakest effects in T-pattern analysis, with less difference between patterns detected in real and randomized data. While in line with predictions, more T-patterns were on average found in the high-presence group, statistical analysis showed that there was no significant effect. With knowledge from existing research, it was assumed that the defined events were apparently not optimal for analysis of behavior in the interactive media environment. The results underline that the main challenge in T-pattern detection is proper event definition. This might hold true especially for interactive stimuli, which enable the user's cognitive system to enter a bidirectional exchange process with the stimulus.

In sum, the results did not confirm hypotheses, but converged with results of ISI distance analyses; this suggests that both methods were sensitive to at least co-occurring, if not comparable or identical facets of blinking behavior, but these facets were not necessarily related to formation of presence. Due to several differences between both methods, this convergence would probably not occur under all circumstances.

First, the ISI distance indicators can be calculated without reference to the stimulus, but T-pattern detection depends on pre-defined media events, in this case peaks in luminance change in experiment 1 and optical flow in experiment 2. While peaks in experiment 1 were predominantly found at cuts in the video, that is precisely defined instants in the stimulus, peaks in experiment 2 could indicate in principle both significant movement in the frame or movement of the camera. In the continuous Birdman video, flow maxima can probably be found in transitions from one set location to another, but these maxima are likely lower in magnitude and less abrupt than the Mr. Bean cuts. If maxima during such transitions were not very pronounced, it could be possible that comparable maxima were also found within scenes, where the major proportion of content presentation takes place (e.g., when the camera spins around the protagonists). Although a separation between cinematic form and content is complicated due to the common correspondence of both features (Ohler, 1994), this event definition might have introduced both content-related and form-related events into T-pattern detection, making the analyses in experiments 1 and 2 even less comparable. This could only be determined by careful content analysis of the stimulus at the identified peaks in flow. However, the convergence of results with the ISI method, which is not susceptible to such influences, suggests that event definition was appropriate.

Second, the implications of both methods differ slightly with respect to the aspects of blinking behavior in their focus: The T-pattern algorithm—at least in the form it was used in this thesis—focuses on blink occurrences, whereas the ISI distance measure is more sensitive to co-occurring changes in blink rate, and not blink coincidences. While the choice of methods in this thesis was following existing research, future studies could combine additional measures: for T-pattern detection, they could also consider blink inhibition, and not only blink occurrences; for spike train synchrony, they could use, for example, the measure of SPIKE distance or one of its later refinements, which are more sensitive for co-occurrences of blinks (Kreuz et al., 2013; Kreuz, Chicharro, Greschner, & Andrzejak, 2011; Mulansky, Bozanic, & Kreuz, 2015; Satuvuori et al., 2017).

Third, T-pattern detection depends on the detection parameters chosen by the researcher. In this thesis, we mostly used the Theme software's default values, but especially the choice of the level of significance for the critical interval can influence which behavior is detected. For example, two groups could show in principle comparable degrees of behavioral organization, but one group with a more loosely defined timing, and one group with tighter temporal relationships. In this case, a strict critical interval setting could reject the loosely timed behavior, and more patterns would be found in the tightly organized group, although equal numbers of temporal event relations were present. Testing with different levels of significance could prevent such incomplete conclusions, and could offer new possibilities for interpreting blinking behavior. Similar circumstances could influence pattern detection with different media events. While cuts in a video can be defined very precisely both mathematically and by observation, optical flow peaks in a continuous stimulus, on the other hand, can also be defined mathematically, but those peaks are nevertheless broader than a peak resulting from an abrupt cut, and are also less obvious in their appearance to the human eye. Consequently, peaks in flow may have been processed by participants in a more loosely timed manner than the extremely well-defined cuts. A looser timing would then be detected less reliably by a relatively strict level of significance for critical intervals, and could lead to fewer detected critical interval relationships, and thus fewer T-patterns. Such different constraints in timing that result from stimulus characteristics could also be accounted for by conducting multiple T-pattern detections with different levels of significance.

Future studies should include a wider variety of theoretically grounded media events from the form and content domains. Nakano et al. (2009) already concluded that blinks occurring immediately after cuts in a video are not the only contributors to behavioral structure. Definition of other form features than cuts or peaks in flow could rely more on findings from psychological research on attention and its dependence on stimulus properties. For example, research suggests that motion is a strong attractor of attention (Al-Aidroos, Guo, & Pratt, 2010), but that the emergence of new perceptual objects, rather than a change in luminance, is crucial for triggering attention allocation (Hillstrom & Yantis, 1994; Yantis & Hillstrom, 1994). The definition of content features, on the other hand, is warranted by theoretical assumptions on presence. Wirth et al. (2007) suggest that processing of content information may contribute to presence formation, as well, possibly mediated by processes such as involvement. In future studies, events such as appearance of new characters, suspenseful plot points, or events with affective or evolutionary relevance in the narrative could be defined as media content events. In addition, it can be concluded from research with video stimuli that social cues are attractors of human attention (Shepherd et al., 2010; Shultz, Klin, and Jones, 2011). When using a broader range of possible events, T-pattern detection could reveal which events are predominantly incorporated into behavioral patterns accompanying content-guided or form-guided processing; together with questionnaire data, researchers could then identify which events are especially relevant for the formation of various media reception processes, including presence. This would lead to analyses of contributions from form and content aspects to the media use experience, and could help clarify the result patterns of observational and self-report data found in this thesis. Such analyses would go beyond existing analyses of contributions from media form and content features between different media environments (e.g., Baños, Botella, et al., 2004), and could offer detailed insights into form and content contributions even within a given media use situation.

Further methodological refinements in future studies could address the randomization procedures in T-pattern validation. In this thesis, two randomization methods were used in the Theme software: event shuffling with random replacement of raw data events, and event rotation with a random, circular shifting of event sequences. A more appropriate approach for randomization of blinking behavior would be shuffling of inter-blink intervals (Nakano et al., 2009), which was used in thesis experiments 1 and 2 for the ISI distance measure, and should lead to more precise estimates of the real behavior's deviation from a hypothetical random behavior. The Theme software also offers to choose which event types are to be randomized in the simulation runs. While the randomization of all event types in a raw data file is an established approach in T-pattern detection studies (e.g., Burgoon, Wilson, Hass, & Schuetzler, 2016), an even more stringent testing for media research purposes could be achieved by randomizing only event types representing user actions, while the observed timing in media event occurrences would be preserved; this would represent the best comparison with hypothetical random user reactions to the exact same media stimulus. Finally, future research could address appropriate normalization of T-pattern occurrences to account for different blink rates, and obtain more reliable indicators for analysis on an individual level. For example, it would be possible that individuals in a media reception situation would blink with high probability after certain media events. If the timing of these blinks was stable enough for blinks to be within the boundaries of the critical interval even for very frequent blink elicitation, then individuals with lower blink rates would be able to produce fewer T-patterns, even though their individual blinking behavior would show a comparable amount of stimulus dependence. Researchers could then, for example, try to normalize individual pattern counts to individual blink rates, use the difference between structure in real and random data, or use the individual percentages of blinks incorporated in media-dependent T-patterns.

In conclusion, the method's applicability to diverse media environments has to be judged as excellent. Due to the adaptive nature of the T-pattern detection algorithm, different stimulus dynamics between participants are no issue for detection performance, making the method appropriate for both non-interactive and interactive media. By using the full potential of the T-system, more complex analyses of human behavior during media use are possible, including the identification of events that trigger blink inhibition. Methodological adaptations, such as uniquely labeled events in analyses with video stimuli and normalization procedures for individual pattern counts, further improve the method's use as an objective indicator on an individual level. With its original conceptualization as a process measure, T-pattern detection can give detailed insights into the behavioral structure exhibited by participants during media use.

9.2.5 Conclusions and Use in Future Research

Based on the collected empirical findings, some conclusions can be drawn for the future use of these methods in presence research. Of the three methods under evaluation, the method of blink interval variability delivered the least convincing objective indicators in this thesis. While the computation of blink interval standard deviations can be achieved with comparably little effort, the information gained from this index is limited by design, and allowed no inferences on the participants' internal processes in this thesis; in its current form, this method's contribution to future research may be limited. It appears more promising to use a combination of spike train synchrony and T-pattern detection methods, especially with implementation of the proposed methodological adaptations (see sections 9.2.3 and 9.2.4). Both measures combined can be used to identify attention-attracting media events, to test how these events influence blink inhibition or blink elicitation, and to reveal how reactions towards such events are related to presence or other reception phenomena. Especially the T-pattern detection method allows for testing of effects of multiple predictor event types in the medium on multiple, discrete outcome event types in the user, and can do so in a variety of non-interactive and interactive media settings. Such outcome events can not only be manually coded behavior, such as blinks, but can also be derived from continuous data, such as psychophysiological and behavioral measures. Studies using a broad range of objective measures have already proven the value of such wide-scoped approaches (e.g., Liebold et al., 2017). In general, this thesis used T-pattern detection only at its most basic level, and future studies could make use of the method's full potential, including more event types, analysis of higher-level structures, analysis of event positions within these event structures, and analysis of co-occurrence probabilities between event types. An example for the latter use can already be seen in inspection of the detected T-patterns in experiments 1 and 2: certain media events were followed by a blink within a critical interval in many or even all participants. Other media events were regularly preceded by blinks, what could suggest an anticipatory process, or the existence of an unknown, blink-eliciting event immediately before these known media events. Such stable reactions across a sample of participants with very different blink rates might indicate highly relevant media events, and subsequent analysis of these relevant events could inform about internal processing during media use. Eventually, future studies on blinking behavior during media use could try to predict stimulus segments with increased or decreased probability of blink occurrences, and then relate the accuracy of these predictions to self-report scores.

We will now briefly discuss the implications of the thesis results for presence research, and will see that future research can benefit from refined measurement methods.

9.3 Theoretical Conclusions

The present thesis aimed at evaluating three measurement methods as alternative measures for subjective presence experiences; more profound theoretical considerations about presence were primarily used to derive the need for objective measurement approaches, and to derive the link between processing of a media stimulus, blinking behavior, and presence experiences. However, the unexpected results of the thesis experiments move the concept of presence itself into the focus, so implications for theorizing on presence will be included in the theoretical conclusions, as well. The conclusions will begin with a discussion of the current understanding of stimulus-dependent structure in blinking, and which advancements of this understanding can be derived from the thesis results. Theoretical conclusions are completed with a discussion of how the found results could fit into the theoretical frame of the presence concept, and how the evaluated methods could be used in future research to test new assumptions.

9.3.1 Stimulus-Dependent Structure in Blinking Behavior

In line with the extensive research on factors of influence for blinking behavior (see section 4), and in line with previous research on blinking behavior during media use (e.g., Brill, 2010; Brill, Jonsson, Magnusson, & Schwab, 2016; Liebold et al., 2017; Nakano et al., 2009; Nomura et al., 2015), it can be concluded that spontaneous eye-blinks observed in the three thesis experiments are far from being a randomly executed behavior. The blinking behavior rather showed a stimulus-dependent temporal structure, which could be found—to a lower or higher extent—in all three experiments, with two different analysis methods and three different stimuli.

In experiments 1 and 2, the different instructions created conditions which both called for attention allocation on the stimulus. In contrast to other paradigms that rely on distracting attention away from the stimulus, this approach in principle offers the opportunity to not only observe if structured blinking behavior can be related to presence experiences, but also to test if the stimulus-dependent structures are different when they result from either stimulus processing in a state of presence, or from stimulus processing without presence. The median split approach represents a straight-forward method to observe different, naturally emerged degrees of presence experiences—and as the experiment results have shown, it more likely yields the desired groups with different levels of presence. When using the effective analysis methods with the suggested improvements in future studies, it should be possible to analyze which stimulus aspects actually capture the participant's attention, what causes media-dependent structure in eye-blink behavior, and if these aspects differ between individuals reporting low or high presence.

While we have learned about numerous possible influences on blinking behavior, it can only be speculated at this point which of these mechanisms are involved during a given media use situation, and then lead to stimulus-dependent structure in blinking behavior. For example, a stimulus dependent timing of blinks could result from a restart of the blink generator from an off-state, as it was found after voluntary blink inhibition (Moraitis & Ghosh, 2014); such a restart with a relatively stable timing in blink elicitation could possibly also occur after involuntary eye-blink inhibition, for example after orienting responses on media content (Liebold et al., 2017). Other explanations could refer to the assumptions by Nakano (2015) on the role of blinks during release and reallocation of attention, to Shultz, Klin and Jones' (2011) assumptions that blinks could be inhibited in anticipation of emotionally relevant events (p. 21273), or to the assumption that blinks indicate changes in cognitive processing and release of information from working memory (Ichikawa & Ohira, 2004; Siegle et al., 2008). Investigation of such mechanisms was outside the scope of this thesis; we rather used the body of research to derive the general rationale that processing of a media stimulus should lead to a higher degree of structure in blinking behavior when users are in a state of presence, because the cognitive processes with a focus on media content should at the same time influence timing of spontaneous eye-blinks. However, this assumption could not be confirmed in the thesis experiments: behavioral structure in blinking was not always higher in participants who were instructed to focus on stimulus content, and not higher in participants who reported higher presence scores. To interpret the results, a more detailed view on stimulus-dependent structure in spontaneous eye-blink behavior is necessary.

Future research could use the review of existing theoretical and empirical evidence from existing research, as well as the findings from this thesis, to conduct studies on the nature of blinking behavior during media use; however, in order to do so, an expanded understanding of stimulus-dependent structure in blinking behavior is necessary.

9.3.2 Stimulus-Dependent Structure in Blinking Behavior— Revisited

Results in this thesis suggest that the degree of stimulus-dependent structure in blinking behavior alone might be an indicator for stimulus processing, but is likely not suitable as a specific indicator for processes during presence experiences. To this end, a more detailed understanding of stimulus-dependent structure is necessary.

The two suitable methods for blink timing analysis used in this thesis, spike train synchrony and T-pattern detection, showed converging results. This suggests that in principle, structure in blinking can be revealed with these methods, despite their different approach to quantification of structure. However, conditions of low and high presence experiences could not be induced as intended, so the degree of behavioral structure could not be related to presence experiences in the way it had been intended. In this thesis, it was derived from existing research on blinking during media use (Nakano et al., 2009; Nomura et al., 2015) that a higher degree of stimulus-dependent structure in blinking should correspond to a higher degree of presence. However, results show that the existence of structure alone is not sufficient to infer on presence experiences: based on the results, we have assumed that stimulus-dependent structure in general was susceptible to influence from accentuated processing of formal features (experiment 1), and was not related to higher presence experiences (experiments 1 and 2). This suggests that there may exist different facets of stimulus-dependent structure with different informative value. As a conclusion, the research question should not so much be if stimulus-dependent structure in blinking is present or to what degree it is present, but rather on what media aspects this structure depends.

Due to the design of this thesis, it was not explicitly tested on what events the found stimulus-dependent structure in both groups depended. It would be possible that the overall degree of structure had been similar, but had resulted from processing of different media aspects. In this case, the form group's structure would have resulted from a focus on formal features, and the content group's structure would have resulted from a focus on content features; due to the close interdependence of form and content media aspects (Ohler, 1994), both behaviors could have led to quantitatively comparable synchrony within groups, but with qualitative differences regarding the events on which this structuring depends.

Consequently, we can suggest that not a content-blind analysis of stimulus-dependent structure in general, but a more in-depth, content-aware analysis approach is needed. Only with appropriate methods and appropriate consideration of the stimulus, it is possible to not only quantify how much attention is directed to the medium, but also to which specific aspects of the medium attention is directed. A closer inspection of such attention-attracting relevant media events appears to be essential in light of Liebold et al.'s (2017) findings, where blinks were elicited after externally triggered orienting responses. Because these triggers were breaks in presence, media events contributed to a structure in blinking behavior that did not indicate a higher level of presence; on the contrary, structure caused by reactions towards such interferences would indicate impairment of presence formation. Such detailed considerations of the media stimulus are a challenge for content-blind analyses of general blinking structure. However, the consideration of media content provides the opportunity to expand research on blinking structure as an indicator for presence experiences by a content-aware facet, so contributing and distracting media events could be distinguished.

9.3.3 Advancing Presence Research

The ultimate purpose of this thesis was the advancement of presence research by evaluating process measures for a more detailed analysis of internal processes during media use. This subsection first recapitulates and acknowledges the complex nature of presence research with inherently complex stimuli and complex theorizing. We derive from this premise a need for sophisticated methods in presence research, and discuss how the methods evaluated in this thesis can contribute to presence research. Due to unexpected results of the applied experimental manipulation of low and high presence conditions, we will also briefly discuss how these methods could help disambiguate findings from the three thesis experiments.

9.3.3.1 Complex Stimuli

Presence research necessarily involves more or less sophisticated, complex media stimuli, and those stimuli themselves are used to present more or less complex content. When using cinematic stimuli as an example, a movie could present an actor engaged in an everyday activity. As research on event segmentation (e.g., Kurby & Zacks, 2008; Zacks, Braver, et al., 2001; Zacks, Tversky, et al., 2001) shows, the perception of basic activities involves both bottom-up processes, influenced by "distinctive sensory characteristics" (Zacks, 2004, p. 979), and top-down processes, influenced by existing knowledge structures, as well as interactions of these processes (Zacks, 2004). In most cases, media do not offer an un-edited, unfiltered representation of such content; the content is rather presented with help of a sophisticated formal language that is not independent of the pre-sented content, but is intended to support content presentation (Magliano & Zacks, 2011; Monaco, 2015; Ohler, 1994; Zacks et al., 2010).

9.3.3.2 Complex Theorizing

This complexity needs to be accounted for in theorizing, as well, and can be acknowledged by, for example, the assumption that mental models are con-structed as a cognitive representation of media content. Mental models are prom-inent elements of recent presence research (Liebold et al., 2015; Liebold et al., 2017; Wirth et al., 2007), of research on other reception phenomena such as nar-rative engagement (Busselle & Bilandzic, 2008, 2009) or transportation (Nomura et al., 2015), and also in research on comprehension of mediated and real-world events (Huff et al., 2014; Magliano & Zacks, 2011). Interestingly, not only con-struction of such mental models, but also inconsistencies and disruptions are in the focus of research in different disciplines. For the domain of presence, con-struction, testing, and accepting or discarding of mental models are seen as es-sential in Wirth et al.'s concept (2007), and model inconsistency is proposed as a key element of a cognitive mechanism for breaks in presence (Liebold et al., 2017). Discontinuities have also been used as events of interest in research on narrative engagement (Sukalla et al., 2016), and the theory of event segmentation sees instances of high prediction errors in event prediction as boundaries for seg-menting streams of incoming event information (Reynolds et al., 2007). All these processes rely on continuous perception and processing of visual stimuli, on con-struction and evaluations of mental models, and see instances of model violations as meaningful events.

9.3.3.3 Benefit of Complex Methods

Research with such complex theorizing, using complex and externally valid stim-uli, calls for sophisticated analysis methods to reveal the complex processes dur-ing media reception, such as attention allocation and stimulus processing. A sufficient temporal resolution and a sensitivity for different event types are nec-essary to identify relevant events in the complex stream of information delivered by a media stimulus. New methods for presence research beyond summative, subjective self-report measures can enable researchers to use more effective research paradigms, and observe users during their experience of the process phenomenon presence. For example, based on assumed relationships between higher cognitive load and higher blink latency (Ichikawa & Ohira, 2004; Ohira, 1996; Siegle, Ichikawa, & Steinhauer, 2008), blinking and pupillary responses could be used to investigate user reactions towards different degrees of model violations during event segmentation (Huff, Meitz, & Papenmeier, 2014) and breaks in presence (Liebold et al., 2017). Blinking behavior can be measured in a relatively unobtrusive manner, and derived indicators appear to be applicable across different cultures (e.g., Ichikawa & Ohira, 2004; Nakano et al., 2009; Nakano, 2015; Nomura et al., 2015; Pivik & Dykman, 2004; Shultz, Klin, & Jones, 2011) and age groups (e.g., Pivik & Dykman, 2004; Shultz, Klin, & Jones, 2011).

The thesis project aimed at comparing structure in blinking behavior in purposefully created conditions of low or high presence, so it could be investigated if structure in blinking behavior, influenced by the very same processes which are relevant for presence formation, could inform about an individual's state of presence. Despite a theoretically and empirically grounded presence manipulation, the manipulation by instruction was not successful in the intended way, which complicates interpretation of results in this thesis. Moreover, there were not only non-significant results, but some results contradicted established presence theories, and make interpretation of results difficult within the boundaries of these theories. If the manipulation by instruction had merely been ineffective, then both groups should have reported roughly equal presence scores, as was found in experiment 1. In contrast, the higher presence scores in the form group in experiment 2 are hard to explain with a traditional view on presence, since these participants had also reported to have paid significantly more attention to the movie's form features. Of course, it would be possible to argue that these participants had not followed instructions during the extended duration of the observation period. However, this would not explain why these participants' structure in blinking behavior differed significantly from the blinking of casual viewers in the content group, what had been confirmed by two objective indicators for stimulus-dependent structure in blinking. A disagreement between objective and subjective measures was also found in experiment 1, where the objective measures detected significant differences in blinking behavior between groups, whereas presence questionnaire scores showed no significant difference. In both experiments, participants in the form group stated that they had paid significantly more attention to formal media aspects than their counterparts in the content group, but this did not lead to a reduction of reported presence experiences.

A relation between different styles of attention allocation and presence has been proposed by Fontaine (1992), who was cited by Witmer and Singer (1998), and assumed that a broad focus on many media aspects could be a facilitator for presence experiences in novel media environments. Fontaine further assumed that everyday activities and well-practiced tasks can be performed without such a broad focus. When interpreting the findings from experiment 2 in this way, a broader focus on more aspects of the video during the form group's careful and uncommon analysis could have supported presence formation. However, we will rather interpret the results from the perspective of Wirth et al.'s (2007) theory.

Referring to the PMSP model (Wirth et al., 2007), and under the assumption that the SPES scale provided valid presence assessments, it can only be assumed that the increased attention on stimulus details in the form group in experiment 2 has led to increased experiences of presence, despite the fact that the medium was probably salient as an artefact. In the thesis experiments, the mental capacities of participants who were instructed to focus on form features were most likely bound by the mediated environment; binding of mental capacities to a media stimulus is a predicted effect in a state of presence:

> Spatial Presence is a binary experience, during which perceived self-location and, in most cases, perceived action possibilities are connected to a mediated spatial environment, and **mental capacities are bound by the mediated environment instead of reality.** (Wirth et al., 2007, p. 497; emphasis added)

However, the binding of mental capacities alone—no matter what media aspects these capacities are focusing on—shouldn't be a sufficient factor for the emergence of presence within this theoretical frame. A second source, Hartmann et al.'s (2015) SPES paper, relates to the role of attention for presence:

> Validity tests showed that **the experience of spatial presence** – that is, scores on the SPES – **increases with the amount of users' attention allocation to the media stimulus,** the conciseness of their spatial mental model, and their cognitive involvement in the media stimulus. (Hartmann et al., 2015, p. 11; emphasis added)

When interpreting these references to the letter, it could be speculated if participants who allocated more attention on the stimulus then reported higher levels of presence, reported at the same time higher focus on stimulus details, and exhibited a stimulus-dependent structure in blinking behavior. However, in the context of Hartmann et al.'s paper and Wirth et al.'s theory, it cannot be suggested that mere attention on the medium directly leads to higher presence, and a contamination of presence by higher levels of attention on the stimulus is not explicated, either.

The observed results in this thesis showed deviations from predictions of presence theories, as well as disagreement of subjective and objective measurement methods. These inconsistencies could be used as a starting point for further investigations of the presence concept, and especially the role of attention for formation and maintenance of presence. A first step should be a more detailed analysis of behavioral structure in the experimental groups of this thesis, using the appropriate methods discussed in this thesis. Results from such analyses could reveal if the differences in both groups' behavior result from different degrees of the same behavior, or rather represent distinct structures caused by different stimulus processing. The results could then be related to established conceptualizations of presence, such as Wirth et al.'s (2007) model, but also to recent approaches to presence, such as Riva et al.'s (2015) concept or Liebold et al.'s (2015) concept of presence as a state of focused attention.

With blinking as an attention-related process measure, more detailed investigations of the attentional component of presence would be possible. For example, Green and Bavelier showed effects from playing of action video games on visual selective attention (2003), not only in existing populations of players and non-players, but also as training effects for non-players engaging in action video games. In another series of experiments (Green & Bavelier, 2007), the authors found similar training effects on spatial resolution of visual processing. Further training effects on stimulus processing have been found by Liu and Pack (2017), who suggest that training can increase performance in motion perception tasks. Future studies could determine possible changes in blink structuring with increasing training time of players as another facet of attentional processes. For example, it could be tested if the range and timing of cognitive processing, manifesting in structural aspects of blinking behavior, changes with increasing expertise, as well.

Process measures for analysis of blinking behavior could also be employed in other fields of media research. For research on narrative processing, Sukalla et al. (2016) used physiological measurements of orienting responses to study narrative processing; the theoretical body of this thesis and the findings by Liebold et al. (2017) on orienting responses and blinks after breaks in presence suggest that analyses of blinking behavior could also be used with a focus on narrative media aspects. For flow research, the neurophysiological reconceptualization of flow by Weber et al. (2009) proposes the involvement of attentional networks and dopaminergic reward networks; blinking parameters are a frequently used indicator for attentional and dopaminergic processes, have been used in research on reward responsivity (Peckham & Johnson, 2016), and could possibly serve as a useful indicator in the domain of flow, as well.

All of these research questions would be difficult to address with summative self-report measures, but can profit from objective process measures with adequate temporal resolution.

10 Thesis Conclusion

We conclude this thesis with a short summary of how the results of this thesis can serve presence research.

The purpose of this thesis was to evaluate if objective indicators for stimulus-dependent structure in blinking behavior could be used as indicators for presence experiences. To this end, a large body of theoretical and empirical evidence on the presence concept and on spontaneous eye-blink behavior had been collected. From this body of research, from existing studies on blinking behavior during media use, and from evaluation studies of alternative presence measures, the general research rationale and procedures were derived. Three laboratory experiments had been conducted to relate three different methods for quantification of behavioral structure to an established presence self-report measure. Results of these experiments do not allow a conclusive answer to the research questions under investigation: the degree of stimulus-dependent structure in blinking behavior was no valid indicator for the degree of self-reported presence experiences. Moreover, manipulation of presence experiences was not successful, and even showed result patterns that are hard to explain within the chosen presence theory.

Nevertheless, several contributions to the research process in media psychology can be derived from the results. First, the findings from this thesis suggest that the approach used for experimental manipulation in this thesis should not be used for future, comparable research. Second, it could be determined that one of the three objective indicators under investigation, the measure for inter-blink interval (IBI) variability, is probably no appropriate indicator for describing stimulus-dependent blinking structure in presence research; both group comparisons and correlations with individual IBI variabilities showed no significant results in any of the experiments. Third, the other two objective measures under investigation, ISI distance and T-pattern detection, showed more promising evidence: indicators calculated with these methods largely showed converging results. Comparisons of pair-wise ISI distances within groups and group comparisons of individual T-pattern frequencies were in agreement in experiments 1 and 2; the comparisons of ISI distances found in real data and randomized data showed less stable results, and this indicator probably needs theoretical reconsideration. Fourth, it can be concluded from the combined results that there are unresolved issues regarding both the concept of presence and the concept of stimulus-dependent structure in blinking behavior. For presence, the unpredicted pattern of self-report scores in experiments 1 and 2 raises questions about the role of attention during formation and sustaining of presence experiences. For behavioral structure, the conclusions suggest that a consideration of overall stimulus-dependent structure is, at least for the purpose of this thesis, insufficient. We conclude that future research needs a more detailed consideration of structure in blinking behavior in order to determine further aspects of stimulus-dependent structure, and most importantly which events in the stimulus are contributing to structure.

In sum, this thesis goes beyond existing research on blinking during media use in terms of exhaustiveness of the theoretical foundation, and in terms of diversity of methods and stimuli. Not all research questions of this thesis could be answered conclusively, and maybe even more new open questions for presence research have been revealed; nevertheless, the findings in this thesis also offer researchers new tools to address these open questions.

11 References

Al-Aidroos, N., Guo, R. M., & Pratt, J. (2010). You can't stop new motion: Attentional capture despite a control set for colour. *Visual Cognition, 18*(6), 859–880. https://doi.org/10.1080/13506280903343085

Alcañiz, M., Rey, B., Tembl, J., & Parkhutik, V. (2009). A neuroscience approach to virtual reality experience using transcranial Doppler monitoring. *Presence, 18*(2), 97–111. https://doi.org/10.1162/pres.18.2.97

Anderson, D. R., Alwitt, L. F., Lorch, E. P., & Levin, S. R. (1979). Watching children watch television. In G. A. Hale & M. Lewis (Eds.), *Attention and cognitive development* (pp. 331–361). Boston, MA: Springer US. https://doi.org/10.1007/978-1-4613-2985-5_12

Anderson, D. R., & Lorch, E. P. (1983). Looking at television: Action or reaction. In J. Bryant & D. R. Anderson (Eds.), *Children's understanding of television: Research on attention and comprehension* (pp. 1–34). New York, NY: Academic Press.

Argilés, M., Cardona, G., Pérez-Cabré, E., & Rodríguez, M. (2015). Blink rate and incomplete blinks in six different controlled hard-copy and electronic reading conditions. *Investigative Opthalmology & Visual Science, 56*(11), 6679. https://doi.org/10.1167/iovs.15-16967

Artal, P., & Guirao, A. (1998). Contributions of the cornea and the lens to the aberrations of the human eye. *Optics Letters, 23*(21), 1713. https://doi.org/10.1364/OL.23.001713

Bakeman, R., & Gottman, J. M. (1997). *Observing interaction: An introduction to sequential analysis* (2nd ed). New York: Cambridge University Press.

Baños, R. M., Botella, C., Alcañiz, M., Liaño, V., Guerrero, B., & Rey, B. (2004). Immersion and emotion: Their impact on the sense of presence. *CyberPsychology & Behavior, 7*(6), 734–741. https://doi.org/10.1089/cpb.2004.7.734

Barbato, G., De Padova, V., Paolillo, A. R., Arpaia, L., Russo, E., & Ficca, G. (2007). Increased spontaneous eye blink rate following prolonged wakefulness. *Physiology & Behavior, 90*(1), 151–154. https://doi.org/10.1016/j.physbeh.2006.09.023

Barbato, G., Della Monica, C., Costanzo, A., & De Padova, V. (2012). Dopamine activation in Neuroticism as measured by spontaneous eye blink rate. *Physiology & Behavior, 105*(2), 332–336. https://doi.org/10.1016/j.physbeh.2011.08.004

Barbato, G., Ficca, G., Beatrice, M., Casiello, M., Muscettola, G., & Rinaldi, F. (1995). Effects of sleep deprivation on spontaneous eye blink rate and alpha EEG power. *Biological Psychiatry, 38*(5), 340–341. https://doi.org/10.1016/0006-3223(95)00098-2

Barbato, G., Ficca, G., Muscettola, G., Fichele, M., Beatrice, M., & Rinaldi, F. (2000). Diurnal variation in spontaneous eye-blink rate. *Psychiatry Research, 93*(2), 145–151. https://doi.org/10.1016/S0165-1781(00)00108-6

Batra, R., & Ray, M. (1985). How advertising works at contact. In L. F. Alwitt & A. A. Mitchell (Eds.), *Psychological processes and advertising effects: Theory, research and applications* (pp. 13–43). Hillsdale, NJ: Lawrence Erlbaum.

Baumgartner, T., Valko, L., Esslen, M., & Jäncke, L. (2006). Neural correlate of spatial presence in an arousing and noninteractive virtual reality: An EEG and psychophysiology study. *CyberPsychology & Behavior, 9*(1), 30–45. https://doi.org/10.1089/cpb.2006.9.30

Benedetto, S., Pedrotti, M., Minin, L., Baccino, T., Re, A., & Montanari, R. (2011). Driver workload and eye blink duration. *Transportation Research Part F: Traffic Psychology and Behaviour, 14*(3), 199–208. https://doi.org/10.1016/j.trf.2010.12.001

Bentivoglio, A. R., Bressman, S. B., Cassetta, E., Carretta, D., Tonali, P., & Albanese, A. (1997). Analysis of blink rate patterns in normal subjects. *Movement Disorders, 12*(6), 1028–1034. https://doi.org/10.1002/mds.870120629

Berliner, T., & Cohen, D. J. (2011). The illusion of continuity: Active perception and the classical editing system. *Journal of Film and Video, 63*(1), 44–63. https://doi.org/10.1353/jfv.2011.0008

Bezdek, M. A., & Gerrig, R. J. (2017). When narrative transportation narrows attention: Changes in attentional focus during suspenseful film viewing. *Media Psychology, 20*(1), 60–89. https://doi.org/10.1080/15213269.2015.1121830

Bezdek, M. A., Gerrig, R. J., Wenzel, W. G., Shin, J., Pirog Revill, K., & Schumacher, E. H. (2015). Neural evidence that suspense narrows attentional focus. *Neuroscience, 303,* 338–345. https://doi.org/10.1016/j.neuroscience. 2015.06.055

Biocca, F., & Delaney, B. (1995). Immersive virtual reality technology. In F. Biocca & F. R. Levy (Eds.), *Communication in the age of virtual reality* (pp. 57–124). Hillsdale, NJ: Lawrence Erlbaum Associates.

Biocca, F., & Levy, M. R. (Eds.). (1995). *Communication in the age of virtual reality.* Hillsdale, NJ: Lawrence Erlbaum Associates.

Birkin, J., Davies, J. H., & Weiland, P. (2014). Mr. Bean - Die komplette TV-Serie. United Kingdom: Universal Pictures.

Böcking, S., Wirth, W., Hartmann, T., Klimmt, C., Schramm, H., & Vorderer, P. (2008). Zur Messung von räumlichem Präsenzerleben: Ein Vergleich von vier alternativen Messmethoden. In J. Matthes, W. Wirth, G. Daschmann, & A. Fahr (Eds.), *Die Brücke zwischen Theorie und Empirie: Operationalisierung, Messung und Validierung in der Kommunikationswissenschaft* (pp. 355–379). Köln: von Halem.

Bonfiglio, L., Sello, S., Carboncini, M. C., Arrighi, P., Andre, P., & Rossi, B. (2011). Reciprocal dynamics of EEG alpha and delta oscillations during spontaneous blinking at rest: A survey on a default mode-based visuospatial awareness. *International Journal of Psychophysiology, 80*(1), 44–53. https://doi.org/10.1016/j.ijpsycho.2011.01.002

Bradski, G. (2000). The OpenCV library. *Dr. Dobb's Journal of Software Tools.*

Brill, M. (2010). *Presence in Computerspielen* (Diploma thesis). Saarland University, Saarbrücken.

Brill, M., Carolus, A., & Schwab, F. (2010). T-Patterns in blinking: Towards an objective measure of presence? Presented at the 6th meeting of the MASI research network, Paris.

Brill, M., Carolus, A., & Schwab, F. (2011). Eye on presence? Blinking and the presence in playing computer games. In Ö. Odag, M. Schreier, & Y. Thies-Brandner (Eds.), *Media Psychology. Focus Theme: Cognitive and Emotional Involvement during Media Reception, Proceedings of the 7th Conference of the Media Psychology Division of the German Psychological Society* (p. 32). Pabst Science Publishers.

Brill, M., Jonsson, G. K., Magnusson, M. S., & Schwab, F. (2016). Immersive dynamics: Presence experiences and patterns of attention. In M. S. Magnusson, J. K. Burgoon, & M. Casarrubea (Eds.), *Discovering hidden temporal patterns in behavior and interaction: T-pattern detection and analysis with Theme™* (pp. 183–193). New York, NY: Springer New York. https://doi.org/10.1007/978-1-4939-3249-8_10

Brill, M., Jonsson, G. K., & Schwab, F. (2014). Being there, acting there: Temporal structure of play as a hint to presence experiences. Presented at the ICA Pre-conference Communication Science - Evolution, Biology, and Brains 2.0: Innovation in Theory and Methods, Seattle, WA.

Bristow, D., Frith, C., & Rees, G. (2005). Two distinct neural effects of blinking on human visual processing. *NeuroImage*, *27*(1), 136–145. https://doi.org/10.1016/j.neuroimage.2005.03.037

Bristow, D., Haynes, J.-D., Sylvester, R., Frith, C. D., & Rees, G. (2005). Blinking suppresses the neural response to unchanging retinal stimulation. *Current Biology*, *15*(14), 1296–1300. https://doi.org/10.1016/j.cub.2005.06.025

Brogni, A., Vinayagamoorthy, V., Steed, A., & Slater, M. (2006). Variations in physiological responses of participants during different stages of an immersive virtual environment experiment. In *Proceedings of the ACM Symposium on Virtual Reality Software and Technology* (pp. 376–382). New York, NY, USA: ACM. https://doi.org/10.1145/1180495.1180572

Broughton, S. A., & Bryan, K. (2009). *Discrete Fourier analysis and wavelets: Applications to signal and image processing*. Hoboken, N.J: Wiley.

Bruner, J. S., & Postman, L. (1949). On the perception of incongruity: a paradigm. *Journal of Personality*, *18*, 206–223.

Bulling, A., & Roggen, D. (2011). Recognition of visual memory recall processes using eye movement analysis. In *UbiComp '11 Proceedings of the 13th international conference on Ubiquitous computing* (pp. 455–464). New York, NY: ACM Press. https://doi.org/10.1145/2030112.2030172

Burgoon, J. K., Wilson, D., Hass, M., & Schuetzler, R. (2016). Interactive deception in group decision-making: New insights from communication pattern analysis. In M. S. Magnusson, J. K. Burgoon, & M. Casarrubea (Eds.), *Discovering hidden temporal patterns in behavior and interaction* (pp. 37–62). New York, NY: Humana Press.

Burton, A., & Radford, J. (Eds.). (1978). *Thinking in perspective: Critical essays in the study of thought processes*. London: Methuen.

Business Insider. (2017, January 17). Mark Zuckerberg reveals that Facebook paid more than we thought for Oculus VR. Retrieved from http://www.businessinsider.de/facebook-actually-paid-3-billion-for-oculus-vr-2017-1

Busselle, R., & Bilandzic, H. (2008). Fictionality and perceived realism in experiencing stories: A model of narrative comprehension and engagement. *Communication Theory*, *18*(2), 255–280. https://doi.org/10.1111/j.1468-2885.2008.00322.x

Busselle, R., & Bilandzic, H. (2009). Measuring narrative engagement. *Media Psychology*, *12*(4), 321–347. https://doi.org/10.1080/15213260903287259

Cardona, G., García, C., Serés, C., Vilaseca, M., & Gispets, J. (2011). Blink rate, blink amplitude, and tear film integrity during dynamic visual display terminal tasks. *Current Eye Research*, *36*(3), 190–197. https://doi.org/10.3109/02713683.2010.544442

Carney, L. G., & Hill, R. M. (1984). Variations in blinking behaviour during soft lens wear. *International Contact Lens Clinic*, *11*(4), 250–253.

Charlton, M., & Borcsa, M. (1997). Thematische Voreingenommenheit, Involvement und Formen der Identifikation. In M. Charlton & S. Schneider (Eds.), *Rezeptionsforschung: Theorien und Untersuchungen zum Umgang mit Massenmedien* (pp. 254–267). Wiesbaden: VS Verlag für Sozialwissenschaften. https://doi.org/10.1007/978-3-663-08111-1_14

Chermahini, S. A., & Hommel, B. (2010). The (b)link between creativity and dopamine: Spontaneous eye blink rates predict and dissociate divergent and convergent thinking. *Cognition*, *115*(3), 458–465. https://doi.org/10.1016/j.cognition.2010.03.007

Chu, C. A., Rosenfield, M., & Portello, J. K. (2014). Blink patterns: Reading from a computer screen versus hard copy. *Optometry and Vision Science*, *91*(3), 297–302. https://doi.org/10.1097/OPX.0000000000000157

Chung, J., & Gardner, H. J. (2012). Temporal presence variation in immersive computer games. *International Journal of Human–Computer Interaction*, *28*(8), 511–529. https://doi.org/10.1080/10447318.2011.627298

Coleridge, S. T. (1817). *Biographia literaria, Vol. 2*. London: Oxford University Press.

Collet, C., Vernet-Maury, E., Delhomme, G., & Dittmar, A. (1997). Autonomic nervous system response patterns specificity to basic emotions. *Journal of the Autonomic Nervous System, 62*(1–2), 45–57. https://doi.org/10.1016/S0165-1838(96)00108-7

Colzato, L. S., Slagter, H. A., Spapé, M. M. A., & Hommel, B. (2008). Blinks of the eye predict blinks of the mind. *Neuropsychologia, 46*(13), 3179–3183. https://doi.org/10.1016/j.neuropsychologia.2008.07.006

Colzato, L. S., Slagter, H. A., van den Wildenberg, W. P. M., & Hommel, B. (2009). Closing one's eyes to reality: Evidence for a dopaminergic basis of Psychoticism from spontaneous eye blink rates. *Personality and Individual Differences, 46*(3), 377–380. https://doi.org/10.1016/j.paid.2008.10.017

Colzato, L. S., van Wouwe, N. C., & Hommel, B. (2007). Spontaneous eyeblink rate predicts the strength of visuomotor binding. *Neuropsychologia, 45*(10), 2387–2392. https://doi.org/10.1016/j.neuropsychologia.2007.03.004

Colzato, L. S., Wildenberg, W. P. M. van den, Wouwe, N. C. van, Pannebakker, M. M., & Hommel, B. (2009). Dopamine and inhibitory action control: evidence from spontaneous eye blink rates. *Experimental Brain Research, 196*(3), 467–474. https://doi.org/10.1007/s00221-009-1862-x

Cong, D.-K., Sharikadze, M., Staude, G., Deubel, H., & Wolf, W. (2010). Spontaneous eye blinks are entrained by finger tapping. *Human Movement Science, 29*(1), 1–18. https://doi.org/10.1016/j.humov.2009.08.003

Cruz, A. A. V., Garcia, D. M., Pinto, C. T., & Cechetti, S. P. (2011). Spontaneous eyeblink activity. *The Ocular Surface, 9*(1), 29–41.

Csikszentmihalyi, M. (1975). *Beyond boredom and anxiety*. San Francisco, Washington, London: Jossey-Bass Publishers. Retrieved from http://psy2.ucsd.edu/~nchristenfeld/Happiness_Readings_files/Class%207%20-%20Csikszentmihalyi%201975.pdf

Cummings, J. J., & Bailenson, J. N. (2016). How immersive is enough? A meta-analysis of the effect of immersive technology on user presence. *Media Psychology*, *19*(2), 272–309. https://doi.org/10.1080/15213269.2015.1015740

Cummins, F. (2012). Gaze and blinking in dyadic conversation: A study in coordinated behaviour among individuals. *Language and Cognitive Processes*, *27*(10), 1525–1549. https://doi.org/10.1080/01690965.2011.615220

Darwin, C. (1859). *On the origin of species by means of natural selection*. London: John Murray.

Depue, R. A., Luciana, M., Arbisi, P., Collins, P., & Leon, A. (1994). Dopamine and the structure of personality: Relation of agonist-induced dopamine activity to positive emotionality. *Journal of Personality and Social Psychology*, *67*(3), 485–498. https://doi.org/10.1037/0022-3514.67.3.485

Dharmawansa, A. D., Fukumura, Y., Kanematsu, H., Kobayashi, T., Ogawa, N., & Barry, D. M. (2014). Introducing eye blink of a student to the virtual world and evaluating the affection of the eye blinking during the e-learning. *Procedia Computer Science*, *35*, 1229–1238. https://doi.org/10.1016/j.procs.2014.08.220

Digi-Capital. (2015). Augmented/virtual reality to hit $150 billion disrupting mobile by 2020 [Blog post]. Retrieved from http://www.digi-capital.com/news/2015/04/augmentedvirtual-reality-to-hit-150-billion-disrupting-mobile-by-2020/#.V_ZFheCLRjU

Digi-Capital. (2017). After mixed year, mobile AR to drive $108 billion VR/AR market by 2021 [Blog post]. Retrieved from https://www.digi-capital.com/news/2017/01/after-mixed-year-mobile-ar-to-drive-108-billion-vrar-market-by-2021/

Doane, M. G. (1980). Interaction of eyelids and tears in corneal wetting and the dynamics of the normal human eyeblink. *American Journal of Ophthalmology*, *89*(4), 507–516. https://doi.org/10.1016/0002-9394(80)90058-6

Doughty, M. J. (2001). Consideration of three types of spontaneous eyeblink activity in normal humans: during reading and video display terminal use, in primary gaze, and while in conversation. *Optometry and Vision Science: Official Publication of the American Academy of Optometry*, *78*(10), 712–725.

Doughty, M. J., & Naase, T. (2006). Further analysis of the human spontaneous eye blink rate by a cluster analysis-based approach to categorize individuals with "normal" versus "frequent" eye blink activity. *Eye & Contact Lens, 32*(6), 294–299. https://doi.org/10.1097/01.icl.0000224359.32709.4d

Draper, J. V., Kaber, D. B., & Usher, J. M. (1998). Telepresence. *Human Factors: The Journal of the Human Factors and Ergonomics Society, 40*(3), 354–375. https://doi.org/10.1518/001872098779591386

Dreisbach, G., Müller, J., Goschke, T., Strobel, A., Schulze, K., Lesch, K.-P., & Brocke, B. (2005). Dopamine and cognitive control: The influence of spontaneous eyeblink rate and dopamine gene polymorphisms on perseveration and distractibility. *Behavioral Neuroscience, 119*(2), 483–490. https://doi.org/10.1037/0735-7044.119.2.483

Drew, G. C. (1951). Variations in reflex blink-rate during visual-motor tasks. *Quarterly Journal of Experimental Psychology, 3*(2), 73–88. https://doi.org/10.1080/17470215108416776

Dua, H. S., Faraj, L. A., Said, D. G., Gray, T., & Lowe, J. (2013). Human corneal anatomy redefined. *Ophthalmology, 120*(9), 1778–1785. https://doi.org/10.1016/j.ophtha.2013.01.018

Eaton, J. W., Bateman, D., Hauberg, S., & Wehbring, R. (2015). *GNU Octave version 4.0.0 manual: A high-level interactive language for numerical computations.* Retrieved from http://www.gnu.org/software/octave/doc/interpreter

Eaton, J. W., & Octave Community. (2015). GNU Octave (Version 4.0.3) [Computer software].

Eclipse (Version 4.5.0) [Computer software]. (2015). Ottawa, Ontario, Canada: Eclipse Foundation, Inc. Retrieved from http://www.eclipse.org/

Esteban, A., Traba, A., & Prieto, J. (2004). Eyelid movements in health and disease. The supranuclear impairment of the palpebral motility. *Clinical Neurophysiology, 34*(1), 3–15. https://doi.org/10.1016/j.neucli.2004.01.002

Evinger, C., Manning, K., Pellegrini, J., Basso, M., Powers, A., & Sibony, P. (1994). Not looking while leaping: the linkage of blinking and saccadic gaze shifts. *Experimental Brain Research, 100*(2). https://doi.org/10.1007/BF00227203

Experiment Suite 360° (Version 2) [Computer software]. (2016). Teltow, Germany: SensoMotoric Instruments GmbH.

Eye tracking glasses (Version 1) [Apparatus]. (2016). Teltow, Germany: SensoMotoric Instruments GmbH.

Eye Tracking on an F1 car [Online video] (2016). Isleworth, United Kingdom: Sky Sports F1. Retrieved from https://www.youtube.com/watch?v=zjkUUMZnTnU

Facebook. (2014). Facebook to acquire oculus [Press release]. Retrieved from http://newsroom.fb.com/news/2014/03/facebook-to-acquire-oculus/

FaceDetect (Custom version) [Computer software] (2016). Erlangen: Fraunhofer Institute for Integrated Circuits IIS, Intelligent Systems Group, Electronic Imaging Department.

Farnebäck, G. (2003). Two-frame motion estimation based on polynomial expansion. In J. Bigun & T. Gustavsson (Eds.), *Image Analysis: 13th Scandinavian Conference, SCIA 2003 Halmstad, Sweden, June 29 – July 2, 2003 Proceedings* (pp. 363–370). Berlin, Heidelberg: Springer Berlin Heidelberg. https://doi.org/10.1007/3-540-45103-X_50

Feinstein, A. R., & Cicchetti, D. V. (1990). High agreement but low Kappa: I. the problems of two paradoxes. *Journal of Clinical Epidemiology, 43*(6), 543–549. https://doi.org/10.1016/0895-4356(90)90158-L

FFmpeg [Computer software]. (2016). Retrieved from http://ffmpeg.org/

Filion, D. L., Dawson, M. E., & Schell, A. M. (1998). The psychological significance of human startle eyeblink modification: A review. *Biological Psychology, 47*(1), 1–43. https://doi.org/10.1016/S0301-0511(97)00020-3

Fogarty, C., & Stern, J. A. (1989). Eye movements and blinks: Their relationship to higher cognitive processes. *International Journal of Psychophysiology, 8*(1), 35–42. https://doi.org/10.1016/0167-8760(89)90017-2

Fontaine, G. (1992). The experience of a sense of presence in intercultural and international encounters. *Presence: Teleoperators and Virtual Environments, 1*(4), 482–490. https://doi.org/10.1162/pres.1992.1.4.482

Forbes. (2014, March 25). Facebook buys Oculus, virtual reality gaming startup, for $2 billion. Retrieved from https://www.forbes.com/sites/briansolo mon/2014/03/25/facebook-buys-oculus-virtual-reality-gaming-startup-for-2-billion/

Ford, C. C., Bugmann, G., & Culverhouse, P. (2010). Eye movement & facial expression in human-robot communication (pp. 717–729). Presented at the International Conference on Kansei Engineering and Emotion Research 2010, Paris.

Ford, C. C., Bugmann, G., & Culverhouse, P. (2013). Modeling the human blink: A computational model for use within human-robot interaction. *International Journal of Humanoid Robotics*, *10*(1), 1350006. https://doi.org/10. 1142/S0219843613500060

Fortune. (2015, December 4). Is 2016 the year of virtual reality? Retrieved from http://fortune.com/2015/12/04/2016-the-year-of-virtual-reality/

Freeman, J. (1999). *Subjective and objective approaches to the assessment of presence* (PhD thesis). University of Essex, Colchester, UK.

Freeman, J., Avons, S. E., Meddis, R., Pearson, D. E., & IJsselsteijn, W. (2000). Using behavioral realism to estimate presence: A study of the utility of postural responses to motion stimuli. *Presence*, *9*(2), 149–164. https://doi. org/10.1162/105474600566691

Freeman, J., Avons, S. E., Pearson, D. E., & IJsselsteijn, W. A. (1999). Effects of sensory information and prior experience on direct subjective ratings of presence. *Presence: Teleoperators and Virtual Environments*, *8*(1), 1–13. https://doi.org/10.1162/105474699566017

Fried, M., Tsitsiashvili, E., Bonneh, Y. S., Sterkin, A., Wygnanski-Jaffe, T., Epstein, T., & Polat, U. (2014). ADHD subjects fail to suppress eye blinks and microsaccades while anticipating visual stimuli but recover with medication. *Vision Research*, *101*, 62–72. https://doi.org/10.1016/j.visres.2014. 05.004

Fritz, T., Begel, A., Müller, S. C., Yigit-Elliott, S., & Züger, M. (2014). Using psycho-physiological measures to assess task difficulty in software development. In *ICSE 2014 Proceedings of the 36th International Conference on Software Engineering* (pp. 402–413). New York, NY: ACM Press. https:// doi.org/10.1145/2568225.2568266

Fukuda, K. (2001). Eye blinks: new indices for the detection of deception. *International Journal of Psychophysiology, 40*(3), 239–245. https://doi.org/10.1016/S0167-8760(00)00192-6

Galley, N., & Andres, G. (1996). Saccadic eye movements and blinks during long-term driving on the autobahn with minimal alcohol ingestion. *Vision in Vehicles, 5,* 381–388.

Galley, N., Andres, G., & Reitter, E. (1999). Driver fatigue as identified by saccadic and blink indicators. *Vision in Vehicles, 7,* 49–59.

Galley, N., Schleicher, R., & Galley, L. (2004). Blink parameters as indicators of driver's sleepiness–possibilities and limitations. *Vision in Vehicles, 10,* 189–196.

Game Informer. (2015, December 8). January cover revealed - the virtual reality issue. Retrieved from http://www.gameinformer.com/b/news/archive/2015/12/08/january-cover-reveal0903975441.aspx

Garau, M., Friedman, D., Widenfeld, H., Antley, A., Brogni, A., & Slater, M. (2008). Temporal and spatial variations in presence: Qualitative analysis of interviews from an experiment on breaks in presence. *Presence, 17*(3), 293–309. https://doi.org/10.1162/pres.17.3.293

Garsoffky, B., Glaser, M., & Schwan, S. (2012). Aufmerksamkeit und Filmerleben. Was uns physiologische Maße über das Empfinden von Transportation beim Filmsehen sagen können. *Rabbit Eye – Zeitschrift für Filmforschung, 4,* 102–117.

Gerrig, R. J. (1993). *Experiencing narrative worlds: On the psychological activities of reading.* New Haven, CT: Yale University Press.

Gerrig, R. J., & Zimbardo, P. (2016). *Psychologie* (20., aktualisierte und erweiterte Auflage). Hallbergmoos/Germany: Pearson.

Gibbons, J. D., & Chakraborti, S. (1991). Comparisons of the Mann-Whitney, Student's *t*, and alternate *t* tests for means of normal distributions. *The Journal of Experimental Education, 59*(3), 258–267. https://doi.org/10.1080/00220973.1991.10806565

Gibson, J. J. (1966). *The senses considered as perceptual systems.* Boston, MA: Houghton Mifflin.

Gibson, J. J. (1979). *The ecological approach to visual perception*. Boston, MA: Houghton Mifflin.

Goldstein, R., Bauer, L. O., & Stern, J. A. (1992). Effect of task difficulty and interstimulus interval on blink parameters. *International Journal of Psychophysiology, 13*(2), 111–117. https://doi.org/10.1016/0167-8760(92)90050-L

Gorini, A., Capideville, C. S., De Leo, G., Mantovani, F., & Riva, G. (2011). The role of immersion and narrative in mediated presence: The virtual hospital experience. *Cyberpsychology, Behavior, and Social Networking, 14*(3), 99–105. https://doi.org/10.1089/cyber.2010.0100

Graham, F. K. (1975). The more or less startling effects of weak pre-stimulation. *Psychophysiology, 12*, 238–248.

Green, M. C., & Brock, T. C. (2000). The role of transportation in the persuasiveness of public narratives. *Journal of Personality and Social Psychology, 79*(5), 701–721. https://doi.org/10.1037/0022-3514.79.5.701

Gregory, R. L. (1952). Variations in blink rate during nonvisual tasks. *Quarterly Journal of Experimental Psychology, 4*, 165–169.

Groen, Y., Börger, N. A., Koerts, J., Thome, J., & Tucha, O. (2017). Blink rate and blink timing in children with ADHD and the influence of stimulant medication. *Journal of Neural Transmission, 124*(1), 27–38. https://doi.org/10.1007/s00702-015-1457-6

Hargutt, V. (2003). *Das Lidschlussverhalten als Indikator für Aufmerksamkeits- und Müdigkeitsprozesse bei Arbeitshandlungen*. Düsseldorf: VDI-Verlag.

Hartmann, T., Böcking, S., Schramm, H., Wirth, W., Klimmt, C., & Vorderer, P. (2005). Räumliche Präsenz als Rezeptionsmodalität: ein theoretisches Modell zur Entstehung von Präsenzerleben. In V. Gehrau, H. Bilandzic, & J. Woelke (Eds.), *Rezeptionsstrategien und Rezeptionsmodalitäten* (pp. 21–37). R. Fischer.

Hartmann, T., Wirth, W., Schramm, H., Klimmt, C., Vorderer, P., Gysbers, A., … Maria Sacau, A. (2015). The Spatial Presence Experience Scale (SPES). *Journal of Media Psychology, 28*(1), 1–15. https://doi.org/10.1027/1864-1105/a000137

Hawkins, R. P., Pingree, S., Hitchon, J. B., Gilligan, E., Kahlor, L., Gorham, B. W., ... Serlin, R. C. (2002). What holds attention to television?: Strategic inertia of looks at content boundaries. *Communication Research, 29*(1), 3–30. https://doi.org/10.1177/0093650202029001001

Heinlein, R. A. (1942). Waldo. In *Astounding Science-Fiction, August 1942* (Vol. 6). New York, NY: Street & Smith Publications, Inc.

Hillstrom, A. P., & Yantis, S. (1994). Visual motion and attentional capture. *Perception & Psychophysics, 55*(4), 399–411.

Hofer, M., Wirth, W., Kuehne, R., Schramm, H., & Sacau, A. (2012). Structural equation modeling of spatial presence: The influence of cognitive processes and traits. *Media Psychology, 15*(4), 373–395. https://doi.org/10.1080/15213269.2012.723118

Holland, M. K., & Tarlow, G. (1972). Blinking and mental load. *Psychological Reports, 31*(1), 119–127. https://doi.org/10.2466/pr0.1972.31.1.119

Holland, M. K., & Tarlow, G. (1975). Blinking and thinking. *Perceptual and Motor Skills, 41*(2), 503–506.

HTC Corporation. (2017). Inside the headset [Website]. Retrieved from http://www.vive.com/us/product/

Huber, K., Holl, E., Liebold, B., Pietschmann, D., & Wolfrum, K. (2017). A modified secondary task reaction time paradigm for research on breaks in presence. Presented at the ICA Annual Conference 2017, San Diego, USA.

Huff, M., Meitz, T. G. K., & Papenmeier, F. (2014). Changes in situation models modulate processes of event perception in audiovisual narratives. *Journal of Experimental Psychology: Learning, Memory, and Cognition, 40*(5), 1377–1388. https://doi.org/10.1037/a0036780

Huff, M., Schwan, S., & Garsoffky, B. (2011). When movement patterns turn into events: Implications for the recognition of spatial configurations from different viewpoints. *Journal of Cognitive Psychology, 23*(4), 476–484. https://doi.org/10.1080/20445911.2011.541152

Hupé, J.-M., Bordier, C., & Dojat, M. (2012). A BOLD signature of eyeblinks in the visual cortex. *NeuroImage, 61*(1), 149–161. https://doi.org/10.1016/j.neuroimage.2012.03.001

Ichikawa, N., & Ohira, H. (2004). Eyeblink activity as an index of cognitive processing: Temporal distribution of eyeblinks as an indicator of expectancy in semantic priming. *Perceptual and Motor Skills*, *98*(1), 131–140. https://doi.org/10.2466/pms.98.1.131-140

IDC. (2016). Worldwide revenues for augmented and virtual reality forecast to reach $162 billion in 2020, according to IDC [Press release]. Retrieved from http://www.idc.com/getdoc.jsp?containerId=prUS41676216

Ijsselsteijn, W. A. (2002). Elements of a multi-level theory of presence: Phenomenology, mental processing and neural correlates. In *Proceedings of PRESENCE, 2002*, 245–259.

IJsselsteijn, W. A., de Ridder, H., Freeman, J., & Avons, S. E. (2000). Presence: Concept, determinants, and measurement. In B. E. Rogowitz & T. N. Pappas (Eds.), *Proceedings of SPIE, Vol. 3959* (pp. 520–529). https://doi.org/10.1117/12.387188

IJsselsteijn, W., Ridder, H. d, Freeman, J., Avons, S. E., & Bouwhuis, D. (2001). Effects of stereoscopic presentation, image motion, and screen size on subjective and objective corroborative measures of presence. *Presence*, *10*(3), 298–311. https://doi.org/10.1162/105474601300343621

Iñárritu, A. G. (2014). *Birdman or (The Unexpected Virtue of Ignorance)* [Motion picture]. Fox Searchlight Pictures.

ISPR. (2009). Presence defined. Retrieved from https://ispr.info/about-presence-2/about-presence/

ITU. (2015). Recommendation ITU-R BT.601-7 (03/2011): Studio encoding parameters of digital television for standard 4:3 and wide-screen 16:9 aspect ratios. *BT Series Broadcasting Service (Television)*. Retrieved from https://www.itu.int/dms_pubrec/itu-r/rec/bt/R-REC-BT.601-7-201103-I!!PDF-E.pdf

JASP (Version 0.8.1.2) [Computer software]. (2017). Retrieved from https://jasp-stats.org/

Jin, S.-A. A. (2011). "I feel present. Therefore, I experience flow:" A structural equation modeling approach to flow and presence in video games. *Journal of Broadcasting & Electronic Media*, *55*(1), 114–136. https://doi.org/10.1080/08838151.2011.546248

Jin, S.-A. A. (2012). "Toward integrative models of flow": Effects of performance, skill, challenge, playfulness, and presence on flow in video games. *Journal of Broadcasting & Electronic Media, 56*(2), 169–186. https://doi.org/ 10.1080/08838151.2012.678516

Johnson, M. E., & Murphy, P. J. (2004). Changes in the tear film and ocular surface from dry eye syndrome. *Progress in Retinal and Eye Research, 23*(4), 449–474. https://doi.org/10.1016/j.preteyeres.2004.04.003

Johnson-Laird, P. N. (1983). *Mental models. Towards a cognitive science of language, inference, and consciousness.* Cambridge: Cambridge University Press.

Jongkees, B. J., & Colzato, L. S. (2016). Spontaneous eye blink rate as predictor of dopamine-related cognitive function-A review. *Neuroscience and Biobehavioral Reviews, 71*, 58–82. https://doi.org/10.1016/j.neubiorev.2016.08. 020

Juniper Research. (2016). VR hardware to be worth over $50bn by 2021, driven by widespread gamer adoption [Press release]. Retrieved from https://www.juniperresearch.com/press/press-releases/vr-hardware-to-be-worth-over-$50bn-by-2021-driven

Kaminer, J., Powers, A. S., Horn, K. G., Hui, C., & Evinger, C. (2011). Characterizing the spontaneous blink generator: An animal model. *Journal of Neuroscience, 31*(31), 11256–11267. https://doi.org/10.1523/JNEUROSCI. 6218-10.2011

Karson, C. N. (1983). Spontaneous eye-blink rates and dopaminergic systems. *Brain, 106*(3), 643–653. https://doi.org/10.1093/brain/106.3.643

Karson, C. N. (1988). Physiology of normal and abnormal blinking. *Advances in Neurology, 49*, 25–37.

Karson, C. N. (1989). Blinking. *Bulletin De La Societe Belge D'ophtalmologie, 237*, 443–457.

Kim, T., & Biocca, F. (1997). Telepresence via television: Two dimensions of telepresence may have different connections to memory and persuasion. *Journal of Computer-Mediated Communication, 3*(2), 0–0. https://doi. org/10.1111/j.1083-6101.1997.tb00073.x

Klasen, M., Weber, R., Kircher, T. T. J., Mathiak, K. A., & Mathiak, K. (2012). Neural contributions to flow experience during video game playing. *Social Cognitive and Affective Neuroscience*, *7*(4), 485–495. https://doi.org/ 10.1093/scan/nsr021

Kleinsorge, T., & Scheil, J. (2017). Integration of advance information about a forthcoming task switch – evidence from eye blink rates. *Frontiers in Psychology*, *8*. https://doi.org/10.3389/fpsyg.2017.00290

Krapp, A. (1993). *The construct of interest. Characteristics of individual interests and interest-related actions from the perspective of a person-object theory*. Munich: Universtiy of the Armed Forces.

Kret, M. E. (2015). Emotional expressions beyond facial muscle actions. A call for studying autonomic signals and their impact on social perception. *Frontiers in Psychology*, *6*. https://doi.org/10.3389/fpsyg.2015.00711

Kreuz, T., Chicharro, D., Greschner, M., & Andrzejak, R. G. (2011). Time-resolved and time-scale adaptive measures of spike train synchrony. *Journal of Neuroscience Methods*, *195*(1), 92–106. https://doi.org/10.1016/j. jneumeth.2010.11.020

Kreuz, T., Chicharro, D., Houghton, C., Andrzejak, R. G., & Mormann, F. (2013). Monitoring spike train synchrony. *Journal of Neurophysiology*, *109*(5), 1457–1472. https://doi.org/10.1152/jn.00873.2012

Kreuz, T., Haas, J. S., Morelli, A., Abarbanel, H. D. I., & Politi, A. (2007). Measuring spike train synchrony. *Journal of Neuroscience Methods*, *165*(1), 151–161. https://doi.org/10.1016/j.jneumeth.2007.05.031

Kreuz, T., Mormann, F., Andrzejak, R. G., Kraskov, A., Lehnertz, K., & Grassberger, P. (2007). Measuring synchronization in coupled model systems: A comparison of different approaches. *Physica D: Nonlinear Phenomena*, *225*(1), 29–42. https://doi.org/10.1016/j.physd.2006.09.039

Kreuz, T., Mulansky, M., & Bozanic, N. (2015). SPIKY: A graphical user interface for monitoring spike train synchrony. *Journal of Neurophysiology*, *113*(9), 3432–3445. https://doi.org/10.1152/jn.00848.2014

Krugmann, H. E. (1965). The impact of television advertising: learning without involvement. *Public Opinion Quarterly*, *29*, 349–356.

Kueblbeck, C., & Ernst, A. (2006). Face detection and tracking in video sequences using the modified census transformation. *Journal on Image and Vision Computing*, *24*(6), 564–572.

Kurby, C. A., & Zacks, J. M. (2008). Segmentation in the perception and memory of events. *Trends in Cognitive Sciences*, *12*(2), 72–79. https://doi.org/10.1016/j.tics.2007.11.004

KZero. (2015a). Virtual reality software revenue forecasts 2014 – 2018 [Blog post]. Retrieved from http://www.kzero.co.uk/blog/virtual-reality-software-revenue-forecasts-2014-2018/

KZero. (2015b). VR HMD and input system device revenue forecasts 2014–2018 [Blog post]. Retrieved from http://www.kzero.co.uk/blog/vr-hmd-and-input-system-device-revenue-forecasts-2014-2018/

Laarni, J., Ravaja, N., & Saari, T. (2003). Using eye tracking and psychophysiological methods to study spatial presence. In *Proceedings of the 6th International Workshop on Presence*.

Lawson, R. W. (1948). Photographic evaluation of blackout indices. *Nature, 162*, 531–532.

Lee, K. M. (2004a). Presence, explicated. *Communication Theory, 14*(1), 27–50. https://doi.org/10.1111/j.1468-2885.2004.tb00302.x

Lee, K. M. (2004b). Why presence occurs: Evolutionary psychology, media equation, and presence. *Presence: Teleoperators and Virtual Environments, 13*(4), 494–505. https://doi.org/10.1162/1054746041944830

Lessiter, J., Freeman, J., Keogh, E., & Davidoff, J. (2001). A cross-media presence questionnaire: The ITC-Sense of Presence Inventory. *Presence: Teleoperators and Virtual Environments, 10*(3), 282–297. https://doi.org/10.1162/105474601300343612

Levenson, R. W. (2003). Autonomic specificity and emotion. *Handbook of Affective Sciences, 2*, 212–224.

Liebes, T., & Katz, E. (1986). Patterns of involvement in television fiction: A comparative analysis. *European Journal of Communication, 1*(2), 151–171. https://doi.org/10.1177/0267323186001002004

Liebold, B., Brill, M., Pietschmann, D., Schwab, F., & Ohler, P. (2017). Continuous measurement of breaks in presence: Psychophysiology and orienting responses. *Media Psychology, 20*(3), 477–501. https://doi.org/10.1080/15213269.2016.1206829

Liebold, B., Koban, K., & Ohler, P. (2015). How to become a race driver at home. The effects of authentic input devices and simulation accuracy on motor skill learning and real world transfer. Presented at the 65th ICA Annual Conference, San Juan, PR.

Liebold, B., Pietschmann, D., & Ohler, P. (2015). Another note on presence terminology: A general model of experiencing virtual environments. Presented at the Annual Conference of the ICA 2015, San Juan, PR.

Liu, L. D., & Pack, C. C. (2017). The contribution of area MT to visual motion perception depends on training. *Neuron, 95*(2), 436–446.e3. https://doi.org/10.1016/j.neuron.2017.06.024

Lombard, M., & Ditton, T. (1997). At the heart of it all: The concept of presence. *Journal of Computer-Mediated Communication, 3*(2), 0–0. https://doi.org/10.1111/j.1083-6101.1997.tb00072.x

Lombard, M., Ditton, T., Crane, D., Davis, B., Gil-Egui, G., Horvath, K., & Rossman, J. (2000). Measuring presence: A literature-based approach to the development of a standardized paper-and-pencil instrument (pp. 2–4). Presented at Presence 2000: The Third International Workshop on Presence, Delft, the Netherlands. Retrieved from https://astro.temple.edu/~lombard/ISPR/Proceedings/2000/Lombard,%20Ditton%20et%20al.pdf

Lozoff, B. (2011). Early iron deficiency has brain and behavior effects consistent with dopaminergic dysfunction. *The Journal of Nutrition, 141*(4), 740S–746S. https://doi.org/10.3945/jn.110.131169

Luckiesh, M. (1944). On the rate of involuntary blinking. *Illumination Engineering, 39*, 69–71.

Lyttle, D., & Fellous, J.-M. (2011). A new similarity measure for spike trains: Sensitivity to bursts and periods of inhibition. *Journal of Neuroscience Methods, 199*(2), 296–309. https://doi.org/10.1016/j.jneumeth.2011.05.005

Magliano, J. P., & Zacks, J. M. (2011). The impact of continuity editing in narrative film on event segmentation. *Cognitive Science, 35*(8), 1489–1517. https://doi.org/10.1111/j.1551-6709.2011.01202.x

Magnusson, M. S. (2000). Discovering hidden time patterns in behavior: T-patterns and their detection. *Behavior Research Methods, Instruments, & Computers, 32*(1), 93–110. https://doi.org/10.3758/BF03200792

Magnusson, M. S. (2005). Understanding social interaction: Discovering hidden structure with model and algorithms. In L. Anolli, D. J. Starkey, M. S. Magnusson, & G. Riva (Eds.), *The hidden structure of interaction: From neurons to culture patterns* (pp. 3–22). Amsterdam, the Netherlands: IOS Press.

Magnusson, M. S. (2016). Time and self-similar structure in behavior and interactions: From sequences to symmetry and fractals. In M. S. Magnusson, J. K. Burgoon, & M. Casarrubea (Eds.), *Discovering hidden temporal patterns in behavior and interaction* (pp. 3–35). New York, NY: Humana Press.

Magnusson, M. S., Burgoon, J. K., & Casarrubea, M. (Eds.). (2016). *Discovering hidden temporal patterns in behavior and interaction.* New York, NY: Springer New York. Retrieved from http://link.springer.com/10.1007/978-1-4939-3249-8

Maier, M., Bacherle, P., Adam, S., & Leidecker-Sandmann, M. (2017). The interplay between parties and media in putting EU issues on the agenda: A temporal pattern analysis of the 2014 European Parliamentary election campaigns in Austria, Germany and the United Kingdom. *Party Politics*, 135406881770053. https://doi.org/10.1177/1354068817700532

Malmstrom, F. V., Rachofsky, S. E., & Weber, R. J. (1977). Effects of illumination and meter on spontaneous eyeblinks. *Bulletin of the Psychonomic Society, 9*(3), 163–165. https://doi.org/10.3758/BF03336961

Mandel, A., Helokunnas, S., Pihko, E., & Hari, R. (2014). Neuromagnetic brain responses to other person's eye blinks seen on video. *European Journal of Neuroscience, 40*(3), 2576–2580. https://doi.org/10.1111/ejn.12611

Mandel, A., Helokunnas, S., Pihko, E., & Hari, R. (2015). Brain responds to another person's eye blinks in a natural setting—the more empathetic the viewer the stronger the responses. *European Journal of Neuroscience*, *42*(8), 2508–2514. https://doi.org/10.1111/ejn.13011

Mantovani, G. (1995). Virtual reality as a communication environment: Consensual hallucination, fiction, and possible selves. *Human Relations*, *48*(6), 669–683. https://doi.org/10.1177/001872679504800604

Mark Zuckerberg. (2014, March 25). https://www.facebook.com/zuck/posts/10101319050523971 [Facebook update]. Retrieved from https://www.facebook.com/zuck/posts/10101319050523971

McMonnies, C. W. (2007). Incomplete blinking: Exposure keratopathy, lid wiper epitheliopathy, dry eye, refractive surgery, and dry contact lenses. *Contact Lens & Anterior Eye: The Journal of the British Contact Lens Association*, *30*(1), 37–51. https://doi.org/10.1016/j.clae.2006.12.002

Media Recorder (Version 2) [Computer software]. (2017). Wageningen: Noldus Information Technologies.

Mehrabian, A. (1976). *The psychology of places*. New York, NY: Basic Books.

Metacritic. (2015). Project Cars PC [Website]. Retrieved from http://www.metacritic.com/game/pc/project-cars

Minsky, M. (1980). Telepresence. *Omni*, *2*(9), 45–51.

Mishima, S. (1965). Some physiological aspects of the precorneal tear film. *Archives of Ophthalmology*, *73*(2), 233–241. https://doi.org/10.1001/archopht.1965.00970030235017

Monaco, J. (2015). *Film verstehen: Kunst, Technik, Sprache, Geschichte und Theorie des Films und der Neuen Medien: mit einer Einführung in Multimedia*. (H.-M. Bock, Ed.) (Deutsche Erstausgabe, überarbeitete und erweiterte Neuausgabe, 4. Auflage). Reinbek bei Hamburg: Rowohlt Taschenbuch Verlag.

Monaco, J., & Bock, H.-M. (2011). *Film verstehen - das Lexikon: die wichtigsten Fachbegriffe zu Film und Neuen Medien* (Überarb. Neuausg., Erstausg.). Reinbek bei Hamburg: Rowohlt.

Moraitis, T., & Ghosh, A. (2014). Withdrawal of voluntary inhibition unravels the off state of the spontaneous blink generator. *Neuropsychologia, 65,* 279–286. https://doi.org/10.1016/j.neuropsychologia.2014.09.010

Morrone, M. C., Ross, J., & Burr, D. (2005). Saccadic eye movements cause compression of time as well as space. *Nature Neuroscience, 8*(7), 950–954. https://doi.org/10.1038/nn1488

Mulansky, M., Bozanic, N., & Kreuz, T. (2015). Time-resolved and parameter-free measures of spike train synchrony: Properties and applications. *BMC Neuroscience, 16*(Suppl. 1), 133. https://doi.org/10.1186/1471-2202-16-S1-P133

Mulansky, M., & Kreuz, T. (2016). PySpike—A Python library for analyzing spike train synchrony. *SoftwareX, 5,* 183–189. https://doi.org/10.1016/j.softx.2016.07.006

Müller, J., Dreisbach, G., Brocke, B., Lesch, K.-P., Strobel, A., & Goschke, T. (2007). Dopamine and cognitive control: The influence of spontaneous eyeblink rate, DRD4 exon III polymorphism and gender on flexibility in set-shifting. *Brain Research, 1131,* 155–162.

Nakamura, J., & Csikszentmihalyi, M. (2014). The concept of flow. In M. Csikszentmihalyi, *Flow and the foundations of positive psychology* (pp. 239–263). Dordrecht: Springer Netherlands. https://doi.org/10.1007/978-94-017-9088-8_16

Nakano, T. (2015). Blink-related dynamic switching between internal and external orienting networks while viewing videos. *Neuroscience Research, 96,* 54–58. https://doi.org/10.1016/j.neures.2015.02.010

Nakano, T., Kato, M., Morito, Y., Itoi, S., & Kitazawa, S. (2013). Blink-related momentary activation of the default mode network while viewing videos. *Proceedings of the National Academy of Sciences, 110*(2), 702–706. https://doi.org/10.1073/pnas.1214804110

Nakano, T., Kato, N., & Kitazawa, S. (2011). Lack of eyeblink entrainments in autism spectrum disorders. *Neuropsychologia, 49*(9), 2784–2790. https://doi.org/10.1016/j.neuropsychologia.2011.06.007

Nakano, T., & Kitazawa, S. (2010). Eyeblink entrainment at breakpoints of speech. *Experimental Brain Research, 205*(4), 577–581. https://doi.org/10.1007/s00221-010-2387-z

Nakano, T., Yamamoto, Y., Kitajo, K., Takahashi, T., & Kitazawa, S. (2009). Synchronization of spontaneous eyeblinks while viewing video stories. *Proceedings of the Royal Society of London B: Biological Sciences*, rspb20090828. https://doi.org/10.1098/rspb.2009.0828

National Eye Institute. (2012). Drawing of the eye [Online image]. Retrieved from   https://www.flickr.com/photos/nationaleyeinstitute/7544457582/ in/album-72157646829197286/

National Eye Institute. (2016a). Structures of the eye, including layers of the cornea [Online image]. Retrieved from https://www.flickr.com/photos/ nationaleyeinstitute/28021474805/in/album-72157646829197286/

National Eye Institute. (2016b). Structures involved in tear production [Online image]. Retrieved from https://www.flickr.com/photos/nationaleye institute/28021474935/

Need for Speed: Shift [Computer software]. (2009). Redwood City, CA: Electronic Arts.

Nielsen, P. K., Søgaard, K., Skotte, J., & Wolkoff, P. (2008). Ocular surface area and human eye blink frequency during VDU work: The effect of monitor position and task. *European Journal of Applied Physiology*, *103*(1), 1–7. https://doi.org/10.1007/s00421-007-0661-y

Nomura, R., Hino, K., Shimazu, M., Liang, Y., & Okada, T. (2015). Emotionally excited eyeblink-rate variability predicts an experience of transportation into the narrative world. *Frontiers in Psychology*, *06*. https://doi.org/10. 3389/fpsyg.2015.00447

Nomura, R., & Okada, T. (2014). Spontaneous synchronization of eye-blinks during story-telling performance. *Cogn. Stud.*, *21*, 226–244.

Núñez Castellar, E. P., Antons, J.-N., Marinazzo, D., & Van Looy, J. (2016). Measuring flow through attentional engagement during game play: Validation of a novel technique. In *Proceedings of the International Communication Association Conference* (pp. 1–9). Washington DC, USA: International Communication Association.

Oculus VR. (2017). The magic of presence [Website]. Retrieved from https://www3.oculus.com/en-us/rift/

Oh, J., Han, M., Peterson, B. S., & Jeong, J. (2012). Spontaneous eyeblinks are correlated with responses during the stroop task. *PLoS ONE, 7*(4), e34871. https://doi.org/10.1371/journal.pone.0034871

Oh, J., Jeong, S.-Y., & Jeong, J. (2012). The timing and temporal patterns of eye blinking are dynamically modulated by attention. *Human Movement Science, 31*(6), 1353–1365. https://doi.org/10.1016/j.humov.2012.06.003

Ohira, H. (1996). Eyeblink activity in a word-naming task as a function of semantic priming and cognitive load. *Perceptual and Motor Skills, 82*(3), 835–842. https://doi.org/10.2466/pms.1996.82.3.835

Ohler, P. (1994). *Kognitive Filmpsychologie: Verarbeitung und Repräsentation narrativer Filme.* Münster: MAkS Publikationen.

Ohler, P., Liebold, B., Pietschmann, D., Valtin, G., & Nieding, G. (2013). Digitale Demenz. Eine wissenschaftliche Verortung der aktuellen Monografie von Manfred Spitzer – Teil I. *Tv Diskurs, (63),* 72–76.

Olsen, T., Arnarsson, A., Sasaki, H., Sasaki, K., & Jonasson, F. (2007). On the ocular refractive components: the Reykjavik Eye Study. *Acta Ophthalmologica Scandinavica, 85*(4), 361–366. https://doi.org/10.1111/j.1600-0420.2006.00847.x

OpenCV (Version 3.0.0) [Computer software]. (2014). Retrieved from http://opencv.org/

OpenCV team. (n.d.). Color conversions [Online manual]. Retrieved from http://docs.opencv.org/3.1.0/de/d25/imgproc_color_conversions.html

Oshima, K. (1998). Rakugo: Japanese sit-down comedy. *Humor & Health Journal, 12*(3).

Ousler, G., Abelson, M. B., Johnston, P. R., Rodriguez, J., Lane, K., & Smith, L. M. (2014). Blink patterns and lid-contact times in dry-eye and normal subjects. *Clinical Ophthalmology,* 869. https://doi.org/10.2147/OPTH.S56783

Patrick Bacherle. (2015). *Eintauchen in narrative Welten - theoretische und empirische Zugänge zum Rezeptionserleben.* Retrieved from https://kola.opus.hbz-nrw.de/frontdoor/index/index/docId/935

PC Games Hardware. (2008, February 9). Videobeweis: "Mikroruckler" zerstören den leistungssteigernden Effekt von Multi-GPU-Lösungen [Website]. Retrieved from http://www.pcgameshardware.de/Grafikkarten-Grafikkarte-97980/Tests/Mikroruckler-Micro-Stuttering-631607/

Peckham, A. D., & Johnson, S. L. (2016). Spontaneous eye-blink rate as an index of reward responsivity: Validation and links to bipolar disorder. *Clinical Psychological Science*, *4*(3), 451–463. https://doi.org/10.1177/2167702615594999

Phan, M. H., Jardina, J. R., Hoyle, S., & Chaparro, B. S. (2012). Examining the Role of Gender in Video Game Usage, Preference, and Behavior. *Proceedings of the Human Factors and Ergonomics Society Annual Meeting*, *56*(1), 1496–1500. https://doi.org/10.1177/1071181312561297

Pivik, R. T., & Dykman, R. A. (2004). Endogenous eye blinks in preadolescents: Relationship to information processing and performance. *Biological Psychology*, *66*(3), 191–219. https://doi.org/10.1016/j.biopsycho.2003.10.005

Posner, M. I. (1980). Orienting of attention. *Quarterly Journal of Experimental Psychology*, *32*(1), 3–25. https://doi.org/10.1080/00335558008248231

Poulton, E. C., & Gregory, R. L. (1952). Blinking during visual tracking. *Quarterly Journal of Experimental Psychology*, *4*(2), 57–65. https://doi.org/10.1080/17470215208416604

Prad. (2012). Testbericht: Asus VG278H [Website]. Retrieved from http://www.prad.de/new/monitore/test/2012/test-asus-vg278h-teil7.html#Latenzzeit

Project CARS. [Computer software] (2015). London, United Kingdom: Slightly Mad Studios.

Project CARS Telemetry [Computer software]. (2016, April 17). Retrieved April 17, 2016, from https://pcarstelemetry.wordpress.com/

Rawlinson, J. (2009). *Kuroshio Sea - 2nd largest aquarium tank in the world* [Online video]. Vancouver, Canada. Retrieved from https://vimeo.com/5606758

Rey, B., V Parkhutik, & Alcañiz, M. (2011). Breaks in presence in virtual environments: An analysis of blood flow velocity responses. *Presence*, *20*(3), 273–286. https://doi.org/10.1162/PRES_a_00049

Reynolds, J. R., Zacks, J. M., & Braver, T. S. (2007). A computational model of event segmentation from perceptual prediction. *Cognitive Science, 31*(4), 613–643. https://doi.org/10.1080/15326900701399913

Riecke, B. E., & von der Heyde, M. (2002). Qualitative modeling of spatial orientation processes using logical propositions: Interconnecting spatial presence, spatial updation, piloting, and spatial cognition. Retrieved from http://www.kyb.tuebingen.mpg.de/publications/pdfs/pdf2021.pdf

Riggs, L. A., Kelly, J. P., Manning, K. A., & Moore, R. K. (1987). Blink-related eye movements. *Investigative Ophthalmology & Visual Science, 28*(2), 334–342.

Riggs, L. A., Volkmann, F. C., & Moore, R. K. (1981). Suppression of the blackout due to blinks. *Vision Research, 21*(7), 1075–1079. https://doi.org/10.1016/0042-6989(81)90012-2

Riva, G., Mantovani, F., Waterworth, E. L., & Waterworth, J. A. (2015). Intention, action, self and other: An evolutionary model of presence. In M. Lombard, F. Biocca, J. Freeman, W. IJsselsteijn, & R. J. Schaevitz (Eds.), *Immersed in media* (pp. 73–99). Springer International Publishing. https://doi.org/10.1007/978-3-319-10190-3_5

Roberts, J. E., Symons, F. J., Johnson, A.-M., Hatton, D. D., & Boccia, M. L. (2005). Blink rate in boys with fragile X syndrome: Preliminary evidence for altered dopamine function. *Journal of Intellectual Disability Research, 49*(9), 647–656. https://doi.org/10.1111/j.1365-2788.2005.00713.x

Robinett, W. (1992). Synthetic experience: A proposed taxonomy. *Presence: Teleoperators and Virtual Environments, 1*(2), 229–247. https://doi.org/10.1162/pres.1992.1.2.229

Rolando, M., & Zierhut, M. (2001). The ocular surface and tear film and their dysfunction in dry eye disease. *Survey of Ophthalmology, 45*, S203–S210. https://doi.org/10.1016/S0039-6257(00)00203-4

Rose, L. M., Paige, R. F., Kolovos, D. S., & Polack, F. A. C. (2008). Constructing models with the human-usable textual notation. In K. Czarnecki, I. Ober, J.-M. Bruel, A. Uhl, & M. Völter (Eds.), *Model driven engineering languages and systems* (Vol. 5301, pp. 249–263). Berlin, Heidelberg: Springer Berlin Heidelberg. https://doi.org/10.1007/978-3-540-87875-9_18

Rosenfield, M., Jahan, S., Nunez, K., & Chan, K. (2015). Cognitive demand, digital screens and blink rate. *Computers in Human Behavior, 51,* 403–406. https://doi.org/10.1016/j.chb.2015.04.073

Roser, C. (1990). Involvement, attention, and perceptions of message relevance in the response to persuasive appeals. *Communication Research, 17*(5), 571–600. https://doi.org/10.1177/009365090017005001

Rusu, C. V., & Florian, R. V. (2014). A new class of metrics for spike trains. *Neural Computation, 26*(2), 306–348. https://doi.org/10.1162/NECO_a_00545

Ruxton, G. D. (2006). The unequal variance *t* test is an underused alternative to Student's *t* test and the Mann-Whitney *U* test. *Behavioral Ecology, 17*(4), 688–690. https://doi.org/10.1093/beheco/ark016

Sanford, A. J., & Garrod, S. C. (1981). *Understanding written language: Exploration of comprehension beyond the sentence.* New York: Wiley.

Satuvuori, E., Mulansky, M., Bozanic, N., Malvestio, I., Zeldenrust, F., Lenk, K., & Kreuz, T. (2017). Measures of spike train synchrony for data with multiple time scales. *Journal of Neuroscience Methods, 287,* 25–38. https://doi.org/10.1016/j.jneumeth.2017.05.028

Sayegh, F. N. (1996). The correlation of corneal refractive power, axial length, and the refractive power of the emmetropizing intraocular lens in cataractous eyes. *German Journal of Ophthalmology, 5*(6), 328–331.

Schleicher, R., Galley, N., Briest, S., & Galley, L. (2008). Blinks and saccades as indicators of fatigue in sleepiness warnings: Looking tired? *Ergonomics, 51*(7), 982–1010. https://doi.org/10.1080/00140130701817062

Schmidt, R. F., & Thews, G. (Eds.). (1997). *Physiologie des Menschen [Physiology of man].* Berlin: Springer.

Schubert, T., Friedmann, F., & Regenbrecht, H. (2001). The experience of presence: Factor analytic insights. *Presence: Teleoperators and Virtual Environments, 10*(3), 266–281. https://doi.org/10.1162/105474601300343603

Schubert, T. W. (2009). A new conception of spatial presence: Once again, with feeling. *Communication Theory, 19*(2), 161–187. https://doi.org/10.1111/j.1468-2885.2009.01340.x

Sechenov, I. M. (1965). *Reflexes in the brain*. (S. Belsky, Trans.). Cambridge, MA: MIT Press (Originally published in 1863, St. Petersburg: Sushchinski).

Shepherd, S. V., Steckenfinger, S. A., Hasson, U., & Ghazanfar, A. A. (2010). Human-monkey gaze correlations reveal convergent and divergent patterns of movie viewing. *Current Biology, 20*(7), 649–656. https://doi.org/10.1016/j.cub.2010.02.032

Sherry, J. L. (2004). Flow and media enjoyment. *Communication Theory, 14*(4), 328–347. https://doi.org/10.1111/j.1468-2885.2004.tb00318.x

Shultz, S., Klin, A., & Jones, W. (2011). Inhibition of eye blinking reveals subjective perceptions of stimulus salience. *Proceedings of the National Academy of Sciences, 108*(52), 21270–21275. https://doi.org/10.1073/pnas.1109304108

Siegle, G. J., Ichikawa, N., & Steinhauer, S. (2008). Blink before and after you think: Blinks occur prior to and following cognitive load indexed by pupillary responses. *Psychophysiology, 45*(5), 679–687. https://doi.org/10.1111/j.1469-8986.2008.00681.x

Skotte, J. H., Nøjgaard, J. K., Jørgensen, L. V., Christensen, K. B., & Sjøgaard, G. (2006). Eye blink frequency during different computer tasks quantified by electrooculography. *European Journal of Applied Physiology, 99*(2), 113–119. https://doi.org/10.1007/s00421-006-0322-6

Slater, M. (2004). How colorful was your day? Why questionnaires cannot assess presence in virtual environments. *Presence: Teleoperators and Virtual Environments, 13*(4), 484–493.

Slater, M., Brogni, A., & Steed, A. (2003). Physiological responses to breaks in presence: A pilot study. In *Presence 2003: The 6th Annual International Workshop on Presence* (Vol. 157). Citeseer.

Slater, M., & Garau, M. (2007). The use of questionnaire data in presence studies: Do not seriously Likert. *Presence: Teleoperators and Virtual Environments, 16*(4), 447–456. https://doi.org/10.1162/pres.16.4.447

Slater, M., Linakis, V., Usoh, M., & Kooper, R. (1996). Immersion, presence, and performance in virtual environments: An experiment with tri-dimensional chess. In *ACM virtual reality software and technology (VRST)* (Vol. 163, p. 72). New York, NY: ACM Press.

Slater, M., Lotto, B., Arnold, M. M., & Sanchez-Vives, M. V. (2009). How we experience immersive virtual environments: The concept of presence and its measurement. *Anuario de Psicología/The UB Journal of Psychology*, 40(2), 193–210.

Slater, M., McCarthy, J., & Maringelli, F. (1998). The influence of body movement on subjective presence in virtual environments. *Human Factors: The Journal of the Human Factors and Ergonomics Society*, 40(3), 469–477. https://doi.org/10.1518/001872098779591368

Slater, M., & Steed, A. (2000). A virtual presence counter. *Presence: Teleoperators and Virtual Environments*, 9(5), 413–434. https://doi.org/10.1162/105474600566925

Slater, M., Usoh, M., & Steed, A. (1995). Taking steps: the influence of a walking technique on presence in virtual reality. *ACM Transactions on Computer-Human Interaction*, 2(3), 201–219. https://doi.org/10.1145/210079.210084

Speer, N. K., Swallow, K. M., & Zacks, J. M. (2003). Activation of human motion processing areas during event perception. *Cognitive, Affective, & Behavioral Neuroscience*, 3(4), 335–345. https://doi.org/10.3758/CABN.3.4.335

Stern, J. A., Walrath, L. C., & Goldstein, R. (1984). The endogenous eyeblink. *Psychophysiology*, 21, 22–33.

Steuer, J. (1992). Defining virtual reality: dimensions determining telepresence. *Journal of Communication*, 42(4), 73–93. https://doi.org/10.1111/j.1460-2466.1992.tb00812.x

Studiobox Premium [Apparatus]. (2017). Walzbachtal, Germany: Studiobox GmbH.

Suckfüll, M. (2004). *Rezeptionsmodalitäten: ein integratives Konstrukt für die Medienwirkungsforschung*. München: R. Fischer.

Suckfüll, M., & Unz, D. (2013). Auf der ‚Suche' nach Zeitmustern in mehrdimensionalen Beobachtungsdaten. Presented at the 15. Tagung der Fachgruppe »Methoden der Publizistik- und Kommunikationswissenschaft« in der DGPuK, Münster, Germany.

Suckfüll, M., & Unz, D. (2016). Understanding film art: Moments of impact and patterns of reactions. In M. S. Magnusson, J. K. Burgoon, & M. Casarrubea (Eds.), *Discovering hidden temporal patterns in behavior and interaction*. New York, NY: Springer New York.

Sukalla, F., Shoenberger, H., & Bolls, P. D. (2016). Surprise! An investigation of orienting responses to test assumptions of narrative processing. *Communication Research*, *43*(6), 844–862. https://doi.org/10.1177/0093650215596363

Tada, H., Omori, Y., Hirokawa, K., Ohira, H., & Tomonaga, M. (2013). Eye-blink behaviors in 71 species of primates. *PLoS ONE, 8*(5), e66018. https://doi.org/10.1371/journal.pone.0066018

Taylor, J. R., Elsworth, J. D., Lawrence, M. S., Sladek Jr., J. R., Roth, R. H., & Redmond. (1999). Spontaneous blink rates correlate with dopamine levels in the caudate nucleus of MPTP-treated monkeys. *Experimental Neurology, 158*(1), 214–220. https://doi.org/10.1006/exnr.1999.7093

Telford, C. W., & Thompson, N. (1933). Factors influencing the eyelid responses. *Journal of Experimental Psychology, 16*, 524–539.

TFA Dostmann. (n.d.). "Comfort Control" Digitales Thermo-Hygrometer [Website]. Retrieved from http://tfa-dostmann.de/index.php?id=78

Thai, L. C., Tomlinson, A., & Ridder, W. H. I. (2002). Contact lens drying and visual performance: The vision cycle with contact lenses. *Optometry & Vision Science, 79*(6), 381–388.

The Observer XT (Version 11.5) [Computer software]. (2017). Wageningen: Noldus Information Technologies.

Theme (Version 6) [Computer software]. (2017). Reykjavík, Iceland: Pattern Vision Ltd.

Thomas, L. E., & Irwin, D. E. (2006). Voluntary eyeblinks disrupt iconic memory. *Perception & Psychophysics, 68*(3), 475–488.

Timberlake, G. T., Doane, M. G., & Bertera, J. H. (1992). Short-term, low-contrast visual acuity reduction associated with in vivo contact lens drying. *Optometry and Vision Science, 69*(10), 755–760.

Tisinger, R. (2004). Dramatized political narratives and belief change. Presented at the Annual conference of the International Communications Association, New Orleans.

TrendForce. (2015). TrendForce forecasts VR market value to hit US$70 billion in 2020 as innovative apps enrich this industry [Press release]. Retrieved from http://press.trendforce.com/press/20151204-2210.html

Tse, P. U., Baumgartner, F. J., & Greenlee, M. W. (2010). Event-related functional MRI of cortical activity evoked by microsaccades, small visually-guided saccades, and eyeblinks in human visual cortex. *NeuroImage, 49*(1), 805–816. https://doi.org/10.1016/j.neuroimage.2009.07.052

Tsubota, K., Egami, F., Ohtsuki, T., & Shintani, M. (1999). Abnormal blinking of newscasters. *The Lancet, 354*(9175), 308. https://doi.org/10.1016/S0140-6736(99)02100-5

Tsubota, K., Hata, S., Okusawa, Y., Egami, F., Ohtsuki, T., & Nakamori, K. (1996). Quantitative videographic analysis of blinking in normal subjects and patients with dry eye. *Archives of Ophthalmology, 114*(6), 715. https://doi.org/10.1001/archopht.1996.01100130707012

Tsubota, K., & Nakamori, K. (1993). Dry eyes and video display terminals. *New England Journal of Medicine, 328*(8), 584–584. https://doi.org/10.1056/NEJM199302253280817

Usoh, M., Catena, E., Arman, S., & Slater, M. (2000). Using presence questionnaires in reality. *Presence: Teleoperators and Virtual Environments, 9*(5), 497–503. https://doi.org/10.1162/105474600566989

Valtin, G., Liebold, B., Pietschmann, D., & Ohler, P. (2011). When situation models fail: The cognitive and emotional processing of "mystery" in TV series and films. In Ö. Odag, M. Schreier, & Y. Thies-Brandner (Eds.), *Proceedings of the 7th Conference of the Media Psychology Division of the German Psychological Society* (pp. 83–84). Bremen: Pabst Science Publishers.

Van Baren, J., & IJsselsteijn, W. (2004). Measuring presence: A guide to current measurement approaches. *Deliverable of the OmniPres Project IST-2001-39237.*

Van Bochove, M. E., van der Haegen, L., Notebaert, W., & Verguts, T. (2013). Blinking predicts enhanced cognitive control. *Cognitive, Affective, & Behavioral Neuroscience*, *13*(2), 346–354. https://doi.org/10.3758/s13415-012-0138-2

Van Opstal, F., De Loof, E., Verguts, T., & Cleeremans, A. (2016). Spontaneous eyeblinks during breaking continuous flash suppression are associated with increased detection times. *Journal of Vision*, *16*(14), 21. https://doi.org/10.1167/16.14.21

Van der Werf, F., Brassinga, P., Reits, D., Aramideh, M., & Ongerboer de Visser, B. (2003). Eyelid movements: Behavioral studies of blinking in humans under different stimulus conditions. *Journal of Neurophysiology*, *89*(5), 2784–2796. https://doi.org/10.1152/jn.00557.2002

Various authors, & Miller, M. (2015). Signal (Version 1.3.2) [Computer software]. Retrieved from https://octave.sourceforge.io/signal/

Victor, J. D., & Purpura, K. P. (1997). Metric-space analysis of spike trains: Theory, algorithms and application. *Network: Computation in Neural Systems*, *8*(2), 127–164. https://doi.org/10.1088/0954-898X_8_2_003

Virtual Reality Society. (2016). 2016: The year of VR? Retrieved from http://www.vrs.org.uk/news/2016-the-year-of-vr

Volkmann, F. C. (1986). Human visual suppression. *Vision Research*, *26*(9), 1401–1416. https://doi.org/10.1016/0042-6989(86)90164-1

Volkmann, F. C., Riggs, L. A., Ellicott, A. G., & Moore, R. K. (1982). Measurements of visual suppression during opening, closing and blinking of the eyes. *Vision Research*, *22*(8), 991–996. https://doi.org/10.1016/0042-6989(82)90035-9

Vorderer, P. (1992). *Fernsehen als Handlung. Fernsehfilmrezeption aus motivationspsychologischer Perspektive.* Edition Sigma.

Vorderer, P, Wirth, W., Gouveia, F. R., Biocca, F., Saari, T., Jäncke, L., Böcking, S., Schramm, H., Gysbers, A., Hartmann, T., Klimmt, C., Laarni, J., Ravaja, N., Sacau, A., Baumgartner, T. & Jäncke, P. (2004). *MEC Spatial Presence Questionnaire (MEC-SPQ): Short Documentation and Instructions for Application.* Report to the European Community, Project Presence: MEC (IST-2001-37661). Online. Available from http://www.ijk.hmt-hannover.de/presence.

Wascher, E., Heppner, H., Möckel, T., Kobald, S. O., & Getzmann, S. (2015). Eyeblinks in choice response tasks uncover hidden aspects of information processing. *EXCLI Journal, 14,* 1207–1218. https://doi.org/10.17179/excli2015-696

Weber, R., Huskey, R., Craighead, B., & Terrazas, M. (2016). Developing and validating an unobtrusive and online measure of the attentional component of flow. Presented at the 66th Annual Conference of the International Communications Association, Fukuoka, Japan.

Weber, R., Tamborini, R., Westcott-Baker, A., & Kantor, B. (2009). Theorizing flow and media enjoyment as cognitive synchronization of attentional and reward networks. *Communication Theory, 19*(4), 397–422. https://doi.org/10.1111/j.1468-2885.2009.01352.x

Wiederhold, B. K., Jang, D., Kaneda, M., Cabral, I., Lurie, Y., May, T., … Kim, S. (2001). An investigation into physiological responses in virtual environments: an objective measurement of presence. *Towards Cyberpsychology: Mind, Cognitions and Society in the Internet Age.*

Wild, T. C., Kuiken, D., & Schopflocher, D. (1995). The role of absorption in experiential involvement. *Journal of Personality and Social Psychology, 69*(3), 569–579. https://doi.org/10.1037/0022-3514.69.3.569

Wirth, W. (2006). Involvement. In J. Bryant & P. Vorderer (Eds.), *Psychology of entertainment* (pp. 199–213). Mahwah, NJ: Lawrence Erlbaum Associates.

Wirth, W., Hartmann, T., Böcking, S., Vorderer, P., Klimmt, C., Schramm, H., Saari, T., Laarni, J., Ravaja, N., Gouveia, F. R., Biocca, F., Sacau, A., Jäncke, L., Baumgartner, P., & Jäncke, P. (2007). A process model of the formation of spatial presence experiences. *Media Psychology, 9*(3), 493–525. https://doi.org/10.1080/15213260701283079

Wirth, W., Hofer, M., & Schramm, H. (2012). The role of emotional involvement and trait absorption in the formation of spatial presence. *Media Psychology, 15*(1), 19–43. https://doi.org/10.1080/15213269.2011.648536

Wirth, W., Schramm, H., Böcking, S., Gysbers, A., Hartmann, T., Klimmt, C., & Vorderer, P. (2008). Entwicklung und Validierung eines Fragebogens zur Entstehung von räumlichem Präsenzerleben. In J. Matthes, W. Wirth, G. Daschmann, & A. Fahr (Eds.), *Die Brücke zwischen Theorie und Empirie: Operationalisierung, Messung und Validierung in der Kommunikationswissenschaft. Köln: von Halem* (pp. 70–95).

Witmer, B. G., & Singer, M. J. (1998). Measuring presence in virtual environments: A presence questionnaire. *Presence: Teleoperators and Virtual Environments, 7*(3), 225–240. https://doi.org/10.1162/105474698565686

Wood, C. L., & Bitterman, M. E. (1950). Blinking as a measure of effort in visual work. *The American Journal of Psychology, 63*(4), 584–588. https://doi.org/10.2307/1418873

Wulff, H. J. (2012a). Sequenz und Szene [Online encyclopedia]. Retrieved from http://filmlexikon.uni-kiel.de/index.php?action=lexikon&tag=det&id=332

Wulff, H. J. (2012b). Szene [Online encyclopedia]. Retrieved from http://filmlexikon.uni-kiel.de/index.php?action=lexikon&tag=det&id=1501

Yantis, S., & Hillstrom, A. P. (1994). Stimulus-driven attentional capture: Evidence from equiluminant visual objects. *Journal of Experimental Psychology. Human Perception and Performance, 20*(1), 95–107.

Yarbus, A. L. (1967). *Eye movements and vision.* (L. A. Riggs & L. H. Ballou, Eds., B. Haigh, Trans.). New York, NY: Plenum Press.

Yee, N. (2017, January 19). Beyond 50/50: Breaking down the percentage of female gamers by genre [Blog post]. Retrieved from http://quanticfoundry.com/2017/01/19/female-gamers-by-genre/

Zacks, J. M. (2004). Using movement and intentions to understand simple events. *Cognitive Science, 28*(6), 979–1008. https://doi.org/10.1016/j.cogsci.2004.06.003

Zacks, J. M., Braver, T. S., Sheridan, M. A., Donaldson, D. I., Snyder, A. Z., Ollinger, J. M., ... Raichle, M. E. (2001). Human brain activity timelocked to perceptual event boundaries. *Nature Neuroscience, 4*(6), 651–655. https://doi.org/10.1038/88486

Zacks, J. M., Kumar, S., Abrams, R. A., & Mehta, R. (2009). Using movement and intentions to understand human activity. *Cognition, 112*(2), 201–216. https://doi.org/10.1016/j.cognition.2009.03.007

Zacks, J. M., Speer, N. K., & Reynolds, J. R. (2009). Segmentation in reading and film comprehension. *Journal of Experimental Psychology: General, 138*(2), 307–327. https://doi.org/10.1037/a0015305

Zacks, J. M., Speer, N. K., Swallow, K. M., Braver, T. S., & Reynolds, J. R. (2007). Event perception: A mind-brain perspective. *Psychological Bulletin, 133*(2), 273–293. https://doi.org/10.1037/0033-2909.133.2.273

Zacks, J. M., Speer, N. K., Swallow, K. M., & Maley, C. J. (2010). The brain's cutting-room floor: Segmentation of narrative cinema. *Frontiers in Human Neuroscience, 4.* https://doi.org/10.3389/fnhum.2010.00168

Zacks, J. M., & Swallow, K. M. (2007). Event segmentation. *Current Directions in Psychological Science, 16*(2), 80–84. https://doi.org/10.1111/j.1467-8721.2007.00480.x

Zacks, J. M., Swallow, K. M., Vettel, J. M., & McAvoy, M. P. (2006). Visual motion and the neural correlates of event perception. *Brain Research, 1076*(1), 150–162. https://doi.org/10.1016/j.brainres.2005.12.122

Zacks, J. M., Tversky, B., & Iyer, G. (2001). Perceiving, remembering, and communicating structure in events. *Journal of Experimental Psychology: General, 130*(1), 29–58. https://doi.org/10.1037/0096-3445.130.1.29

Zaman, M. L., & Doughty, M. J. (1997). Some methodological issues in the assessment of spontaneous eyeblink frequency in man. *Ophthalmic and Physiological Optics, 17,* 421–432.

Zimmerman, D. W. (1987). Comparative power of Student *t* test and Mann-Whitney *U* test for unequal sample sizes and variances. *The Journal of Experimental Education, 55*(3), 171–174. https://doi.org/10.1080/00220973.1987.10806451

Zimmerman, D. W. (1998). Invalidation of parametric and nonparametric statistical tests by concurrent violation of two assumptions. *The Journal of Experimental Education, 67*(1), 55–68. https://doi.org/10.1080/00220979809598344

Zimmerman, D. W. (2000). Statistical significance levels of nonparametric tests biased by heterogeneous variances of treatment groups. *The Journal of General Psychology, 127*(4), 354–364. https://doi.org/10.1080/00221300009598589

Zimmerman, D. W. (2003). A warning about the large-sample Wilcoxon-Mann-Whitney test. *Understanding Statistics, 2*(4), 267–280. https://doi.org/10.1207/S15328031US0204_03

12 Appendix A

The instruction texts for experimental manipulations in experiment 1 are presented on the following pages.

12.1 Experimental Manipulation

Manipulation of experimental conditions in experiment 1. The instructions were read to participants in a video, and key aspects of the instruction were repeated as text on the screen. Emphasis has been added to highlight the differences between both texts.

12.1.1 Instruction to focus on stimulus form

Hallo und erst einmal vielen Dank für deine Teilnahme. In diesem Versuch interessieren wir uns für die Wahrnehmung von Videos, oder genauer gesagt dafür, wie gut sie **von der Filmtechnik oder Machart her** für unsere Studien geeignet sind. Deshalb zeigen wir dir gleich einen kurzen Ausschnitt aus Mr. Bean - ohne Ton - und stellen dir danach ein paar Fragen zu **deiner Analyse der Machart**. Zuerst wird gleich für circa zwei Minuten ein schwarzes Bild mit einem weißen Kreuz angezeigt. Bitte schaue dann einfach auf das weiße Kreuz und nutze die Zeit, um ruhig zu werden und dich auf deine Aufgabe vorzubereiten. Danach beginnt automatisch das Mr. Bean Video. Deine Aufgabe ist es, **dich voll und ganz auf die Filmtechnik und die Machart des Videos zu konzentrieren. Bleib' mit deinen Gedanken immer völlig hier und jetzt im Labor und analysiere das Video, um nachher die Fragen zur Filmtechnik gut beantworten zu können.** Es kommt also darauf an, **wie du die äußere Form des Videos nach deiner Analyse bewertest.** Gleich startet der schwarze Bildschirm und danach kommt das Video.

12.1.2 Instruction to focus on stimulus content

Hallo und erst einmal vielen Dank für deine Teilnahme. In diesem Versuch interessieren wir uns für die Wahrnehmung von Videos, oder genauer gesagt dafür, wie gut sie **vom Inhalt her** für unsere Studien geeignet sind. Deshalb zeigen wir dir gleich einen kurzen Ausschnitt aus Mr. Bean - ohne Ton - und stellen dir danach ein paar Fragen zu **deinem Erleben**. Zuerst wird gleich für circa zwei Minuten ein schwarzes Bild mit einem weißen Kreuz angezeigt. Bitte schaue dann einfach auf das weiße Kreuz und nutze die Zeit, um ruhig zu werden und dich auf den Filmgenuss einzustimmen. Danach beginnt automatisch das Mr. Bean Video. Deine Aufgabe ist es, **dich voll und ganz auf den Inhalt des Videos einzulassen. Bleib' mit deinen Gedanken immer völlig im Film bei Mr. Bean und lass dich einfach mitreißen, um erst danach die inhaltlichen Aspekte einschätzen zu können.** Es kommt also darauf an, **wie du den Inhalt des Videos ganz normal beim Anschauen erlebst.** Gleich startet der schwarze Bildschirm und danach kommt das Video.

13 Appendix B

The instruction texts for experimental manipulations in experiment 2 are presented on this page.

13.1 Experimental Manipulation

Manipulation of experimental conditions in experiment 2. The instructions were read to participants by the experimenter. Emphasis has been added to highlight the differences between both texts.

13.1.1 Instruction to focus on stimulus form

Hallo und danke für Eure Teilnahme. In diesem Versuch interessieren wir uns für die Wahrnehmung von **Filmtechnik**. Deshalb zeigen wir euch gleich einen Ausschnitt aus einem Film, **bei dem ihr möglichst genau auf die Filmtechnik achtet**. Danach stellen wir ein paar Fragen zu **eurer Analyse der Machart**. Zum Einstimmen und ruhig werden gibt es erst für zwei Minuten einen Film ohne Ton von einem Aquarium zu sehen. Danach beginnt automatisch der Film.

13.1.2 Instruction to focus on stimulus content

Hallo und danke für eure Teilnahme. In diesem Versuch interessieren wir uns für Wahrnehmung von **Filmen**. Deshalb zeigen wir euch gleich einen Ausschnitt aus einem Film, **den ihr einfach nur anschauen müsst, wir ihr das im Kino auch machen würdet**. Danach stellen wir euch ein paar Fragen zu **eurem Erleben**. Zum Einstimmen gibt es erst für zwei Minuten einen Film ohne Ton von einem Aquarium zu sehen. Danach beginnt automatisch der Film.

14 German Synopsis

Die vorliegende Dissertation befasst sich mit alternativen Messzugängen zum Rezeptionsphänomen des räumlichen Präsenzerlebens (engl.: spatial presence), genauer gesagt mit der Eignung struktureller Aspekte des spontanen Lidschluss-verhaltens als Indikatoren für Präsenzerleben.

Präsenz wird als ein Zustand beschrieben, in dem MediennutzerInnen sich nicht mehr vollkommen bewusst sind, dass ihnen die wahrgenommenen Inhalte durch ein Medium vermittelt wurden; wie die International Society for Presence Research definiert (ISPR, 2009), zeichnen sich Präsenzzustände durch eine Reihe von Eigenschaften aus, unter anderem dadurch, dass (1) die vermittelnde Rolle der Medientechnologie ganz oder teilweise übersehen wird, dass (2) Präsenz ein Nutzerphänomen ist, das nur durch Technologie ermöglicht und unterstützt wird, dass (3) Präsenzzustände fluktuieren können, und dass (4) Präsenz nur während einer Mediennutzungssituation auftreten kann.

Die Einleitung in Kapitel 1 führt kurz in die Thematik ein und betont die anhaltende Relevanz der Präsenzforschung, besonders angesichts sich immer weiter entwickelnder Medientechnologien wie etwa Geräten zur Virtual-Reality-Nutzung.

Zur Untersuchung des alternativen Messzugangs werden in Kapitel 2 zunächst der Medienbegriff definiert, theoretische Grundlagen des Präsenzerlebens erörtert, sowie Abgrenzungen zu benachbarten Mediennutzungsphänomenen vorgenommen. Zur Vorbereitung der späteren Argumentation wird bei der Beschreibung jeder Theorie die angenommene Rolle von Aufmerksamkeitsprozessen besonders diskutiert. Als theoretische Grundlage für den Präsenzbegriff in dieser Dissertation wird schließlich ein Modell zur Entstehung räumlichen Präsenzerlebens, das Process Model of the Formation of Spatial Presence Experiences von Wirth et al. (2007), ausgewählt.

In Kapitel 3 werden existierende Messmethoden für Präsenzerleben vorgestellt. Präsenz als subjektives Erleben wird für gewöhnlich durch Selbstauskünfte in Fragebögen erhoben—ein Vorgehen, das Vorteile und Nachteile in sich vereint. Um Einschränkungen wie die sehr geringe zeitliche Auflösung der Verfahren oder ihre Anfälligkeit für subjektive Verfälschungen zu vermeiden, wurde in der Forschung eine Reihe von objektiven Messzugängen vorgeschlagen und evaluiert. Die Vorstellung solcher alternativen Messzugänge leitet über zum spontanen Lidschlussverhalten als zentralem Aspekt dieser Dissertation.

Kapitel 4 befasst sich detailliert mit physiologischen Grundlagen des spontanen Lidschlussverhaltens und diskutiert ein umfangreiches Korpus von theoretischen Annahmen und empirischen Befunden zu Einflussfaktoren auf den spontanen Lidschluss. Diese Forschungserkenntnisse werden anschließend genutzt, um existierende Annahmen über spontanes Lidschlussverhalten als Indikator für benachbarte Rezeptionsphänomene zu präzisieren und auf den Bereich der Präsenzforschung zu übertragen. Dabei geht es vor allem um eine belastbare Begründung für die potenzielle Eignung struktureller Aspekte des Lidschlussverhaltens als Indikator für räumliches Präsenzerleben. Es wird hergeleitet, dass die angenommene intensivere Aufmerksamkeitszuwendung zum Stimulus und intensivere Verarbeitung der Inhalte des Stimulus in einem Präsenzzustand zu einem höheren Grad an Stimulus-abhängiger Struktur im spontanen Lidschlussverhalten führt.

Aus einer Zusammenfassung der bis dahin zusammengetragenen Erkenntnisse wird in Kapitel 5 das Vorgehen für den empirischen Teil der Dissertation präzisiert. Als leitende Forschungsfrage soll untersucht werden, ob ein höheres Maß an Stimulus-abhängiger Struktur im spontanen Lidschlussverhalten mit höheren Präsenz-Selbsteinschätzungen in einem etablierten Fragebogeninstrument einhergeht. Zur Untersuchung dieser Fragestellung werden drei empirisch-experimentelle Untersuchungen geplant, in denen drei verschiedene Methoden zur Erfassung von Struktur in bis zu drei verschiedenen Medienumgebungen erprobt werden sollen. Um die Anwendbarkeit in einem breiten Medienspektrum zu untersuchen, werden aus existierender Forschung drei unterschiedliche Stimuli abgeleitet, die in gleicher oder vergleichbarer Form bereits als geeignet befunden wurden, eine Stimulus-abhängige Struktur im Lidschlussverhalten auszulösen. Diese Stimuli sind erstens ein konventionell geschnittener Videostimulus, in diesem Fall ein Auszug aus einer *Mr. Bean* Episode; zweitens ein Videostimulus, der durch Kameraführung und Schnitt den Eindruck erweckt, aus einer einzigen kontinuierlichen Einstellung zu bestehen, in diesem Fall ein Auszug aus dem Film *Birdman oder (Die unverhoffte Macht der Ahnungslosigkeit)*; drittens ein interaktives Videospiel mit ebenfalls kontinuierlicher Darstellung, in diesem Fall die Rennsimulation *Project CARS*. Drei Methoden werden aus existierender Forschung abgeleitet, um Stimulus-abhängige Struktur im Lidschlussverhalten zu quantifizieren. Als erste Methode dient die *Variabilität der Intervalle zwischen aufeinanderfolgenden Lidschlüssen*, unter der Annahme, dass ein natürliches, vom Stimulus unbeeinflusstes Lidschlussverhalten zu regelmäßigeren Lidschlüssen führt. Als zweite Methode dienen Indikatoren der *Spike-train-synchrony*, in diesem Fall ein Synchronitätsmaß zur Erfassung gleichartig gelagerter Veränderungen in der Lidschlussfrequenz zwischen MediennutzerInnen, unter der Annahme, dass sich das Lidschlussverhalten von MediennutzerInnen, die stark vom selben Stimulus beeinflusst werden, einander angleicht. Diese Methode wurde in den Experimenten 1 und 2 angewendet, in denen allen Probanden identische Stimuli präsentiert wurden. Als dritte Methode dient die *T-pattern detection* zur Entdeckung von Strukturen in überzufälligen Koinzidenzen von Ereignisdaten, unter der Annahme, dass sich ein Stimulus-beeinflusstes Lidschlussverhalten in häufigeren, überzufälligen zeitlichen Beziehungen zwischen Medienereignissen und Nutzerereignissen zeigt. In Anlehnung an bestehende Evaluierungsstudien zu alternativen Messzugängen für Präsenzerleben sollen experimentelle Bedingungen geschaffen werden, die Präsenzerleben entweder fördern oder behindern, um eine größere Bandbreite von unterschiedlich starkem Präsenzerleben während der gegebenen Mediennutzung analysieren zu können. Auf Grundlage von Präsenztheorien wird eine Manipulation durch verschiedene Instruktionen hergeleitet, um eine Manipulation mit möglichst geringen Störeinflüssen auf das Lidschlussverhalten einzusetzen: Probanden sollen instruiert werden, sich entweder auf Aspekte des Stimulusinhalts oder der Stimulusform zu konzentrieren. Damit sind die Vorbereitungen für die drei durchzuführenden Experimente abgeschlossen.

Durchführung und Ergebnisse der drei Experimente werden in den Kapiteln 6 bis 8 beschrieben. In Experiment 1 wurden insgesamt 62 Probanden in einem experimentellen 2 × 1 Versuchsdesign getestet. Allen Probanden wurde in Einzelsitzungen ein identischer Ausschnitt aus einer Mr. Bean Episode auf einem Computerbildschirm präsentiert, jedoch wurde eine Gruppe instruiert, ihre Aufmerksamkeit auf den Inhalt des Videos zu richten („Inhalt-Gruppe"), während die andere Gruppe instruiert wurde, ihre Aufmerksamkeit auf formale Aspekte des Videos zu richten („Form-Gruppe"). Diese Manipulation sollte den Versuchsteilnehmern in der Form-Gruppe stets vor Augen halten, dass sie sich in einer Mediennutzungssituation befinden, wodurch das Auftreten von Präsenzerleben verringert werden sollte. Es wurde entsprechend erwartet, dass die Inhalt-Gruppe im subjektiven Maß höhere Fragebogenwerte zum Präsenzerleben berichten würde und in den objektiven Maßen einen höheren Grad von Stimulus-abhängiger Struktur im spontanen Lidschlussverhalten zeigen würde. Die Lidschlüsse der Probanden wurden von zwei unabhängigen Kodierern aus Videoaufnahmen kodiert. Die Ergebnisse zeigten, dass Inhalt- und Form-Gruppe ein vergleichbar hohes Präsenzerleben berichteten, obwohl die Form-Gruppe gleichzeitig einen signifikant stärkeren Fokus auf formale Aspekte des Mediums berichtete. In den objektiven Maßen fand sich kein Effekt für die Variabilität der Lidschlussintervalle; die restlichen objektiven Maße ergaben übereinstimmend, dass das Lidschlussverhalten der Form-Gruppe ein signifikant höheres Maß an Stimulus-abhängiger Struktur aufwies.

In Experiment 2 wurden insgesamt 61 Probanden in einem experimentellen 2 × 1 Versuchsdesign getestet. Allen Probanden wurde in Kleingruppen ein identischer Ausschnitt aus dem Film Birdman als Projektion auf einer Leinwand präsentiert; wieder wurden beide Gruppen verschieden instruiert. Die Instruktion der Inhalt-Gruppe wurde leicht verändert, da vermutet wurde, dass das Präsenzerleben der Inhalt-Gruppe in Experiment 1 durch die starke Instruktion, bewusst auf den Inhalt des Videos zu achten, beeinträchtigt worden sein könnte. Daher wurde die Inhalt-Gruppe instruiert, den Film möglichst natürlich so zu rezipieren, wie sie es auch im Kino tun würde; die Form-Gruppe wurde weiterhin instruiert, ihre Aufmerksamkeit auf formale Aspekte des Videos zu richten. Es wurde wieder erwartet, dass die Inhalt-Gruppe im subjektiven Maß höhere Fragebogenwerte zum Präsenzerleben berichten würde und in den objektiven Maßen einen höheren Grad von Stimulus-abhängiger Struktur im spontanen Lidschlussverhalten zeigen würde. Die Lidschlüsse der Probanden wurden von einem Kodierer aus Videoaufnahmen kodiert und durch eine unabhängige Zweitkodierung von zufällig ausgewählten Intervallen der Beobachtung jedes Probanden überprüft. Die Ergebnisse zeigten, dass die Form-Gruppe ein signifikant höheres Präsenzerleben berichtete, obwohl die Form-Gruppe gleichzeitig einen signifikant stärkeren Fokus auf formale Aspekte des Mediums berichtete. Für die Variabilität der Lidschlussintervalle fand sich kein Effekt; die restlichen objektiven Maße stimmten überwiegend darin überein, dass das Lidschlussverhalten der Inhalt-Gruppe ein signifikant höheres Maß an Stimulus-abhängiger Struktur aufwies.

In Experiment 3 wurden insgesamt 48 Probanden in einem quasi-experimentellen 2 × 1 Versuchsdesign getestet. Die Probanden spielten die Rennsimulation Project CARS und wurden für die Auswertung entlang des Medians ihres berichteten Präsenzerlebens in eine Gruppe mit hohem und eine Gruppe mit niedrigem Präsenzerleben aufgeteilt, da der Ansatz, das Präsenzerleben durch verschiedene Instruktionen zu manipulieren, in den vorherigen Experimenten keine Erfolge zeigte. Es wurde erwartet, dass die Gruppe mit höherem Präsenzerleben in den nun zwei objektiven Maßen einen höheren Grad von Stimulus-abhängiger Struktur im spontanen Lidschlussverhalten zeigen würde. Die Lidschlüsse der Probanden wurden mit Hilfe einer Eye-Tracking-Brille kodiert. In der Auswertung der objektiven Maße fand sich kein Effekt für die Variabilität der Lidschlussintervalle. Für die Ergebnisse der T-pattern Detektion wurde nur ein Trend in der vorhergesagten Richtung, aber kein signifikantes Ergebnis gefunden; außerdem zeigte die Analyse, dass die Güte der detektierten Verhaltensmuster deutlich geringer war als in den vorherigen Experimenten.

Die empirischen Befunde der drei Experimente werden in Kapitel 9 zusammengefasst und hinsichtlich methodenbezogener und theoriebezogener Schlussfolgerungen diskutiert. In den methodenbezogenen Schlussfolgerungen werden die Ergebnisse zum eingesetzte Manipulationsansatz und den drei Messmethoden bewertet.

Insgesamt zeigte sich, dass die angewendete Manipulation durch verschiedene Instruktionen nicht zum beabsichtigten Ergebnis geführt hatte. In Experiment 1 zeigte sie keinen Effekt auf das berichtete Präsenzerleben; in einer modifizierten Form führte sie in Experiment 2 entgegen den Vorhersagen der Theorie zu gegenteiligen Effekten. Durch diesen Widerspruch zur theoretischen Grundlage konnten die objektiven Maße nicht in der geplanten Form evaluiert werden. Die alternativen Messmethoden wurden trotzdem analysiert, um eventuelle Diskrepanzen zwischen subjektiven und objektiven Messzugängen aufzudecken.

Die erste Methode, die Variabilität der Lidschlussintervalle, wurde in allen drei Experimenten angewendet, zeigte aber keinerlei Effekte in Vergleichen zwischen den Experimentalgruppen. Die anderen beiden Methoden zeigten in den Experimenten 1 und 2 übereinstimmende Ergebnisse, jedoch nicht immer im Sinne der inhaltlichen Forschungsfrage, da die höhere Struktur in der jeweiligen Gruppe entweder aufgrund der Instruktion oder des berichteten Präsenzerlebens nicht vorhergesagt wurde. Die T-pattern Detektion zeigte im dritten Experiment kein signifikantes Ergebnis.

Aus den Studienergebnissen werden Verbesserungsvorschläge für zukünftige Anwendungen in der Präsenzforschung, aber auch in der Erforschung benachbarter Mediennutzungsphänomene abgeleitet. Für zukünftige Studien über das Lidschlussverhalten oder Aufmerksamkeitsprozesse in Mediennutzungssituationen wird der Einsatz von Synchronitätsmaßen und T-pattern Detektion empfohlen, je nach Fragestellung einzeln oder auch in Kombination. Mit Blick auf die Ergebnisse aus Experiment 3 wird in der Diskussion auch auf eine angemessene Auswahl von Medienereignissen für die T-pattern Detektion eingegangen.

In den theoriebezogenen Schlussfolgerungen wird zunächst auf das Konzept der Stimulus-abhängigen Struktur im spontanen Lidschlussverhalten eingegangen. Die beiden brauchbaren Methoden konnten solche Struktur in den Experimenten überwiegend zeigen. Dabei wurden Unterschiede im Grad der Strukturierung zwischen Gruppen von Probanden gefunden, denen exakt derselbe Stimulus mit nur unterschiedlicher Aufgabenstellung präsentiert wurde. Die Ergebnisse standen damit jedoch nicht in Einklang mit den Selbstauskünften über Präsenzerleben. Aufgrund der nicht eindeutigen Befundlage durch die unerwarteten Effekte der Präsenzmanipulation ist eine abschließende Bewertung der alternativen Messmethoden schwierig. Einen Anhaltspunkt könnten die Ergebnisse des Synchronitätsmaßes und der T-pattern Detektion geben, welche trotz unterschiedlicher Methoden zur Abbildung von Verhaltensstruktur übereinstimmende Ergebnisse zeigten. Dies legt nahe, dass Stimulus-abhängige Struktur vorhanden war, diese aber nicht notwendigerweise Verhaltensaspekte abbildete, die mit der Entstehung von Präsenzerleben—oder zumindest mit der im Fragebogen berichteten retrospektiven Selbsteinschätzung von Präsenzerleben—einhergingen. Unter der Annahme, dass die Fragebogenwerte eine valide Einschätzung des Präsenzerlebens lieferten, müsste geschlussfolgert werden, dass das bisherige Verständnis von Stimulus-abhängiger Struktur in spontanem Lidschlussverhalten unzureichend ist. Basierend auf bisheriger Forschung zum Lidschlussverhalten während der Mediennutzung sah die Untersuchungsanlage in dieser Dissertation vor, das generelle Ausmaß an Stimulus-abhängiger Struktur im spontanen Lidschlussverhalten als Informationsquelle zu benutzen. Eine Interpretation der Ergebnisse unter Rückbezug auf den theoretischen Hintergrund legt jedoch nahe, dass vielleicht nicht quantitative Unterschiede im Ausmaß der Struktur, sondern qualitative Unterschiede in der Struktur informativer sein könnten. Aus ihnen könnten Rückschlüsse darauf gezogen werden, welche Medienereignisse ursächlich für die Ausbildung der Struktur waren, womit exaktere Rückschlüsse auf die Verarbeitungsprozesse während der Mediennutzung und gegebenenfalls die Nutzung als Präsenzindikator möglich wären.

Anschließend wird auf das Konzept Präsenz eingegangen. Dabei wird zunächst die Angemessenheit komplexer Prozessmaße für die Präsenzforschung diskutiert. Theorien zum Präsenzerleben nehmen an, dass Präsenz ein Zustand ist, der während der Mediennutzung auftreten kann, woraus sich ergibt, dass Präsenzforschung in diesem theoretischen Rahmen notwendigerweise auf mehr oder weniger komplexe mediale Stimuli angewiesen ist. Da Präsenz häufig als fluktuierender Zustand konzipiert wird, sind für eine detaillierte Betrachtung des Phänomens weiterhin prozessabbildende Messmethoden mit angemessener zeitlicher Auflösung und Sensitivität für präsenzrelevante Nutzervariablen notwendig. Eine abschließende Bewertung darüber, ob die in dieser Dissertation untersuchten Messmethoden diese Voraussetzungen vollständig erfüllen, ist bei der gegebenen Ergebnislage nicht möglich. Daher wird abschließend diskutiert, wie die beiden vielversprechenden Messzugänge in zukünftigen Studien genutzt werden könnten, um zunächst die unklaren Befunde der vorliegenden Dissertation aufzuklären. Daraus könnte ein besseres Verständnis der Eigenschaften und Determinanten Stimulus-abhängiger Struktur im Lidschlussverhalten gewonnen werden. Bezüglich der Befunde, die den Vorhersagen aus Präsenztheorien widersprechen, werden ebenfalls empirische Untersuchungsanlagen diskutiert, die zur weiteren Erforschung besonders der Rolle von Aufmerksamkeitsprozessen während der Mediennutzung dienen sollen.

Kapitel 10 schließt die Dissertation mit einer kurzen Zusammenfassung der erbrachten Leistung ab.